REORIENTING THE PURE LAND

INTERSECTIONS

Asian and Pacific American Transcultural Studies

RUSSELL C. LEONG
DAVID K. YOO
MARY YUU DANICO
Series Editors

REORIENTING THE PURE LAND

Nisei Buddhism in the Transwar Years, 1943–1965

Michael K. Masatsugu

University of Hawai'i Press
Honolulu

In Association with
UCLA Asian American Studies Center, Los Angeles

First printing, 2023

Library of Congress Cataloging-in-Publication Data

Names: Masatsugu, Michael K., author.

Title: Reorienting the Pure Land : Nisei Buddhism in the transwar years, 1943–1965 / Michael K. Masatsugu.

Other titles: Intersections (Honolulu, Hawaii)

Description: Honolulu : University of Hawai'i Press, [2023] | Series: Intersections: Asian and Pacific American transcultural studies | Includes bibliographical references and index.

Identifiers: LCCN 2023005005 (print) | LCCN 2023005006 (ebook) | ISBN 9780824894306 (hardback) | ISBN 9780824895532 (paperback) | ISBN 9780824896577 (pdf) | ISBN 9780824896584 (epub) | ISBN 9780824896591 (kindle edition)

Subjects: LCSH: Shin (Sect)—United States—History—20th century. | Shin Buddhists—United States—History—20th century. | Japanese Americans—Religion. | Buddhism and culture—United States.

Classification: LCC BQ8712.9.U6 M37 2023 (print) | LCC BQ8712.9.U6 (ebook) | DDC 294.3/92609730904—dc23/eng/20230216

LC record available at https://lccn.loc.gov/2023005005

LC ebook record available at https://lccn.loc.gov/2023005006

Cover illustration: Funeral ceremony for Pvt. 1st Class George Gushiken, Nishi Hongwanji Temple, Los Angeles, CA, May 1, 1948. Reproduced courtesy of the Los Angeles Times Photographic Archive, Library Special Collections, Charles E. Young Research Library, UCLA

*Wiebke Ipsen (1970–2009), my partner, colleague, and wife,
was a historian of gender and nation building in late-nineteenth-century
Brazil. Wiebke lived courageously with cancer until the end of her days.
Her keen insights, her passion for historical research, and her kindness,
gentleness, and concern for social justice live on in this work,
which is dedicated to her memory.*

CONTENTS

ACKNOWLEDGMENTS

Research for this book was initiated as a result of my participation in the Buddhist Church of San Francisco Oral History project. I am grateful to Ben Kobashigawa and Reverend LaVerne Sasaki for involving me in the project. I am deeply appreciative to Reverend John and Koko Doami, Isao Fujimoto, Patty Hirota, Kimi and Clarence Hisatsune, Ryo Imamura, Hiroshi Kashiwagi, Keith Kojimoto, Albert Saijo, Gary Snyder, Tomiye Sumner, Taitetsu Unno, and Haruo Yamaoka for generously sharing their time. Our conversations have been an illuminating and humbling reminder that history is not simply recorded, edited, interpreted, and written but also, irreducibly, lived.

This book has benefited greatly from colleagues who reviewed numerous versions of the manuscript, offering their encouragement and suggestions. I am immensely grateful to Linda Cummings Akiyama, Michihiro Ama, Jane Iwamura, Christian Koot, Lon Kurashige, Christopher Lee, Tomoe Moriya, Fiona I. B. Ngo, Akim Reinhardt, Duncan Ryūken Williams, Chiou-Ling Yeh, and David Yoo. A number of scholars have provided invaluable feedback and guidance at various stages in the research and writing of this book. Thank you to Eiichiro Azuma, Sharon Block, Rebecca M. Brown, Lisa Marie Cacho, Carolyn Chen, Yong Chen, Cindy I-Fen Cheng, Mary Dudziak, Dave Johnson, Tetsuden Kashima, George Lipsitz, James Kyung-Jin Lee, Eileen Luhr, Meghan Mettler, Tunde Oduntan, Stella Oh, James Paligutan, Arnold Pan, Lori Anne Pierce, Kenneth Pomeranz, Liam Riordan, Greg Robinson, Erik Ropers, Nayan Shah, Martin Summers, Linda Trinh Vo, Ann Walthall, R. Bin Wong, Carl Yamamoto, and Ayanna Yonemura.

I am forever indebted to Jon Wiener for his longstanding guidance, feedback, mentorship, and support for this project. I am also grateful to the ongoing exchanges and support from my wonderful colleagues at Towson University who have participated in the History Seminar Reading Group. I am especially indebted to my editor, Masako Ikeda, and the anonymous reviewers at the University of Hawai'i Press for their guidance, which has improved this study immeasurably. Thank you also to Santos Barbasa, Susan Campbell, Lani Meyer, Mary Mortensen, and Mary Ribesky for their invaluable assistance in completing the production of this book.

I have also been fortunate to have had wonderful mentors and colleagues whose insights, feedback, and support have sustained my work on this book over the years. Thank you to Jose Alamillo, Omar Ali, Diem-My Bui, Joseph Cheah, Gilbert Chen, Wilson Chen, Robert W. Cherny, Terry Cooney, Rita Costa-Gomes, Andrew Diemer, Nicole Dombrowski-Risser, Susannah Duerr, Ben Fisher, Thelma Foote, Dorothy Fujita-Rony, Thomas Fujita-Rony, Alhena Gadotti, Kelly Gray, Lane Hirabayashi, Jane Hseu, William Issel, Russell Jeung, Anne Joh, Kimberly Katz, Mimi Khúc, David Kyuman Kim, Soo Kim, Miriam Beevi Lam, Jeff Larson, Barbara Loomis, Martin Manalansan, John Mancini, La Shonda Mims, Xóchitl Mota, Jennifer Murray, Mimi Thi Nguyen, Genevieve Erin O'Brien, Kent Ono, Karen Oslund, Jocelyn Pacleb, Su Yon Pak, Edward J. W. Park, Steve Phillips, Ronn Pineo, Junaid Rana, Bob Rook, Steven Rosales, Heather Rounds, Nichole Sanders, Alan Shima, Marcio Siwi, Elizabeth Stinson, Donna T. Tong, Linda Trinh Vo, Amanda Walter, Janelle Wong, Yutien Wong, and Ben Zajicek.

Many archivists and librarians have supported my research. I am deeply appreciative to the archivists who were critical in guiding me through the BCA Collection for the many years that it was housed at the Institute for Buddhist Studies and the Japanese American National Museum, including Robert Dirig, Debbie Malone, Marie Masumoto, Cristine Paschild, Aileen Tu, and Lauren Zuchowsky. I also wish to thank Megan Browndorf, Elizabeth DeCoster, and the ILL staff at the Cook Library, Towson University, for enduring my unending requests for obscure materials. Thank you to John Skarstad at Special Collections at the General Library at the University of California, Davis; Michael Henry and Jim Baxter, Special Collections and University Archives, at the University of Maryland, College Park; Molly Haigh, Special Collections at the Charles E. Young Research Library, UCLA; Emma Saito Lincoln, Japanese American Service Committee Archives, and the many archivists and librarians at the Library of Congress, and the National Archives, College Park, Maryland.

I wish to extend a heartfelt thanks to Dean Chris Chulos, the Department of History, and the College of Liberal Arts at Towson University for their financial support for the completion of this book. Thank you as well to the Shinso Ito Center for Japanese Religions and Culture at the University of Southern California for sponsoring me as a visiting scholar.

My family has been a source of enduring love and support during good times and difficult ones, particularly with the passing of Wiebke Ipsen, to whom this book is dedicated. I am forever grateful to Marian and James Masatsugu, Glen and Barbara Blaser, Miles and Bernadette Masatsugu, Lani and Jason Meyer,

Maren and Jeff Tusing, Dirk and Irene Seifert-Ipsen, Ken and Donna Hine, and the Higa, Hioki, Kaplan, Krietenstein, Licnikas, Masatsugu, Sato, and Shima families. In addition to family, I would also like to acknowledge those colleagues and friends whose unflinching support, during a difficult period of my life, I will never forget, including Akim Reinhardt, Martha NcNamara, Jim Bordewick, Liam Riordan, Susan Thibedeau, Suzie and Sally Ho, Carolyn Krasner, Diana Terrill, Andy Matinog, Karlin Sloan, George Domontay, Carrie Paterson, Tom Duda, Steve Folta, Amelia Lyons, Steve Bubar, Darin Salazar, Greg Semancik, Mary Carpentier, Amy Maloof, Bob Rook, Scott See, Tonya Smith Laycock, Stefano and Sandra Tijernina, Yuki Kato, Keith Finlay, and Nathan Wilson. I am also deeply indebted to James N. Green, Marc Hertzman, and Theresa Cribelli.

Kristen Anne Hine has been my anchor in this transitory world in which we live. I am forever grateful for her love, compassion, kindness, support, and patience. Her work in ethical theory has influenced my thinking about this book more than she probably realizes. Our children Kai and Benjamin arrived in the late stages of this project. Their curiosity, sense of humor, and sweetness has been a source of joy, inspiration, and sustenance.

Abbreviations

American Academy of Asian Studies (AAAS)
Asian American Political Alliance (AAPA)
Buddhist Churches of America (BCA)
Buddhist Life Program (BLP)
Buddhist Mission of North America (BMNA)
Buddhist Study Center (BSC)
Central California Young Buddhist Association (CCYBA)
Chicago Inter-Agency Council (IAC)
Department of Justice (DOJ)
Federal Bureau of Investigation (FBI)
Institute for Buddhist Studies (IBS)
Japanese American Citizens League (JACL)
Japanese American Evacuation and Resettlement Study (JERS)
Japanese American National Museum (JANM)
Ministerial Training Center, Kyoto (MTC)
National Young Buddhist Association (NYBA)
National Young Buddhist Coordinating Council (NYBCC)
New York Buddhist Church (NYBC)
Office of Naval Intelligence (ONI)
Office of War Information (OWI)
Special Projects Fund (SPF)
Supreme Commander for Allied Powers (SCAP)
Varsity Victory Volunteers (VVV)
Veterans of Foreign Wars (VFW)
War Relocation Authority (WRA)
Wartime Civil Control Administration (WCCA)

Western Adult Buddhist League (WABL)
Western Young Buddhist League (WYBL)
World Fellowship of Buddhists (WFB)
Young Adult Buddhist Association (YABA)
Young Buddhist Association (YBA)
Young Men's Buddhist Association (YMBA)
Young Men's Christian Association (YMCA)
Young Men's and Women's Buddhist Association (YMWBA)
Young Women's Christian Association (YWCA)

REORIENTING THE PURE LAND

Introduction

In August 1948, Nikkei (Japanese American) Buddhists held a Golden Jubilee Festival in San Francisco, California, to celebrate the fifty-year anniversary of the establishment of Shin Buddhism (Jōdo Shinshū) in the United States. The festival was planned just three years after the end of World War II and detainees' release from US-government sponsored "internment" camps, and organizers hoped it would serve to revitalize American Shin Buddhist communities and advance Nisei (second-generation children of Issei immigrants) to positions of leadership. Golden Jubilee chairman Toshio Yoshida, a Nisei, proclaimed that the festival commemorated "50 years since our parents brought Buddhism into this country." Yoshida continued, "To those who have departed and cannot see and enjoy the fruits of their toil, we bow our heads in deep reverence. To those still with us, we express our sincerest appreciation for carrying the torch for us." "But," he added, "we cannot expect them to carry it for us forever."[1]

Given the recent wartime experience of racial and religious discrimination faced by Nikkei Buddhists, Nisei believed that in order to carry on the legacy of Issei Buddhism, improved race relations, particularly between Nikkei Buddhists and white Americans, was a necessity. They also believed that their bicultural background and status as American citizens could serve as a bridge between Nikkei Buddhists and the broader American public. An integral aspect of the Golden Jubilee Festival was the roster of invited outside guests, which included journalists, representatives from the American military, and civic leaders, including George Christopher, a member of the San Francisco Board of Supervisors who would serve as the city's future mayor.[2]

On the final Sunday of the festival, organizers staged a *bon odori,* a folk dance associated with the summer Obon ceremony in honor of deceased ancestors. For many Nikkei, *bon odori* evoked memories of prewar Issei Buddhist traditions that connected them to communities both in the United States and across the Pacific to Japan. Yet, in addition to bringing Nikkei together, the dance was also planned with the broader American public in mind. In an effort to highlight Buddhism's resonance with American political and economic values, the *bon odori* was moved from its prewar location near Nihonmachi (Japanesetown) to the civic center in front of San Francisco City Hall and paired with a raffle drawing for a new automobile. Those in attendance witnessed men, women, and children dressed in *yukata* (Japanese summer robes) moving in rhythm to Japanese folk songs as they circled the *yagura* (central tower stage) accompanied by the beat of *taiko* drumming. San Franciscans in attendance were not the only ones to witness this spectacle. With the media invited to the event, the Nisei Buddhist vision on display was also made accessible to millions of readers of *LIFE* magazine. In a three-page article that included photos of Shin Buddhist religious ceremonies and festival events, including the *bon odori*, *LIFE* noted that, "Japanese-American Buddhists in San Francisco . . . dressed in traditional costumes, danced ancient steps at the city's Civic Center, then raffled off a Chevrolet."[3]

The Nisei vision on display for San Franciscans and *LIFE*'s readers highlighted Buddhist tradition as a part of Japanese American ethnic heritage. This presentation sought to counter wartime portrayals of Nikkei Buddhists as unassimilable adherents of a foreign religion associated with a recent wartime enemy. Significantly, the performance also challenged the cultural assimilation programs advocated by the US government during and immediately following World War II. These government programs advocated ethnic dispersal and assimilation into white middle-class Christian communities. Under these programs, Buddhists were pressured to downplay signifiers associated with Buddhism. In promoting Buddhism as part of their religious heritage, then, Nisei organizers also sought to claim for Buddhists basic protections of religious freedom guaranteed under the first amendment to the US Constitution. The struggle to associate with fellow Buddhists and practice Buddhist rituals and tradition was viewed by Nisei ministers and lay leaders not only in relation to the American democratic tradition of religious freedom, but also as a continuation of a longer Issei Buddhist tradition of *bukkyō tōzen,* or the eastward spread of Buddhism to the West.[4]

Buddhist festivals represented one among a number of religious and cultural sites wherein Nisei Buddhism, a new form of Shin Buddhist organization, practice, and identity, came to prominence among Nikkei Buddhists and in the American public consciousness in the years between World War II and the first two decades of the Cold War. During this period, Nisei Buddhism emerged as a complex, multifaceted set of adaptations to Shin Buddhism in America, to meet the changing social and spiritual needs of Nikkei Shin Buddhists.[5] Led by a new generation of Nisei leaders, the Buddhist Churches of America (BCA), representing Shin Buddhism in the United States and its affiliated churches and temples, adapted Buddhist cultural forms and practices, even as the organization worked to maintain core Shin Buddhist teachings. The Nisei imprint on Nikkei Shin

Buddhist communities emerged over time in a patchwork of organizations, programs, cultural and religious events, and activities.

Nisei Buddhism emerged during a period when American racial liberal ideology increasingly defined official US government policy on race relations, both at home and abroad.[6] In contrast to the virulent biological racism of the prewar years that had defined Japanese Americans as unassimilable aliens, racial liberals in the federal government, together with academics and mainstream media outlets, increasingly characterized Japanese Americans and other Asian American ethnic groups as assimilable yet racially distinct from white Americans.[7] Japanese Americans and other groups of Asian Americans actively engaged in the creation of this new racial image.[8]

As adherents of a non-Christian religious tradition with roots in Asia, Nikkei Buddhists faced both challenges and new possibilities, as they sought to claim Buddhism as part of their ethnic heritage. Racial liberal conceptions of cultural assimilation were shaped by sociological theories that had roots in earlier American missionary discourse, which emphasized conversion to Christianity as vital in bridging racial divides.[9] In this regard, the presence of Nikkei Buddhists disrupted imaginings of America not only as a white nation, but also as a Christian nation that was distinctly situated to uplift non-Christian groups in the United States as well as beyond its borders.[10] At the same time, religious tolerance emerged as a new touchstone for gauging national character, and global leadership, in the aftermath of the Nazi Holocaust and amid Cold War competition for hearts and minds, particularly in the decolonizing "third world."[11] Nisei Buddhism sought to bridge the gap between Christian nationalism and religious pluralism by, on the one hand, demonstrating cultural assimilation to American values and norms, while also, on the other, maintaining religious difference, claiming Buddhism as a part of an American tradition of religious freedom.

Even as they claimed Buddhism as ethnic American heritage, Nisei also presented Buddhism as a world religion and emphasized its global reach and importance. For many Nisei Buddhists, the identification of Buddhism as a world religious tradition was more than a rhetorical strategy for sustaining Buddhist communities in America. Indeed, Nisei extended their vision of the sangha (community of Buddhists) to include interested American "convert" Buddhists, Shin Buddhists in Japan with whom they reconnected, and lay Buddhists in South and Southeast Asia, whose efforts to build a global Buddhist movement challenged the emergent competing Cold War models of global integration established by the United States and Soviet Union.[12]

Shin Buddhism (Jōdo Shinshū), a Japanese development of Pure Land Buddhism founded by Shinran (1173–1263), was a branch of the Mahayana tradition.

In contrast to other Buddhist traditions, Pure Land Buddhism emphasized enlightenment after death, when one was reborn in Amida Buddha's Pure Land (Western Paradise). Central to Shin Buddhist practice was the recitation of the *nembutsu*, an expression of gratitude to the Amida Buddha. Shinran broke with the Japanese monastic tradition of his day by marrying and having children, and his disciples followed his example.[13] Shin Buddhist communities first developed in Hawaiʻi and North America in the late nineteenth century, following routes forged by Issei immigrants. In 1899, the North American Buddhist Mission (NABM) was established in San Francisco, California, as a branch of Nishi Honganji, one of two head temples for Shin Buddhism in Japan. Issei Shin Buddhist priests gave dharma talks, led ritual services on important Buddhist holidays, conducted funeral rites, and provided other social services for Buddhist communities. They also engaged in outreach with the general American public by providing classes on general Buddhism and publishing an English-language newsletter.[14]

The growth of an organized anti-Japanese exclusion movement during the early 1900s accelerated the process of Issei Buddhist family and community formation. Pressure from anti-Japanese exclusionists led to the creation of the Gentlemen's Agreement, arranged between the United States and Japan in 1907. Japan agreed to restrict new emigration of Japanese laborers, while the United States agreed to accept those Issei already in the United States and allow for the immigration of their spouses, children, and parents. Over the next two decades, the first wave of a second generation of Nisei children was born. The formation of Issei Buddhist families, together with the passage of the 1924 Immigration Act, which ended Asian immigration to the United States, increased pressure on Issei Buddhist institutions to introduce adaptations to meet the needs of Nisei while insulating Nikkei Buddhist communities from racial and religious discrimination.[15]

Raised within the bicultural world of Issei Buddhist churches and communities, Nisei were uniquely situated to usher in the transition from Issei to Nisei Buddhism. In contrast to Issei, who were banned from becoming naturalized citizens by US law, Nisei were American citizens by birth under the Fourteenth Amendment to the US Constitution. Most had been raised in local Buddhist churches and temples, where they attended Sunday Buddhist services, participated in Sunday School, and enrolled in Buddhist-sponsored Japanese-language schools. They joined their local Young Buddhist Associations and Buddhist sports leagues, formed Buddhist Scout troops, and took classes in Japanese cultural arts, ranging from *kendo* and other martial arts to *ikebana* (flower arrangement).[16] A small number of Nisei became Buddhist priests. Sent to Japan for ministerial training,

Nisei priests would come to play a critical role in bridging generational divisions among Nikkei and in serving as liaisons between Nikkei Buddhists and the general American public.[17]

Nisei Buddhist priests and lay leaders drew from their status as citizens and their bicultural upbringing in guiding Nikkei Buddhist communities through the wartime crises of forced incarceration and resettlement and into the postwar years, when these communities faced new challenges shaped by changing community demographics as well as emerging Cold War domestic and international politics. In their efforts to provide for evolving Nikkei communities, in introducing more Americans to Buddhist concepts and teachings, and in creating ties with Buddhists overseas, Nisei drew from their familiarity with American democratic traditions and the history and traditions of Issei Buddhism, as well as their contacts with Asian Buddhists, in crafting new adaptations to American Shin Buddhism.

Reorienting the Pure Land highlights points of continuity and divergence with the Issei Buddhism of the prewar years and contributes to the scholarly study of Nikkei Buddhist acculturation in America during the transwar period.[18] As with Issei Buddhism, the process of acculturation for Nisei Buddhism involved modifications to external forms of practice amid efforts to maintain core Shin Buddhists teachings. For Nisei, these efforts were complicated by a number of internal factors, including weakened ties with Shin Buddhists in Japan, a broadening language divide between Japanese-speaking Issei Shin ministers and a growing generation of Nisei and Sansei with limited or no Japanese-language skills, and by increased contact with American Buddhist "converts" and Asian Buddhists from other sects and traditions. At the same time, Nisei Buddhist acculturation was shaped by external factors. Most significant among these were American domestic and foreign policy.[19]

The story of Nisei Buddhism also contributes to the discussion of postwar Japanese Americans and of Buddhism in America. The focus on Buddhism highlights the largely overlooked impact of religion in shaping Japanese American postwar resettlement and the gradual acceptance and remaking of Japanese Americans into a "model minority." While Zen Buddhism would come to be embraced by countercultural figures as an alternative to American social and religious norms, Nisei Shin Buddhism was gradually accepted and promoted, by status quo elites, as a religion possessing teachings and "cultural" values comparable to Protestantism.

Finally, the focus on Nisei Buddhism as both a domestic and transnational development also contributes to recent studies that have sought to broaden Nisei histories beyond national boundaries. Nikkei Buddhists utilized emerging postwar transpacific economic and cultural exchange networks in embarking on spiritual journeys to Asia and in developing and promoting transpacific religious networks and community with Buddhists in Asia and other parts of the world.[20]

The chapters that follow trace the evolution of Nisei Buddhism in relation to the shifting needs of Nikkei Buddhist communities and in response to unfolding domestic and international developments as they engaged with shifting ideas about race and religious pluralism. The first two chapters examine the longer history of Shin Buddhism in America that would give rise to Nisei Buddhism. Chapter 1 examines the nascent roots of Nisei Buddhism that were cultivated within Issei Shin Buddhist communities, highlighting the role that Issei immigrants working with the Nishi Honganji head temple in Japan played in creating the North American Buddhist Mission (NABM) and in crafting new forms of Shin Buddhist affiliation in the United States.

Chapter 2 situates the rapid rise of Nisei Buddhist leadership during a period of wartime crisis, as Japanese Americans were forcibly removed and imprisoned in "assembly centers," run by the US military, and, later, in "internment camps" led by the War Relocation Authority (WRA), a US civilian agency under the Department of the Interior. The chapter examines Nisei Buddhist responses to WRA programs for the recruitment of American-born Nikkei for military service and for government sponsored "resettlement" programs. The WRA's policies, which stressed cultural assimilation, played a central role in the rapid rise of Nisei Buddhist leaders and influenced adaptations made to Buddhist organizations and programs. While Shin Buddhist teachings and rituals continued, many of the external cultural markers, particularly those that signified associations with Japan, were significantly modified.

Wartime Nisei-led adaptations to Buddhist organizations and programs continued to evolve from the resettlement period into the late 1940s. Chapters 3 through 5 consider the strategies adopted by Nisei-led Buddhist organizations and communities to meet their shifting needs, given the growing prominence of racial liberalism as well as debates over the sectarian orientation of the organization. Chapter 3 focuses on postwar efforts in the mid-to-late 1940s to link Nisei Buddhist martial patriotism and sacrifice to arguments for the inclusion of Buddhists through the memorialization of Nisei Buddhist soldiers. The chapter highlights how long-standing predominant understandings of America as a culturally Christian nation shaped struggles for Buddhist inclusion. The promotion of ethnic American Buddhism sought to broaden racial liberalism to include religious difference, thus challenging Christian conversion formulations that supported assimilationist programs for inclusion.

By the 1950s, the growing recognition of Shin Buddhism as an ethnic American religion that was part of a world religious tradition facilitated new domestic and international developments among Nisei Buddhists. Chapter 4 examines the early transition from Issei Buddhism to Nisei Buddhism through an examination of institutional and cultural politics of the Buddhist Churches of America (BCA) from the late 1940s through the 1950s. As Nisei rose to leadership positions within BCA, they were divided over how best to support and promote Nikkei Buddhist communities and Buddhism in America. A cohort of older Nisei, with stronger ties to the prewar Issei Buddhist community, emphasized Shin sectarianism as critical to the revitalization of Nikkei Buddhist communities. In contrast, a younger cohort of Nisei emphasized the importance of transmitting Buddhist teachings beyond the Shin Buddhist ethnic community in ways that would influence both Nikkei and the broader general public. The chapter considers the role that the rapid transformation of Japan—from wartime enemy to Cold War partner during the US occupation of Japan between 1945 and 1952—played in elevating the sectarianists within BCA. Growing recognition of Nikkei Buddhists as ethnic Americans facilitated BCA efforts to reconstitute ties with the Nishi Honganji head temple in Japan. Adapting racial liberalism to emerging Cold War political rhetoric, both BCA leadership and Nishi Honganji posited Shin Buddhism as in line with democratic values and anticommunism. By the 1950s, BCA introduced recruitment and funding campaigns for Shin-focused ministerial training programs. Coordinated efforts with the Nishi Honganji culminated in the founding in 1967 of the Institute of Buddhist Studies in Berkeley, California, the first graduate ministerial training center outside of Japan recognized by Nishi Honganji. Having lost the battle within the BCA, trans-sectarian advocates turned their energies toward the promotion of Buddhist study groups and in serving BCA's public relations departments, where they were best situated to interface with the general American public.

Chapter 5 extends the discussion of the domestic institutional development and cultural politics of Nisei Buddhism to a transpacific stage as Nisei participated in, and increasingly viewed themselves as part of, a broader Buddhist sangha that extended beyond the borders of the nation-state. The chapter first explores Nisei participation in the World Fellowship of Buddhists (WFB), an organization that grew during a period of rapid decolonization and postcolonial nation building and amid an increasingly polarized Cold War world. Led by Asian lay Buddhists in South and Southeast Asia, WFB sought to end systemic racial and religious discrimination, and promoted Buddhism as an alternative "middle path" during the Cold War. In presenting themselves as ethnic American "cultural ambassadors" on behalf of a long-standing Asian world religion, Nisei sought to serve as a bridge between the United States and Buddhists in Asia. The chapter next examines the extension of the sectarian impulse within Nisei Buddhism, as BCA lay leaders and members participated in 700th Memorial Services for Shinran, held in Kyoto, to reforge transpacific sectarian bonds. It argues that Shin Buddhist leaders in the United States and Japan viewed memorial services and the coordination of more than one thousand BCA members in a "pilgrimage" to Kyoto as an opportunity to reconstitute transpacific ties and resuscitate their respective institutions.

The final two chapters return to the US domestic context of the late 1950s to 1960s to consider diverging responses to a rapidly changing social and political landscape. The greater visibility and acceptance of Buddhism among the general American public contributed to greater social and spatial mobility, as Nisei Buddhists accessed higher-paying white-collar jobs and middle-class suburban housing, and joined in the postwar domestic family revival. In the face of these social and spatial shifts, Buddhist leaders and ministers' priorities shifted toward meeting the demands of its more widely dispersed communities and the growing needs of emerging Nisei Buddhist families. Chapter 6 examines BCA's family Buddhism programs, as a response to the spatial and life-stage demographic shifts of its members. Driven by concerns raised among older membership about a perceived breakdown of Buddhist community and "juvenile delinquency" among Buddhist teenagers, these programs sought to develop mentoring programs and provide forums for youth to address social issues.

Chapter 7 addresses debates revolving around Nisei Buddhism from the mid-1950s through the 1960s. The chapter examines competing visions of how the sangha was to be defined, and of the authenticity and politics of ethnic and family Buddhism. Both proponents of Nisei Buddhism and their critics were driven by varying responses to the Cold War domestic containment ideology. Nisei Buddhism and its various adaptations and programs came under increasing scrutiny and criticism, by white convert Buddhists and some Nisei, in the mid-to-late 1950s, who charged that programs in support of temple and family Buddhism departed from Buddhism's original tenets and practices.

By the 1960s, in the midst of social movements for racial and gender equality, antiwar protests, and critiques of the antidemocratic hierarchical nature of institutions, including religious ones, a new cohort of (often) younger progressive Nisei and Sansei activists, joined by convert Buddhists, began to question the Cold War racial liberalism at the heart of Nisei Buddhism. These critics pointed to BCA's complicity with Cold War policy in Vietnam and portrayed BCA leadership as patriarchal, authoritarian, and out of touch with the social changes that had transformed the United States. Inspired by the mass social movements for civil rights and women's rights, and the antiwar movements, non-ethnic and progressive groups of younger Nisei and Sansei increasingly sought to pressure Nisei Buddhist leadership to take a more critical position on US foreign policy and to undo the hierarchical and patriarchal style of BCA governance. While some sought to reform the organization, others decided to leave in search of more progressive communities in which to channel their social activism.

The story of Nisei Buddhism highlights the struggle of Japanese Americans for racial and religious inclusion during a period when the shift toward racial liberalism highlighted religion as a marker of racial difference. It presents the history of a Buddhist religious community that has often been overlooked in a society in which "American Buddhism" continues to be identified with white practitioners of an Asian religion. Most importantly, it highlights the continued central role of Shin Buddhism as a form of practice, and as a source of community and cultural identity, in the lives of Nikkei Buddhists.

CHAPTER ONE

Issei Buddhism to World War II

In a memoir published thirty years after her forced incarceration, Shinobu Matsuura recalled the turbulent and unsettling period at the end of World War II, when her family was released and returned to the small coastal town of Guadalupe, California. Matsuura noted, "Life was a continuous series of adversities and hapless worries. The camp was to close, so we were told to leave. Those who had a place to return to were fortunate, but few. Most were in daily apprehension and anxiety about where to go, what to do, and where to find jobs."[1]

Matsuura, an Issei (first-generation Japanese immigrant) Shin Buddhist, and her three American-born Nisei children had been imprisoned, without due process of law, in the spring of 1942 at the Gila River Relocation Center, a concentration camp run by the United States government and located thirty miles southeast of Phoenix, Arizona. Her husband, Issei Matsuura, an Issei Buddhist priest, had been arrested earlier by the FBI. Held in a series of Department of Justice prison camps, he was misdiagnosed with an ulcer. Suffering from what would later be revealed to be terminal cancer, he was finally allowed to rejoin his family two years later at Gila River.[2]

At war's end, the Matsuuras applied for a permit to return to Guadalupe. The War Relocation Authority (WRA), the US government agency charged with overseeing the camps, and later Nikkei resettlement, had initially denied their request on the grounds that racial tension in the town was high. Indeed, Buddhists faced sporadic episodes of violence as they returned to the West Coast to reestablish temples and communities. Yet WRA officials also distrusted Issei, whom the federal government had recently categorized as "alien enemies," and Buddhists, whom the WRA viewed as less assimilated, and thus less trustworthy, than Christians. Undaunted, Reverend Matsuura pleaded with officials to allow the family to return to Guadalupe. He explained that several hundred graves were there that had likely not been attended to for the past four years. The WRA eventually conceded, and the Matsuura family was allowed to board a train for Los Angeles. The family arrived at the deserted train stop late in the evening and walked to the local Buddhist temple, carrying a statue of Amida Buddha along with their few possessions. Shinobu Matsuura recalled, "We opened the altar, which had been nailed shut, and entered from the back. When we placed the Amida [Buddha] in the altar, our great relief and delight were emotions I shall never forget." Early the next morning, the family visited the cemetery. Matsuura recalled, "Voiceless voices beckoned to let us know that all of those buried there were awaiting our return, and we spent a peaceful and quiet time there with them."[3]

Shinobu Matsuura's story of her family's release provides some sense of what the world looked like from the perspective of Issei Shin Buddhists, who interpreted their experiences of uprooted and unsettled lives through the lens of Buddhist teachings and who sought to respond to their predicament through an affirmation of faith and gratitude in the Amida Buddha. At the same time, Matsuura's recounting reveals the level of uncertainty that revolved around the reestablishment of prewar Buddhist communities. Under what circumstances would Buddhists be allowed to reconstitute communities? How would the wartime legacy of racial and religious discrimination affect the plans for their reconstitution? What forms of congregation and religious practice would be deemed acceptable by the federal government and the American public? For Issei Buddhist priests and lay members, these vexing questions offered few clear answers. However, what most Issei and Nisei understood was that, by virtue of their status as American citizens and their bicultural upbringing, the American-born Nisei would play a critical role in efforts to reestablish Buddhist communities in postwar America.

This chapter examines the prewar history of Issei Buddhist immigrant communities up to World War II. The adaptations that would come to be associated with Nisei Buddhism were first discussed and debated in prewar Issei immigrant communities in response to racial and religious discrimination, questions revolving around biculturalism and national belonging, and as a generation of Nisei came of age. War between the United States and Japan upended Nikkei Buddhist communities, rapidly propelling Nisei to positions of leadership. In the weeks and months following the bombing of Pearl Harbor, the United States government and American press summoned the xenophobic and white settler-colonialist discourse of American Orientalism in raising the specter of Nikkei as a domestic "fifth column" threat from within. In doing so, the government relied on long-standing Western Orientalist constructions of Asians, including Asian immigrants, as a "yellow peril" threat to the American nation. Buddhism's "foreignness"—that is, its perceived cultural difference and distance from American Christianity—was highlighted in order to magnify this threat and justify forced removal and imprisonment.[4]

Nisei Buddhism first emerged in direct response to US-government-mandated forced relocation, incarceration, and resettlement policies between 1942 and 1945.

Figure 1.1. Shinobu Matsuura (top right), Issei Matsuura (center), and their five Nisei children. Reproduced courtesy of the Guadalupe Buddhist Church.

These policies thoroughly uprooted and disrupted Nikkei Buddhist communities. The attitudes toward Buddhists of the government officials placed in charge of these programs ranged from hostile to ambivalent. Many of these officials viewed Buddhism as an alien and foreign religion that was incompatible with American Christianity. As a result, they maintained a suspicion and distrust of Buddhists. In this climate, Nisei played a central role in advocating on behalf of Buddhist communities for time, space, and resources to carry on their activities.

Nisei leadership and Nisei Buddhism remained prominent during the equally challenging period of release and resettlement from the camps. As they planned for the rapid release and dispersion of Nikkei back into the general American populace, WRA officials, joined by civic and Christian charity organizations, defined "successful" mass resettlement through the lens of cultural assimilation. Nisei responded to WRA pressure to assimilate to white middle-class Christian norms by presenting themselves as ethnic American representatives of an Asian world religion that was in line with American political and religious values. The rise of Nisei among Shin Buddhist communities would have a profound impact on the form and content of Buddhist organizations and practice in the early postwar years.

Early Issei Buddhist Communities

Forged amid the crisis of World War II, the ideas, programs, and adaptations that would come to be associated with Nisei Buddhism first took root and germinated in Issei immigrant communities in Hawai'i and North America. In 1898, two Shin Buddhist priests—Reverend Eryu Honda and Reverend Ejun Miyamoto—arrived in San Francisco. A year later they founded the Hokubei Bukkyōdan or Buddhist Mission of North America (BMNA) as a branch office of the Nishi Honganji, one of two head temples for Shin Buddhism, located in Kyoto, Japan. The founding and establishment of a branch office resulted from the requests of small numbers of devout Issei Buddhist immigrants but also reflected the home temple's interest in *bukkyō tōzen,* or the eastward transmission of Buddhism through an engagement with Western audiences.[5]

A small group of Japanese laborers were recruited to work in the sovereign kingdom of the Hawaiian Islands in 1869. However, not until the 1880s did significant recruitment of Japanese immigrant labor begin in earnest. Between 1884 and 1894, approximately thirty thousand Japanese immigrants had arrived in North America as a result of demand for new sources of cheap agricultural labor created in the aftermath of the passage of a series of Chinese exclusion laws. By 1900, some 24,236 Japanese were living in the continental United States. A decade later, their numbers had risen to 72,157.[6]

The vast majority of Issei had emigrated from Hiroshima, Yamaguchi, Kumamoto and Fukuoka, four prefectures in Japan in which Jōdo Shinshū Buddhism predominated. Although smaller numbers of adherents from Jōdo, Kegon, Nichiren, Shingon, and Zen Buddhist sects were also present among early Issei communities, the sheer numbers of adherents ensured that Shin Buddhism had a disproportionate impact in the development of Issei Buddhism in America.[7] Shin Buddhism (Jōdo Shinshū), was a Japanese development of Pure Land Buddhism, a branch of the Mahayana tradition, founded by Shinran (1173–1263). Central to the Shin Buddhist tradition was the concept of a "mind of faith" (*shinjin, anjin*) and the associated practice of the *nembutsu,* the recitation of *"Namu Amida Butsu,"* translated as "I take refuge in the *Amida Buddha.*"[8]

As an adaptation to Japanese Shin Buddhism, Issei Buddhism developed in Hawai'i in the 1880s, and on the continental United States beginning in the 1890s, to meet the spiritual and social needs of Issei Buddhists. Early groups of Issei emigrated for various reasons, but many viewed themselves as sojourners in search of economic opportunity, with the goal of returning to Japan having accrued some savings. This *dekasegi* or sojourning mentality often aimed to improve one's economic and social condition back in Japan. Others were drawn by the prospects of greater political liberty. For these immigrants, the physical distance from Japan, together with America's democratic traditions, were viewed as creating a haven for political perspectives that were outside the mainstream of Meiji political culture.[9]

Shaped by an exploitative ethnic contract labor system and a *dekasegi* mentality among ordinary workers, early Issei immigrant society stood in stark contrast to the web of premigration social and religious networks that, for Buddhists, were rooted in local temples and maintained by resident priestly families. Devout Issei Buddhists communicated the absence of Shin Buddhism in their daily lives to the Nishi Honganji head temple in Kyoto.[10] In 1898, eighty-three Issei who resided in San Francisco, California, sent a petition to Abbot Myoyo Ohtani, head of Nishi Honganji, requesting the services of a Buddhist priest. An excerpt from their petition read,

> For those of us living in the United States, there is no possibility of basking in the Compassionate Life [Light] of Buddha. Not only are we unable to hear about the Buddhadharma in general, we are cut off from enlightenment through the Teaching of Jodo Shinshu. Thus, we are unable to understand and appreciate the heart and mind of Shinran Shonin.[11]

The sense of isolation expressed by these Issei reflected a spiritual separation from Shin Buddhist teachings that was magnified by the vastness of the Pacific Ocean and physical distance from Japan.

Compounding the sense of isolation was the predominance of Christian missionaries among early Issei immigrant communities. Drawing from their earlier experiences in Japan and among Chinese immigrant populations in the United States, Christian missionaries played an important role in the early formation of Issei immigrant communities. They and their denominations sponsored and worked with small groups of dedicated Issei Christians to provide housing, employment services, and English-language classes alongside Bible study and church services.[12]

Issei Buddhists responded by requesting similar resources from the Nishi Honganji home temple. When devout Shin Buddhist Nisaburo Hirano arrived in San Francisco in 1891, he reportedly received support from Methodist missionaries, accompanied by efforts to convert him. Hirano expressed gratitude to the missionaries for their services but refused to be baptized. Instead, he returned to

Japan in 1896 and appealed to Nishi Honganji to send Shin Buddhist missionaries to San Francisco. Hirano's efforts resulted in the deployment of the two Shin Buddhist missionaries Honda and Miyamoto to investigate conditions in 1898. That same year, Issei Buddhist immigrants in San Francisco formed a *Bukkyō Seinenkai* or a Young Men's Buddhist Association (YMBA) and petitioned Shin Buddhist institutions for support to develop parallel institutions and services for Buddhists. In doing so, Issei immigrants were engaging in Buddhist lay activities that mirrored the responses of Buddhists in Japan and South Asia to Christian missionary efforts by organizations like the Young Men's Christian Association.[13]

Nishi Honganji's decision to send Buddhist scholar-priests to San Francisco to establish a North American branch office was not solely in response to the requests of Issei immigrants; an equally significant factor driving the decision was the opportunity that a branch office would provide to engage with Western scholars and proselytize to a general American audience. Having experienced persecution during Japan's Meiji Restoration, Japanese Buddhist institutions viewed this engagement and related overseas missionary work as an important aspect in recovering institutional power in Japan.[14]

Along with other Buddhist institutions, Nishi Honganji sent scholar-priests on information-gathering trips to Europe and the United States beginning in the 1870s to learn more about Christianity in relation to Western society.[15] By the 1880s, Nishi Honganji was engaged in substantive reforms of Shin Buddhist institutions, rituals, and doctrine. It eliminated a hierarchical temple-ranking system and, in 1881, introduced a representative assembly (*shūe*). Following the model of a Western constitutional monarchy, the abbot remained the spiritual authority, while the *shūe* was tasked with administrative decisions. Meanwhile, Nishi Honganji was engaged in efforts to systematize Shin doctrine following Western academic approaches to the study of religion.[16] Efforts to engage with Western religious scholarship and to revise and reform Shin Buddhism in Japan were complemented by efforts to present Japanese Buddhism to the West. Scholars view the World's Parliament of Religions held in 1893 as the first major opportunity for Shin Buddhists (together with other Asian Buddhists) to reach a mass American audience.[17]

The first Issei Shin Buddhist priests to North America thus arrived with engagement in mind for both Issei Buddhist immigrants and Western theologians, scholars, and the general American public. Nishi Honganji sent some of its most promising scholar-priests to serve as superintendents (*kantoku*) in San Francisco beginning with Dr. Shūe Sonoda and Kakuryo Nishimura in September 1899. A graduate of Tokyo Imperial University, Sonoda was head of the Academy of Literature at the Bukkyō Daigaku (present-day Ryukoku University) prior to his arrival in San Francisco. Following his tenure as *kantoku,* Sonoda would go on to study in Germany before returning to Kyoto to serve as president of Bukkyō Daigaku. Nishimura was an ordained priest and former student of Sonoda's whose bilingual skills would prove invaluable in efforts to engage with the general American public.[18]

Sonoda and Nishimura engaged in a range of activities that supported Issei immigrants while addressing the interest of a broader American audience. On Saturdays, they presented sermons in Japanese for a Shin Buddhist audience. On Sundays they taught general Buddhism to European American audiences in the afternoon, followed by evening lectures in Japanese to a general Issei audience. Every other Thursday, they also held gatherings of the Buddhist Women's Association. Sonoda and Nishimura also oversaw the publication of both a Japanese language journal, *Beikoku bukkyō,* in 1900, and an English language journal, *The Light of Dharma,* from 1901 to 1906. The later publication drew from Shin Buddhist knowledge and engagement with Western scholarship in presenting Buddhism in ways that would appeal to American audiences.[19]

This approach by Issei Buddhist priests in North America—to support Issei immigrants while also engaging the general American public—would persist and have as much of an imprint on the form and content of Issei Buddhism as would emerging anti-Japanese sentiment. Rather than using terminology specific to Jōdo Shinshū, Issei Shin Buddhists adopted the term *bukkyōkai,* which they translated as "Buddhist church." As Michihiro Ama has explained, the naming of Nishi Honganji overseas branch offices reflected geopolitics that mirrored Japanese diplomatic relations. The Buddhist Mission in North America (BMNA) was designated by Kōyō Uchida, its fourth bishop, as *bukkyōkai,* a term devoid of the colonial or territorial designations assigned to branch offices in Japan's colonies in Asia, or in areas like Hawai'i and Siberia where Japan held imperial ambitions.[20]

From *Dekasegi* to Permanent Settlement

As a branch office of Nishi Honganji, BMNA was cognizant of its important informal cultural diplomatic role on behalf of Japanese Buddhism and the Meiji government. Even so, as Buddhist church and temple membership in the United States grew, Issei Buddhist immigrant communities would emerge as the primary force shaping BMNA's future activities and direction. BMNA's importance increased significantly after Issei began to settle roots in America in the midst of a rising anti-Japanese movement.

Between the 1910s and 1924, the *dekasegi* or sojourning mentality typical of many Issei gave way to calls by leaders for permanent settlement.[21] The shift toward permanent settlement emerged during a period of heightened anti-Japanese sentiment. A wide range of labor organizations including the American Federation of Labor and politicians throughout the West Coast targeted Japanese immigrants for exclusion and sought to marginalize their economic foothold. Nativists pointed to the sojourning mentality, together with cultural attributes including the non-Christian religious background of a majority of immigrants, as "proof" that the Japanese represented an unassimilable race. The early push for Japanese exclusion on the continental United States resulted in the Gentlemen's Agreement between the United States and Japan. Signed in 1907 the agreement limited Japanese migration to the continental United States to merchants, students, diplomats, and tourists, as well as parents, wives, and children of Japanese residents.[22]

The shift toward permanent settlement during a period of heightened anti-Japanese sentiment led to greater efforts among Issei Buddhist leaders to adapt and frame Buddhism in ways that would highlight its engagement with American religion and culture. Issei Buddhists selectively adopted rituals and practices to suit conditions in the United States. In contrast to Japan, where Buddhist services were conducted on Buddhist religious ceremonial days, Issei held regular Sunday services and Sunday School and, in areas with European American Buddhist sympathizers, held English-language services and study groups and special services and annual commemorative events for Sākyamuni.[23] In doing so, they were following prescriptions in the larger Issei community for *gaimenteki dōko,* a form of external assimilationist practice. Issei increasingly tried to conform to the practice following the Gentlemen's Agreement negotiated between the United States and Japan in 1907.[24] *Gaimenteki dōko* involved adopting white Anglo Saxon Protestant middle-class social norms including styles of dress, living arrangements, and adherence to prescribed gender roles. For Buddhists, *gaimenteki doko* also involved the incorporation of American religious and cultural practices such as observing the Sabbath as a day of rest and celebrating American national holidays, while eschewing external signifiers of Japanese culture.[25]

The centrality of Christianity to the rhetorical and performative adaptive strategies of Issei is unsurprising, considering that many of the allies of Japanese immigrants in America came from the ranks of Christian ministers and congregations. In the first two decades of the twentieth century, both white Christian ministers and Issei Christian converts increasingly emphasized cultural assimilation. They did so in response to both the shift in permanent settlement and a rising anti-Japanese exclusion movement, as well as in reaction to the growing presence of Buddhist missionaries in America.[26]

Shaped by the formation of Issei Buddhist communities, nativist anti-Japanese sentiment, and competition with white missionaries and Issei Christians, Issei

Buddhist adaptations were complex, involving, in Michihiro Ama's phrasing, acculturative processes of Japanization and Americanization. Thus, in addition to practices that reflected the *gaimenteki dōko* approach, Issei Buddhists also maintained recently developed traditions that underscored a modern Japanese Buddhist sensibility that corresponded with the Meiji state. They offered special services for Shinran while also celebrating imperial Japanese holidays marking the beginning of Emperor Jinmu's rule and the birthday of Emperor Meiji. Buddhist priests and lay leaders also played a central role in running Japanese-language schools, held after American public school and on Saturdays, where Nisei were taught the Japanese language and Japanese history and culture.[27]

While some modifications continued to be designed with Western audiences in mind, others reflected the centrality of an evolving membership of Issei Buddhist communities. As Tetsuden Kashima has explained, the expansion of networks of Issei Buddhist communities was premised on a cycle that began with the gathering of a critical mass of Issei, the founding of Bukkyō Seinenkais (Young Men's Buddhist Associations, YMBAs), the establishment of churches and temples, the arrival of more immigrants, and the additional founding of new Bukkyō Seinenkais.[28]

Issei Shin Buddhist priests and lay leaders adapted BMNA and its related organizations to the immigrant population, establishing a new pattern that diverged from the family-centered temples in Japan. To better coordinate among its churches, BMNA purchased land and built an institutional headquarters in San Francisco's Western Addition neighborhood in 1913. A year later, BMNA held its first general meeting of lay representatives and ministers. Approximately twenty-five temples or branch temples existed by that time. Representatives officially established BMNA and drafted a constitution.[29]

As it grew in complexity, in the midst of growing anti-Japanese sentiment in the United States, BMNA's relationship with Nishi Honganji also evolved. The home temple continued to play a central supporting role in the development of Issei Buddhism. Nishi Honganji selected BMNA's bishop (*kantoku*), sent matching funds to support an annual stipend for the bishop, and generally entrusted the bishop to serve as its representative and authority in North America.[30] It also trained and approved the assignments of most Buddhist priests to America. In contrast to Japan, where local temples were managed and held by a single family and passed on for generations from father to son, temples and churches in the United States employed Buddhist priests who had volunteered to minister overseas. Many served for a limited time before returning to Japan, where they might serve in a family temple, as a traveling minister, or retire. New ministers would be sent to the United States, and the cycle would begin again. These ministers relied on Nishi Honganji for sponsorship for their visas, which became essential after the Gentlemen's Agreement in 1907.[31]

Over time, several factors increased the self-dependence of local Buddhist membership in ways that were distinct from temples in Japan. Distance from the head temple and from local temples in Japan, the logistics of operating within the legal jurisdiction of the United States, and a complex and evolving immigrant community meant that priests and lay leaders were ever reliant on a dedicated membership to maintain the vibrancy of local temples and churches.[32] Issei priests were also beholden to their members, who were critical for raising funds and providing voluntary support for the ministers and the temple. Church funds were raised in a variety of ways. Churches collected regular membership dues and language-school fees from enrolled students. In addition, organizations like the Fujinkai or Women's Auxiliary Organization and Young Buddhist Associations (YBAs) collected membership dues.[33] Buddhist ministers were also paid for conducting funeral and memorial services, but as they were salaried by their local churches, the funds that they earned went directly to their churches.

The Issei Buddhist Roots of Nisei Buddhism

From the 1920s to World War II, Issei Buddhism was increasingly influenced by the growing presence of an American-born Nisei generation, and the roots of what would become Nisei Buddhism were cultivated in this environment. Issei grappled with how their institutions, organizations, and rituals could be adapted in ways that would meet the emerging needs of the Nisei even as they continued to serve Issei. Nisei were increasingly viewed as representing the future of Buddhism in America as the anti-Japanese exclusion movement grew in strength. In 1922, the US Supreme Court ruled, in *Ozawa vs. the United States,* that the plaintiff, Takeo Ozawa, could not become a naturalized citizen, based on his race. After the passage of the 1924 Immigration Act, which ended immigration from Japan, many Issei Buddhists increasingly viewed the Nisei as key to their future in America.[34]

Concern about Nisei among Issei Buddhists first emerged amid the formation of families that grew in the aftermath of policies encouraged by the 1907 Gentlemen's Agreement, which led to the arrival of Issei family members and "picture brides." By 1912, Issei educators in California had shifted from an emphasis on preparing Nisei for returning to Japan to preparing them for a life in the United States.[35] From the late 1920s to the 1930s, similar concerns among Issei Buddhists about the growing Nisei membership led to programs designed to better facilitate the transmission of Shin and general Buddhist teachings to Nisei as well as the general American public. In 1927, BMNA's Bishop Hōshō Sasaki required recently arrived Buddhist priests from Japan to enroll in English-language training programs.[36] Upon his arrival to the United States in 1930, Sasaki's successor Bishop Kenju Masuyama, a former professor from Ryukoku University, began recruiting the first generation of Nisei for the priesthood. Among those Nisei sent to Japan for training were Kenryu Kumata who would play a critical role as public relations director during World War II.[37]

The institutional vision, programs, strategies, and teachings that would come to be associated with Nisei Buddhism from the 1940s forward were first inculcated in Issei Buddhist-sponsored temples, churches, and organizations. As David Yoo has explained, given the persistence of racial discrimination and segregation, Buddhist temples and affiliated organizations were important in forging social ties and a sense of community and belonging among an emerging Nisei subculture. Nisei first encountered both Buddhist teachings and social networks in Sunday School and Japanese-language school classes.[38] For many young Bussei (Nisei Buddhists) Japanese-language school and Sunday School served as a place for socializing and identifying as bicultural in an environment free of anti-Japanese sentiment. Despite the additional hours of schooling, students often looked forward to attending Buddhist-sponsored school programs. For Hiroshi Kashiwagi, who attended language school in the small town of Penryn, outside of Sacramento, California, Japanese-language school was a space where he could feel comfortable with his Japanese cultural heritage. He recalled,

> For most of us we did our required lessons, but it was a less pressurized respite from our regular school. Even our lunches were different. On Saturdays my mother would pack my lunch of *onigiri* (rice ball) or *makizushi* (sushi roll) or leftover *okazu* (cooked meat and vegetables) and other Japanese dishes I wouldn't dare take to the American school. These lunches made Saturday school special.[39]

In the decade prior to the US entry into World War II, an adapted form of Shin Buddhism had become an established and central facet of Japanese American life. An internal report from 1931 noted that the Buddhist Mission of North America oversaw thirty-three Buddhist temples, as well as numerous branch temples. Fifty-nine BMNA Buddhist priests ministered to 11,757 registered members, and 332 Sunday School teachers taught 6,874 Nisei students. Another 1,875 older Nisei were members of the YBA, and 3,308 women were members of the Fujinkai or Ladies Auxiliary.[40]

If Sunday Schools and Japanese-language schools were a point of entry into a Nisei Buddhist subculture, the Young Buddhist Associations were, in David Yoo's words, "the primary vehicles for drawing Nisei." Founded in the late nineteenth century by Issei immigrants, by the 1920s and 1930s they had been transformed into primarily Nisei organizations as the American-born generation came of age. During the 1920s, under the leadership of the Reverend Herbert Tansei Terakawa, various young men's and young women's Buddhist organizations formed leagues and united, first as the YMWBA and later as the YBA.[41]

YBA leagues initiated a tradition of regional and statewide conferences that allowed Nisei to develop social ties as well as a deeper understanding of Shin Buddhism. Nisei Buddhists turned to social networks and religious faith, while also invoking America's founding documents, in reconciling their bicultural and non-Christian background with American society. In the face of continued racial and religious discrimination, they argued that America's tradition of religious tolerance meant that Buddhism and American national identity were not irreconcilable.[42]

War and the Rise of Nisei Leadership

World War II had a profound and lasting impact on the political and social dynamics of Nikkei Shin Buddhist communities, setting them on a path that would lead to ascendance of Nisei leadership and the emergence of Nisei Buddhism. US government policies that racially profiled individuals using religious affiliation, along with other signs of ethnic criteria deemed suspect, resulted in the segregation of much of the Issei Buddhist clergy and lay leadership for the duration of the war. In this setting, a small number of Nisei Buddhists priests along with Nisei lay leaders quickly rose to prominent positions of leadership and initiated programs for what they called the Americanization of Buddhism.

The bombing of Pearl Harbor on December 7, 1941, by Imperial Japan, and the US declaration of war the following day, resulted in the severing of all ties between the Nishi Honganji head temple and BMNA for the duration of the war and into the early postwar period. As discussed earlier, institutional ties were important not only because BMNA relied primarily on trained Issei priests from Japan but also because Nishi Honganji and its head abbot were respectively the institutional and religious authority for both Issei priests and lay leaders.[43] In addition to undermining the major source of their cultural and religious authority, the wartime policies of the US government, in combination with the historic status of

Issei as "aliens ineligible for citizenship," immediately affected first-generation Issei. BMNA's Issei bishop, priests, and lay leaders were all legally categorized as alien residents. Franklin Roosevelt's Presidential Proclamation No. 2525 effectively designated all "natives, citizens, denizens or subjects of the Empire of Japan being fourteen years and upwards, who shall be within the United States, or within any territories in any way the jurisdiction of the United States and not actually naturalized" as "alien enemies," and severely restricted their movements. Meanwhile, the US Treasury Department froze Issei bank accounts and canceled licenses of Issei-owned businesses.[44]

Proclamation 2525 also authorized the attorney general and secretary of war to conduct interrogations and arrests of suspected alien-enemies. Government arrests of Issei relied on a government compiled "ABC list" of some two thousand Japanese that included Buddhist priests and lay leaders. According to Tetsuden Kashima, the creation of the list was probably first initiated by the Office of Naval Intelligence (ONI) in 1938. The FBI and the Department of Justice had compiled similar lists prior to World War II. As Duncan Williams noted, the ONI issued a report that it shared with the FBI, army intelligence, and the State Department just days before the bombing of Pearl Harbor that "emphasized Buddhism as an alien religion whose entire leadership collectively posed a threat to national security."[45]

As a result of the presidential proclamation and the use of the ABC list, from the end of 1941 through the first two months of 1942, Issei Buddhist priests and lay leaders were among those who were targeted and arrested in sweeps coordinated by the FBI, ONI, and the Department of Justice.[46] Curiously, BMNA's bishop and priests in San Francisco and Oakland were not arrested; however, identification as a Buddhist combined with other activities such as membership in a suspected organization or status as a Japanese-language instructor raised the chances of becoming targeted. Those arrested were taken to nearby city or county jails before being sent to "enemy alien" detention facilities.[47] Amid the arrests, rumors began to spread among Japanese American communities that all Issei would be incarcerated in prison camps.[48]

As FBI raids continued on the West Coast of the United States, and later as President Roosevelt and other policy makers began to debate and then develop plans for movement and imprisonment, sensationalized stories portraying Nikkei as part of an invading "fifth column" appeared in major daily newspapers across the country. Buddhist affiliation was one among a number of characteristics offered as "evidence." A series of raids covered by major newspapers, conducted near Monterey, California, in early February 1942, showcased unsubstantiated associations created by the FBI and the media in efforts to link Japanese ancestry and Buddhism with a "fifth column" in the minds of the American public. The FBI, working together with US Naval Intelligence and local and county law enforcement, raided Buddhist temples along with Japanese American homes, businesses, and workplaces. Following the raid of Ellis H. Spiegl's ranch in Chualar, California, and the arrest of Japanese American foreman Shunso Matsuda, Nat J. L. Pieper, chief of the San Francisco office of the FBI, described the ranch as "the mystery Japanese colony of the Pacific" and named Matsuda the "Emperor of Chualar."[49] Similarly, the *New York Times* described the federal government's raids of Japanese "colonies" as intended "on preventing a repetition of Pearl Harbor in Northern California." The *Times* noted, "Buddhist temples did not escape the F.B.I. raiders. In one, which yielded an assortment of items including maps and radios as well as microphones and mimeograph machines used to conduct services and produce newsletters, the Rev. Koyo Tamanaka, 43, and the Rev. Bunyu Fujimura and the Rev. Hoshin Fujikado, both 32 were arrested."[50]

A month later, FBI raids of a Japanese American club in Los Angeles were justified by the FBI and the press by alleged connections to spies for the ultranationalist Kokuryūkai or Black Dragon Society, which had long been associated in the American press with the activities of Buddhists in Japan. The *New York Times* described the Black Dragon Society as "an organization of Buddhist priests and Japanese army officers so powerful that it even threatened Prince Konoye when that statesmen was making peace overtures to this country in the pre-war days." Nat J. L. Pieper claimed that those arrested in the raids admitted that they had been members of the organization. The *New York Times* claimed that the society operated on the Pacific Coast in connection with the LA-based Tokyo Club, which "has had an unsavory reputation in Los Angeles. One of the prisoners Kyashi Uyeda served five years in San Quentin for a killing at the club."[51] In his study, *Judgement without Trial,* Tetsuden Kashima found no evidence of Issei or Nisei joining the organization, nor evidence to indicate that the Black Dragon Society was a viable organization in the United States.[52]

In the midst of the freezing of Issei assets and cancellation of their business licenses, mass arrests of Issei priests, and increasingly xenophobic media coverage, Nisei Buddhist priests and lay leaders quickly emerged to play a prominent leadership role. Reverend Kenryo Kumata, a Nisei Buddhist priest, was hastily chosen to serve as the public relations director and spokesperson on behalf of BMNA. Part of a small cohort of Nisei Shin Buddhist priests who received training as a result of the efforts of Bishop Masuyama in the 1930s, Kumata was relatively inexperienced in administration at the time of his appointment. He had served as a resident priest at the Hongwanji Buddhist Temple in Los Angeles and as executive secretary of the National Young Buddhist Association.

Kumata consulted and formed ties with the Japanese American Citizens League (JACL), hiring Saburo Kido, JACL's attorney, and inviting executive secretary Mike Masaoka to a series of YBA emergency meetings to seek his advice and to stay updated on ongoing government decision making regarding the fate of Japanese Americans. Prior to the war, JACL comprised primarily middle-class professionals, most of whom were Christian, and rose steadily in influence during the period from an outlier organization with little influence among Nikkei to one with a prominent role as liaison to US military and government officials. The organization's unflinching dedication to unconditional loyalty and martial patriotism ensured that its rise was not without controversy.[53]

Between January and March of 1942, Kumata produced bulletins for the mainstream press and for Nikkei Buddhist communities. Under orders from ONI, BMNA communications and newsletters were submitted to both ONI and the FBI. Kumata's speedy transition from young resident priest to public relations spokesman on behalf of BMNA foreshadowed the critical role that citizenship and bilingual and bicultural background would play over the course of the war.[54] In public rallies, addresses, and publications, as well as through internal community bulletins, Nisei Buddhists emphasized their status as American citizens and loyalty to their country of birth.[55]

In January and February 1942, Young Buddhist Association leaders in California called a series of emergency meetings in which they discussed incorporation of BMNA headquarters and all member Buddhist temples as nonprofit religious entities with the state of California. With BMNA funds frozen, participants agreed that major Nisei-led organizations including the National Young Buddhist Federation, the California Young Buddhist League, the Sunday School Federation, and two other regional YBA district organizations would need to pool their resources in order for BMNA policies and programs to continue to carry on basic functions.[56]

The movement toward incorporation of BMNA under the names of Nisei and the funding of BMNA by Nisei organizations begged the question of the standing of Issei leadership, a question that would be addressed only gradually as the war progressed. During the February emergency meeting, Nisei were divided over the issue, with some arguing that "actual administration" should be conducted "by those with American citizenship."[57] Reverend Kumata was one of the strongest proponents of this position, arguing that transfer of administration meant that Nisei would be responsible for the continued propagation of Shin Buddhism. Kumata noted that an "Americanization program" required affiliated churches to "incorporate under Nisei name, where such has not been done previously" and, further, "that the actual running responsibilities of their local churches must be borne by the citizen believers."[58]

As Nisei Buddhist leaders proclaimed loyalty and promoted the transference of leadership, Buddhist members sought to distance themselves from religious practices and artifacts that might drive suspicion from an increasingly hysterical American media and public. During the months following the onset of war, some Buddhists began attending Christian religious services. Temples removed Buddhist religious symbols such as the *manji,* which resembled but predated the Nazi swastika from their buildings.[59] Meanwhile concerned that Japanese Buddhist religious items would target them as enemies, some Nikkei burned Buddhist sutras or concealed cherished *butsudan* (family home altars).[60]

Efforts to transfer administration of Issei Buddhist institutions to Nisei would prove critical, as the Issei Buddhism that had existed prior to the war as a flexible, transnational strategy for both acculturation and cultural retention was rendered impossible by the war.[61] President Franklin Roosevelt implemented a series of measures targeting those of Japanese ancestry and leading to the forced movement and incarceration of more than 110,000 people, two-thirds of whom were American citizens by birth. Meanwhile, government officials and the national media continued to reference Buddhism along with other aspects of Japanese culture in representing Japanese Americans as an alien-enemy race. The racialization of Buddhism and the characterization of those of Japanese ancestry as un-American and racially suspect was then utilized to justify the wartime forced removal and incarceration.[62]

CHAPTER TWO

Forced Incarceration, Resettlement, and the Rise of Nisei Buddhism

As Nikkei were corralled into the War Department's Wartime Civil Control Administration (WCCA) "assembly centers," from March to August of 1942, fears of racial and religious persecution spread among Buddhists. Buddhists were forbidden to maintain aspects of their religious rituals and practices, and many were understandably hesitant to engage in permitted activities. As Duncan Williams explained, "the WCCA barely tolerated the practice of Buddhism, and [it] banned groups associated with State Shinto completely," despite an official policy against religious discrimination. WCCA staff monitored religious activities and camp newsletters, and some managers censored announcements of religious services. The absence of Issei Buddhist priests and lay leaders was compounded by WCCA policies banning spoken Japanese and books printed in the Japanese language, including Buddhist sutras and service books, which affected Issei Buddhist services. Only Christian sacred and service books were excepted from the ban on written material in the Japanese language, a fact that signaled the WCCA's suspicion of non-Christian Nikkei.[1]

By the summer of 1942, Nikkei were transferred from the WCCA centers to more permanent internment "camps." In these camps, under the authority of the War Relocation Authority (WRA), a majority of internees would be held for the duration of the war. It was within the context of imprisonment in WRA camps that Nisei Buddhists first ascended to positions of formal leadership. Under the WRA, Buddhism was more tolerated than in the WCCA centers. In response to repeated requests of laypersons, Buddhists were provided with some space to carry on limited activities. The WRA permitted religious activities to be conducted by leaders of all faiths in August 1942. Under the watchful eye of the WRA, Buddhists were also allowed to organize services, hold Sunday School and Japanese-language school, conduct funeral services, and print newsletters for circulation in the camps. Given limited space, the WRA strongly encouraged the various Buddhist sects to form united "federations" of Buddhist organizations. While some efforts to form trans-sectarian organizations were made, these organ-

Figure 2.1. Buddhist funeral, Manzanar Buddhist Church, circa 1943–1946. Reproduced courtesy of the Shizuko and Shigenori Oiye Collection, Densho Digital Repository.

izations often broke down. Most Buddhists formed parallel congregations utilizing shared space at different times for services, meetings, and events.[2]

Even as they tolerated Buddhism, over the course of the period of forced incarceration and the period of "resettlement" that followed, WRA officials increasingly demarcated Buddhism as a marker of suspect loyalty. Driven by wartime priorities, US government policy during the incarceration period shifted from one driven by "vulgar racism" to one motivated by "polite racism," to use Takashi Fujitani's phrasing. The new emphasis on racial liberalism occurred within the context of propaganda battles with the Axis powers, and Japanese co-prosperity propaganda in particular. The Office of War Information (OWI) came to view Nikkei internment as a public relations problem, even as key figures in the Roosevelt administration grew increasingly worried about the constitutionality of confinement.[3] As a result, the US government sought to transform its concentration camps from spaces of confinement to "rehabilitative" spaces designed to prepare Nikkei, in accordance with white Christian middle-class cultural norms, for re-entry into the American nation. The WRA followed, in Mae Ngai's words, "a kind of benevolent assimilation which used cultural assimilation to both measure and produce Japanese Americans' loyalty."[4]

By early 1943, the WRA was actively preparing for the postwar closing of the internment camps. By this time, both civilian and military officials placed in charge of Nikkei had shifted their official view of the Japanese in America from an unassimilable, biologically differentiable race to an ethnic group who were best assessed for loyalty on an individual basis.[5] What came to be known as the program of "resettlement" involved WRA promotion of the eastward dispersal of Japanese Americans from the camps. President Roosevelt and key WRA leaders, including WRA director Dillon Myer, viewed dispersal of Japanese Americans and cultural assimilation to Christian European American middle-class norms as key to solving the "Japanese problem" of resettlement.[6]

The WRA issued a loyalty questionnaire for leave clearance that favored Nisei Christians and other characteristics that they associated with cultural assimilation. The questionnaire, and two questions in particular—Q27, expressing a willingness to serve in the armed forces or WAAC, and Q28, swearing unqualified allegiance to the United States—proved contentious among Nikkei. For Issei, question 28 violated international law because it would leave them stateless citizens. Officials later changed the wording to asking whether they would "abide by" American law. Service in the armed forces and WAAC also divided Nikkei. Some groups, such as members of the Japanese American Citizens League, had advocated for military service as proof of loyalty. Many who were ambivalent or opposed to military service questioned making the ultimate sacrifice for a government that had forcibly imprisoned them without due process of law.[7]

The WRA's questionnaire served as the basis for a point system that presumed to ascertain the loyalty of each Nikkei individual. The questionnaire's assessment of loyalty was based on the faulty reasoning and cultural bias inherent in formulas created to assess the cultural assimilation of internees. As Eric Muller has shown, religious background was one among a number of significant factors considered in filtering out those the WRA deemed suspect. Those who identified as Christian received two additional points, whereas those who identified as Buddhist received one less point. Meanwhile, Shintoists were automatically rejected from consideration. Both the point system and the color-coded system that replaced it five months later—which similarly elevated Nisei Christians and other markers the government associated with cultural assimilation—served as the basis for the government's early leave clearance policy.[8] The religious bias inherent in the point system had the effect of providing preferential early release to Christians over Buddhists and other non-Christian groups.

The government's preferential view and treatment of Christian Nisei also appeared in propaganda efforts to promote Japanese American resettlement to the general American public. In 1944, the WRA, in coordination with the Office of War Information and Office of Strategic Services, produced the short film, *Challenge to Democracy*. Scenes of life in the concentration camps along with a narrated story about Japanese Americans that highlighted their patriotism and potential for assimilation into the general American society were presented. In discussing religion, *Challenge to Democracy* suggested that the camps promoted freedom of religion and that Japanese were choosing to convert to Christianity. The film noted that "most of the alien Japanese are Buddhist but almost half their American born children belong to some Christian denomination [such as] Catholic, Methodist [or] Presbyterian." This was despite the fact that, "except for State Shinto, involving Emperor worship, there [was] no restriction on religion in relocation centers."[9]

The film's exaggerated claim of rates of conversion to Christianity was intended to assure viewers that American-born Japanese were increasingly assimilated to white Christian norms. Meanwhile, in preparing internees for resettlement, the WRA actively discouraged Buddhists from congregating in large numbers and sought to restrict their activities to religious rather than social meetings.[10]

The WRA's policy of cultural assimilation established middle-class Christian Nisei citizens with few ties to Japan or Japanese culture as a normative model by which each individual's "loyalty" was gauged and assessed for "successful" reentry and acceptance into American society. Still, directors of the various WRA camps understood that significant numbers of the incarcerated continued to identify as Buddhist, and that they needed to prepare them for release. Short of Christian conversion, which most WRA officials would likely have preferred, Buddhists were charged with demonstrating cultural assimilation by distancing themselves from external signifiers of Japanese culture.

At the same time, WRA recognition of its Buddhist constituency created space for Nisei to push the boundaries of WRA policies to include a cultural ambassador role on behalf of Buddhism. A small handful of Nisei Buddhist priests together with Bussei (Nisei Buddhist) lay leaders were hastily elevated to the forefront of Shin Buddhist leadership. Their efforts to preserve BMNA and its affiliated networks of churches, temples, and organizations would usher in institutional reforms, programs, and adaptations that I have identified in this book as central to Nisei Buddhism. With the WRA driving the message to prepare for the closing of the camps, Buddhist lay leaders including two Nisei, Reverend Kenryo Kumata and Tadashi (Tad) Hirota, were instrumental in initiating plans for the organization of a national postwar Buddhist association that could maintain control of BMNA's property and assets in order to aid in the resettlement of Japanese American Buddhists.

Reverend Kumata and Hirota were well positioned to lead the push for a post-war Nisei-driven Buddhist movement. Both served at the Topaz War Relocation Center on the center's Interfaith Council and were recognized and respected among Nisei Buddhist circles. As discussed earlier, Reverend Kumata had been hastily promoted as BMNA spokesperson following the bombing of Pearl Harbor. Hirota volunteered for Military Intelligence School at Camp Savage, Minnesota, while Kumata volunteered to serve as a chaplain for the 442nd Regimental Combat Team, which was in the process of being formed. As one of the few bilingual Nisei priests, Kumata was frequently asked to conduct services and to serve as a guest speaker for Buddhist-sponsored events. Hirota was also bilingual, having developed a fluency in conversational Japanese as a result of speaking Japanese at home and attending Japanese language school.[11] Hirota had long served in prewar and wartime YBA leadership positions and was elected as president of the emergency organization. He was described in the Topaz internment camp paper *Bussei Life* as "a well-known and popular Bussei."[12] The cover of the August 29, 1943, issue of *Bussei Life* featured a sketch of Hirota and his new bride Hisako Kuroiwa, followed by a description of the Buddhist wedding service, which was performed by Reverend Kumata.[13]

Working with the assistance and support of Issei Bishop Matsukage, a handful of Buddhist priests, and a large contingent of Nisei lay leaders, Reverend Kumata and Hirota relied heavily on the social and religious networks that they had developed in the prewar years through the YBAs. Indeed, during planning for reorganization, many Nisei leaders viewed the YBAs as the foundation for the development of a new national Buddhist organization that would replace BMNA.

In May 1943, Buddhists from WRA relocation centers as well as those located in "free zones"—which included Ogden, Salt Lake City, and Longmont, Utah, and Denver and Fort Lupton, Colorado—were permitted to organize a five-day conference in Salt Lake City.[14] Free zone YBAs had been reconstituted through the efforts of Kumata and Hirota, working with the Japanese American Citizens League (JACL) and with the approval of the WRA.[15] Seventy-eight delegates attended the emergency meeting to determine the future direction of BMNA's Japanese American Buddhist temples and churches in the United States. Bussei officers and lay leaders, together with Buddhist priests from the ten WRA relocation centers and seven free-zone chapters, were joined by representatives of the WRA, Christian organizations, and the JACL.[16]

Buddhist leaders were under pressure to remake BMNA and its affiliated temples, churches, and organizations in a way that addressed the WRA's emphasis on cultural assimilation. In doing so, they had to balance efforts to maintain aspects of what had largely been an Issei Buddhist organization with the constraints placed on them by the WRA. As discussed earlier, war and US government policy had an indelible impact on the ability of BMNA to maintain its Issei character. Ties with the Japanese home institution were cut off by the war, and Issei remained categorized as "alien enemies," with many Issei priests and lay leaders imprisoned in separate DOJ and military prison camps. Meanwhile, WRA's preference for culturally assimilated Nikkei in their release programs meant that Issei Buddhists faced greater challenges in being granted leave and reestablishing themselves. Even those Nisei Buddhists the WRA viewed as relatively culturally assimilated, such as Kumata and Hirota, continued to be marked as more suspect and intrinsically un-American in both WRA's assessment and among the general public because they identified as Buddhist. As a result, Nisei Buddhist leaders were expected to report to government officials both to expedite the transition and resettlement of Japanese American Buddhist communities and to assure that individuals and communities were following the directions of government officials.

Working within these constraints, Nisei Buddhist representatives to the May 1943 meeting elected Hirota to serve as president of the emergency group, drafted proposals for the resettlement plans of Buddhists, and submitted their plans for approval by WRA administrators. Emergency meeting representatives proposed the creation of a new national Buddhist headquarters. The headquarters would serve as a coordinating office for the various Young Buddhist Associations located in both the internment camps and the free zones. The headquarters would report directly to WRA officials; it was tasked with creating awareness of Buddhism in the Midwest and eastern United States, in communities where the WRA approved Japanese American resettlement. At the same time, it would work to develop group and individual contacts beyond the Japanese American Buddhist community and through the compilation and publication of religious material related to Buddhism. The Buddhist headquarters was initially housed at the Topaz camp, with Reverend Kumata serving as its director. Kumata was charged with resettling the headquarters in Ogden, Utah, shortly thereafter.[17]

Significantly, representatives to the meeting sought to clarify the sectarian orientation of the national headquarters. As discussed earlier, because a majority of Japanese immigrants to the United States were affiliated with Nishi Honganji, BMNA's prewar churches and temples had often served communities that included smaller numbers of members of other schools of Japanese Buddhism including Higashi Honganji, another denomination of Jōdo Shinshū, along with members affiliated with the Zen, Nichiren, and Shingon schools. Separation of ties with Nishi Honganji and tensions that emerged under pressure from the WRA to form transsectarian camp services help to illuminate why delegates at the emergency meeting sought to affirm the sectarian nature of the headquarters and its affiliated

Figure 2.2. Reverend Kenryo Kumata, Ogden, Utah, circa 1940s. Reproduced courtesy of the Umeyo Sakagami Collection, Densho Digital Repository.

organizations.[18] Delegates proposed that the organization be "primarily Shinshu." At the same time, it was to be "broad enough to welcome any group using the *onembutsu*." This technically could include Higashi Honganji and Jōdo Shu schools. While affirming sectarian orientation, leaders noted that their sectarian orientation did not "restrict any [Buddhist] group from uniting." Delegates also mentioned cooperation with Reverend Julius Goldwater's nonsectarian Buddhist Brotherhood of America. Goldwater had been affiliated with BMNA prior to the war. While serving as caretaker for the Los Angeles Nishi Honganji temple on behalf of interned BMNA leaders, he began to form his own organization during the war.[19]

Even as delegates emphasized the Shin Buddhist orientation of the organization, they also emphasized Buddhism as a world religion in their engagements with the general American public. In doing so, they could draw from BMNA's history dating back to its inception of presenting general Buddhist tenets to the American public. Yet, they also did so under the conditions of forced confinement and the watchful eyes of WRA administrators. In June, WRA director Dillon Myer wrote to Reverend Kumata to signal his approval of the plans drawn up at the emergency meetings. He noted, "We appreciate your offer to cooperate with the War Relocation Authority and other federal agencies and national organizations in carrying out the relocation program, and wish you every success in your work."[20]

Charles Ernst, director of the Topaz internment camp, stated that the WRA had "signaled its willingness and its desire to cooperate with leaders of the Buddhist Church in their plans for providing opportunities for persons who relocate from the centers to continue their worship as Buddhists." More open-minded than many of his fellow administrators, Ernst framed resettlement of Buddhists to the midwestern and eastern United States as an opportunity for the spread of Buddhism. Ernst noted, "Americans living in these sections of the United States know very little about the Japanese or about Buddhism." As a result, "men and women of character and courage are having their chance to now introduce themselves to America." Ernst concluded that "the extension of persons of the Buddhist Faith and the extension of the relocation of persons of Japanese ancestry will go hand in hand in the joint effort to develop a stronger America."[21]

Most administrators were not as supportive. Instead, they encouraged dispersion and distance from anything that would cast suspicion on the resettlers, including traditional Japanese culture and religion. Thus, despite their insistence on maintaining the sectarian character of the Shin institution and affiliated organizations, Nisei lay leaders and priests presented Buddhism to the WRA and the general public as a modern world religion that was compatible with American values and deserving of the protections of religious freedom under the US Constitution. When a reporter who was invited to visit the Rohwer WRA center in the summer of 1943 described Buddhism as comparable to "the neo-paganism which the Nazi's have devised to oust the Christian faiths in Germany," a *Rohwer Outpost* columnist (using the initials B. S., likely *Outpost* editor Barry Saiki) responded that Buddhism was "neither neo-pagan in concept nor an outgrowth of totalitarian beliefs. It is rather a spiritual belief, based upon the teachings of Buddha, who was born in India roughly about 2,400 years ago." The editorial continued, "As an international religion, Buddhism ranks in the numbers of adherents with Christianity and Mohammedanism. As a philosophy, it is recognized by some of the greatest minds in the world today." The editorial argued that the temples and altars used by Buddhists were comparable to those used by Catholics and likened Buddhism's Eight-Fold Path to the Ten Commandments. The editorial concluded,

> A majority of the Center people profess Buddhism as their creed and it is true that most of them are the older residents (Issei). Over half of the Nisei are Buddhist in background, and the trust that can be placed in a

Christian Nisei can just as safely be placed on a Buddhist Nisei. Let us not forget that it was religious intolerance that aided in peopling the North American continent and that the right to profess any religion (as long as it is not contrary to the welfare of the nation) is one of the basic ideals of democracy.[22]

While camp paper editorials were directed to fellow internees along with the War Relocation Authority officials, the WRA's interest in promoting positive public relations to facilitate resettlement created some opportunities for Buddhists to address a national and international audience when the media was invited to cover the Buddhist emergency meetings. In an interview with *Newsweek,* Reverend Kumata underscored his organization's American rather than Japanese ethnic background. He also focused on the compatibility of general Buddhism with Western society but went even further, suggesting that Buddhism's insights and teachings could aid everyone as they emerged from a war-weary world. Kumata noted that "even under the stress of war, American Buddhism was flourishing." Kumata described the teachings of Siddhartha Gautama, the historical Buddha, as in harmony with Western economic and cultural values and as inclusive, emphasizing "the oneness of all men and all life and all things." He concluded,

> The citizens of the world, more than half of whom are now Buddhists have never in the 2,500 years since Gautama Buddha lived had more need of his philosophy and his religion than they had today. The Buddha found that life in this world was suffering. Isn't it? He found that happiness was temporary. Isn't it? He found the achievement of Karma, the force that carries on personality, the only answer to this impermanence, both of sorrow and of happiness. And you build Karma by self-improvement, by good deeds, by meditation, mounting on and on until you achieve Nirvana, which [means] the annihilation of everything but the personality.[23]

Like Saiki's editorial, Kumata emphasized Buddhism as a world religion with distinct insights for a war-weary world. At the same time, Kumata framed Buddhist teachings with an American audience in mind. Despite running counter to basic Buddhist doctrine, his emphasis on the retention of "personality" after Nirvana worked to situate Buddhism within the realm of Western psychological discourse, while avoiding comparisons to Christian eschatology. Kumata thus sought to reassure the American public that they need not fear Japanese Americans or Buddhism in American society.

At the conclusion of the emergency meeting, delegates returned to the internment camps and free zones to discuss and ratify the national headquarters proposal. In doing so, they knew that they faced the sensitive task of presenting a vastly different organization from the one founded and cultivated by Issei over the previous decades. In October 1943, Reverend Kumata was permitted to relocate to Ogden, Utah, to serve as resident minister while preparing logistics for the national organization when it was allowed to return to San Francisco.[24] Delegates agreed to raise funds to send Reverend Kumata on a tour of the camps and free zones, where he would work to build support for the proposal. Bishop Ryotai Matsukage endorsed the campaign, writing letters to Issei priests and lay leaders in support of Reverend Kumata.[25]

Bussei delegates to the emergency meeting wrote editorials in camp papers, addressed members at Sunday services, created registration membership drives, and raised funds in an effort to gain endorsement of the new headquarters. Writing in the Topaz WRA camp publication *Bussei Life* shortly after the emergency meeting, Nisei minister Newton Ishiura noted that Buddhists had "lost sight of our Brethren in other relocation centers and free zones . . . because we did not have a strong central coordinating office" and noted that it was time for Nisei to "take over the responsibilities in 'Carrying On.'"[26] Barry Saiki, president of the YBA at the Rohwer, Arkansas, internment camp, argued that postwar plans for resettlement "could promise the Nisei a chance in post war America, it seems, but it would also disperse the Busseis throughout a wide area without the benefit of their religion." Saiki supported the new national headquarters, stating that he "believe[d] plans should be formulated to tie the Young Buddhists together—a centralized clearing house from which information, news and religious matter could be sent out for a moderate sum."[27]

WRA staff were also included in conversations, particularly among Young Buddhist Associations, to endorse and discuss the proposal for a Nisei-led national headquarters. Harold Boltrell, director of Adult Education at Heart Mountain, was invited to address the YBA Sunday service on the topic, "The Future Youth Movement." His talk was followed by two delegates from the emergency meeting, Noburo Ishitani and Kiyono Wakaye, who discussed their impressions of the conference.[28] Speaking on the topic "Relocation and the Future" at a YBA Sunday Service, Director Charles Ernst asked, "Where will the end of the war find us, not only physically and geographically, but socially and economically? Will we have been assimilated in the normal American life? Will Buddhism be accepted as one of the religions of this country, free from doubt and suspicion?" Ernst concluded that a new Nisei-led organization was key to addressing these questions. He stated, "The Bussei of today have a very definite duty and responsibility placed upon their shoulders; that of dissemination of the Teachings of Buddha among the American public... [which] should be accomplished with a broad, far reaching and well organized program."[29]

With minimal financial support from the WRA, and lacking the outside denominational support enjoyed by Nikkei Christians, fundraising was a critical component of restarting the national headquarters. At the same time, it also provided an opportunity to spread awareness and build support for a Nisei-led Buddhist organization that could transcend generational, cultural, and ideological divisions among Nikkei. Having long sustained BMNA projects, fundraising appeals now presented Nisei canvassers with an opportunity to converse with Nikkei, to inform them about the new organization, and to answer any questions that they might have. The national fund drive was led by Tad Hirota and organized across the WRA camps and free zones through the Young Buddhist Associations. Between July and December 1943, each YBA group set a goal of $300. YBA members canvassed individuals and families in all of the camps and free zones. At Topaz, for example, YBA leaders divided the camp by section and went barrack to barrack, canvassing. Those visited by YBA members were provided with an opportunity to acknowledge or endorse the new organization through a monetary donation, and to voice their support or concerns.[30]

In June 1944, the WRA permitted Buddhist leaders to leave the camps once again to participate in a meeting held in Salt Lake City. At the meeting, Nisei leaders gathered with Bishop Matsukage, Reverend Kumata, and a number of Buddhist priests to endorse the Buddhist Churches of America (BCA), a new organization that signaled the arrival of Nisei Buddhism. The concretization of the new organization represented the culmination of plans first suggested by Nisei during the emergency meetings held two and a half years earlier, following the bombing of Pearl Harbor and the US declaration of war with Japan. Leaders renamed the Buddhist Mission of North America as the Buddhist Churches of America, and approved the incorporation of the BCA in the name of American-born Nisei citizens. In a move designed to meet WRA qualifications for resettlement, participants in the emergency meeting also voted to establish English as the official language of the BCA and included a provision explicitly severing all ties between BCA and the nation of Japan. The renamed Buddhist Churches of America was to be run by a forty-seven-member board of directors comprising exclusively American citizens.[31]

The measures approved at the Salt Lake City emergency meeting were then sent to the Buddhist congregations at the ten WRA camps and four free zones. These measures and the new constitution were approved despite opposition from some Issei laypersons and from a majority of Issei priests. The reappointment of Issei Bishop Matsukage served as a significant compromise, though tensions between Issei priests and Nisei laypersons would persist into the postwar era. Bishop Matsukage's election as president was the one major exception of total Nisei leadership on the board of directors.[32] In July, a third meeting of the National Young Buddhist Associations was held in Salt Lake City. Bussei YBA members ratified the proposed change of title to the Buddhist Churches of America.[33] On May 2, 1944, a Nisei citizen, Henry Shibata, filed articles of incorporation with the State of California on behalf of the newly named Buddhist Churches of America.[34]

Reconstituting Buddhist Communities outside the Camps: Wartime Chicago

The establishment of resettlement in Chicago prior to the end of the war highlights the challenges faced by Buddhists and the debates and strategies that Nisei developed in navigating the rules and surveillance of WRA and Christian relief organization officials.[35] The experience of Buddhists in Chicago also foreshadowed challenges to come for all returning Buddhist Nikkei in the postwar years: limited financial resources, persistent distrust among the general public, surveillance by both government officials and private benevolent organizations, and intra-ethnic fissures along generational, cultural, linguistic, sectarian, and personal lines.

Amid the reconstitution of a national organization, Kumata, Hirota, and Bishop Matsukage, working with Buddhist priests and lay leaders, sought to establish Buddhist hostels and churches in communities where early resettlement was under way. Chicago began receiving resettlers as early as 1943. As Charlotte Brooks observed, the WRA and Christian organizations in Chicago actively pressured resettlers to assimilate into white society and urged that they avoid interactions with fellow Nikkei. Concern by these officials and their Christian allies were heightened as a wave of Buddhists and Nikkei, viewed as more suspect and with less potential to assimilate, began to arrive by mid-1943.[36]

By the end of March 1944, Reverend Kumata had sent YBA leader Mike Maruyama to Chicago to develop plans for the establishment of a Buddhist church. Maruyama attended a luncheon on April 4, held by Dr. Isamu Tashiro, an established dentist and longtime resident of Chicago. Also in attendance were Mrs. Elmer L. Sherrill, wife of the first WRA acting director of the Tule Lake Relocation Center, who was now working in the WRA field office in Chicago. Mrs. Sherrill was joined by Japanese American Evacuation and Resettlement Study (JERS) field workers Frank Miyamoto, Charles Kikuchi, and Tamotsu Shibutani, along with two early resettled students, Beatrice Takeuchi and Louise

Suski, who was also a prewar *Rafu Shimpo* journalist and a current employee of JERS.[37] According to Shibutani's account, Maruyama's role was to encourage fellow Buddhists to organize while placating "Caucasians." In fact, when he attended the luncheon, the Japanese Americans present at the meeting also cautioned him. Maruyama was undaunted and continued to reference the centrality of freedom of religion to democracy in making the case for the creation of Buddhist organizations and congregations. Shibutani recalled, "No one at the luncheon questioned his right to organize but he was cautioned about the possibilities of an adverse public opinion and the possible repercussions upon all Nisei in the area should the Buddhists receive unfavorable publicity."[38]

As a result of concerns about bad publicity, Maruyama was pressured to tentatively agree to restrict the direction and structure of the organization in a number of ways. These included restrictions on social activities including dances for Nisei, sole financial dependence on Caucasians rather than Nisei, restrictions from creating a strictly ethnic group, maintenance of independence from the national YBA, exclusion of Issei influence, English-language services only, and participation in interfaith meetings.[39]

Buddhist leaders in Chicago faced further scrutiny by the WRA and civic and religious leaders in July 1944. By this time, they were in the midst of plans for the creation of a Young Buddhist Association and two Buddhist churches. While the YBA was ostensibly to be led by its own lay leader, Barry Saiki, services and the organization were increasingly influenced by the Reverend Gyodo Kono, an Issei who had arrived from the Rohwer War Relocation Center. Kono and Saiki were joined by Arthur Takemoto, who was sent by Bishop Matsukage in June of 1944 to assist Kono.[40] Saiki, Kono, and Takemoto had participated in the 1943 emergency meetings.[41] Saiki met with a group of Nisei at the home of Mr. and Mrs. Elmer Sherrill on July 28. Shibutani, again present as an observer, noted that as the only Buddhist, Saiki felt compelled to defend the YBA organization from criticism by those at the meeting. According to Shibutani, the Sherrills and Niseis expressed concern that Buddhists were leaving themselves vulnerable to public relations attacks by right-wing conservative Hearst reporter Ray Richards, who had just arrived in Chicago. They noted that Richards had published an article the day before the meeting in which he claimed that former West Coast Japanese subversive organizations were now reorganizing in Chicago. Those attending the meeting charged that Buddhists were "courting danger" by organizing a local YBA, permitting a priest who did not speak English to deliver sermons, and meeting on the South Side of Chicago, in a predominantly African American neighborhood. Mrs. Sherrill noted that most Americans remembered Japanese wartime propaganda targeting African Americans in efforts to spread racial war.[42]

As a result of pressure from the WRA and civic, Christian, and JERS field workers, internal debates emerged among priests and lay leaders as to the aims of their organization and what kinds of interactions members would have, as well as about the external content and presentation of their services and meetings. The primary debates concerning structure and social organization revolved around the question of whether the YBA would be primarily a religious organization or would include a social component. Those who advocated for an exclusively religious organization either expressed an interest in developing a deeper understanding of Buddhist teachings and a Buddhist perspective or cited pressure from the WRA and civic organizations to avoid socialization. Chicago YBA organizer Helen Sasaki envisioned gatherings of small groups of dedicated Nisei Buddhists. She noted, "I would like to see a small organization primarily interested in the philosophy of Buddhism with followers who really believe in the religion. If we had 15 or 20 people who lived a Buddhist life, I wouldn't want any more." These groups could "just get together in a home" and "could invite Caucasians and explain our religion to them," something she viewed as "an integration program, giving as well as receiving."[43]

By contrast, Barry Saiki noted that the group had agreed to define itself as an exclusively religious organization in response to criticisms of being primarily a social organization. He explained, "We want something to outlast the war. We don't want to get stopped by a riot or something. That's why we want to de-emphasize all socials because they would make the group conspicuous."[44]

While arguments against including a social dimension were generally acknowledged as valid by Chicago's YBA organizers, most also agreed that the majority of Bussei were drawn to the organization for social reasons. Thus, despite fear of attacks by right-wing columnists and criticism by the WRA and civic and church leaders, Chicago's YBA leaders pushed for maintaining some kind of social aspect in the church, tethered to a more pragmatic issue of the budget required to sustain a religious organization. Organizers believed that they would need $300 as a minimum monthly budget just to support a priest and executive assistant. Given the standard request for membership of one dollar, this would require a membership of between three hundred to five hundred members.[45] Many concluded that the only way to gain those kinds of numbers would be by adding some kind of social element.[46]

Finally, Chicago YBA organizers also debated to what extent Buddhist religious services themselves should be modified. These discussions were couched in the language of Americanization, reinforced by terms and goals set by the WRA and civic and Christian religious organizations aiding in the resettlement. The issue of language and aspects of the Buddhist service were exacerbated by a growing rivalry between two priests who were each seeking to develop congregations in Chicago. The Reverend Gyodo Kono, an Issei, whose primary language was Japanese, was ordained as a Nishi Honganji minister and had been sent to the United States prior to the war by the Nishi Honganji home temple in Kyoto in coordination with the North American Buddhist Mission. In contrast, Reverend Gyomei Kubose was a Kibei (American born Nisei but raised for a number of years in Japan) who was bilingual. While he had been affiliated with Higashi Honganji during the prewar years, beginning in the camps, he committed to a nondenominational Buddhism and aligned himself with Reverend Julius Goldwater's Buddhist Brotherhood.

Bussei organizers agreed that language was a major barrier to understanding Buddhist teachings and chants. Still, they were divided over how and to what extent Buddhist services should be modified. Here again, Barry Saiki, feeling pressure from the WRA and other white liberal organizations, pushed for the elimination of those aspects of Buddhist services that signified Japaneseness. He pointed to the chanting of the Junirai (Twelve Adorations) *gatha* as one example of what could be cut. Saiki stated, "I think we should cut all things pertaining to Nihon (Japan). For instance, the Junirai chant should be eliminated. They (the Nisei), don't understand it anyway. We all read in Japanese and it doesn't sound good. We should have English readings instead."[47]

Saiki's suggestion was met with significant resistance from other organizers including Akira Yebisu, who was a Kibei, and two Nisei, Arthur Takemoto and Roy Higashi. The conversation was noted by Tamotsu Shibutani:

> *Mr. Yebisu:* "Oh, but you can't change [the Junirai] overnight just because it is no use anymore."
>
> *Mr. Takemoto:* "I'd just gotten used to it. It's become a part of me."
>
> *Mr. Yebisu:* "Rev. (Kenryo) Kumata had a service without it and there was quite a fuss about it."[48]

At the conclusion of the discussion, Roy Higashi noted "The Junirai gives a lot of atmosphere though. It makes you feel as though it is a Buddhist church." Arthur Takemoto reiterated his call to not cut the Junirai: "We shouldn't leave out the sutra chanting though. I miss it." Saiki responded, "There are a lot of things we miss. . . . The question is whether we're going to Americanize or follow old Japan methods."[49]

Written by Nāgārjuna (second to third century CE), the Twelve Adorations described and praised Amida Buddha and Amida's Pure Land. Shinran named

Nāgārjuna the first of seven patriarchs of Shin Buddhism. For Saiki and other pre-dominantly English-speaking Nisei, the primary trouble caused by Junirai was that they believed that it was chanted in Japanese. Even those Nisei who supported its inclusion stated that they did so for familiarity, not necessarily because of content. For most of those involved in the discussion, barriers of language and religious history rendered the Junirai as a central aspect of the Japanese ethnic form of Buddhist practice. In fact, it was this very aspect that provided a sense of the familiar that other members found important, whether they understood the words that were being chanted or not.

Given the practical need for members, the important role that the Buddhist Church would continue to play for social relations among Bussei, and the Reverend Kono's increasing influence in the development of plans for the YBA and Midwest Buddhist Church, Saiki and others who took the most extreme approach to Americanization eventually consented to a more moderate approach. As a result, Saiki, the YBA, and the Midwest Buddhist Church continued to be monitored by civic and religious organizations. For example, Buddhist leaders were called to report to the Chicago Inter-Agency Council (IAC) in September, 1944. The council comprised representatives of the American Baptist Home Mission Society, the American Friends Service Committee, Brethren Service Committee, the Church Federation of Greater Chicago, the Japanese American Citizens League, the War Relocation Authority, the YMCA, and the YWCA.[50]

Anticipating the need for caution in addressing the Inter-Agency Council, Buddhists sent Barry Saiki in place of Arthur Takemoto, believing that he was "far more articulate and was much more familiar with the kinds of things the people in the IAC 'wanted to hear.'"[51] Saiki was asked a number of probing questions about the demographic makeup of the membership and organizational structure, where meetings were held, whether services were in English, whether the organization had socials and publications, the relation of the Young Buddhist Association to the Buddhist Church, and trends in terms of growth of membership and regular attendance. These questions reiterated the WRA and IAC's concerns that Buddhists maintain an assimilationist policy (which they called "integration") and that they avoid socializing and restrict their activities to religious ones.

When Saiki responded that the organization held its meetings at the Parkway Community House, he noted, "that's in the Black Belt and we want to show the colored people that we have no prejudice against them." The IAC followed up by asking why they meet at the Parkway House, to which Saiki responded that they were "meeting there because it is impossible to go elsewhere."[52] In response to a question about language spoken during services, Saiki acknowledged that Reverend

Kono spoke only Japanese but reassured IAC that the organization was seeking to recruit an English-speaking priest. Meanwhile, he suggested that interested Caucasians could attend Reverend Kubose's services. Finally, in responding to the question of holding socials, Saiki stated, "We are opposed to socials." He noted that they had held mixers to allow people to get acquainted with board members early on, but did not plan on holding more. Shibutani believed that Saiki's responses reflected his personal goals for the YBA. However, it is clear that Saiki was equally interested in placating IAC members who, while being liberal allies, were also very much interested in containing the activities of Buddhists for strategic and ideological reasons. Shibutani noted that Saiki's remarks, "about keeping the group small, avoiding socials, and helping promote integration brought out warm smiles of approval from Christian church leaders present at the meeting."[53]

Postwar National Resettlement

The experiences of Buddhists in Chicago provided the most extreme version of the cultural assimilationist paradigm framed by the WRA as it coordinated with organizations such as the Inter-Agency Council. The continuing war with Japan, combined with a disproportionate population of Bussei and a national Buddhist organization thoroughly lacking in funds or organization, led to only a modest gesturing toward assimilation. Even in the most repressive period, Buddhists joined together—granted, not without developing fissures—for social events and religious services.

In the aftermath of the Supreme Court's decision in *Ex parte Endo vs. U.S.*, on December 18, 1944, with justices unanimously ruling that citizens who had demonstrated loyalty to the United States could not be detained, the US government opened up mass resettlement to the West Coast on January 1, 1945. With the WRA planning to close all camps except Tule Lake by the end of 1945, by September, thousands were leaving the camps each month. As Scott Kurashige observed, "although the federal government had created a mass population of homeless Japanese Americans, neither the WRA nor local officials desired taking responsibility for their public welfare." As a result, securing housing emerged as the most significant challenge affecting Nikkei.[54]

Nikkei Buddhist temples and Christian churches established hostels for resettlers. Local Buddhist community hostels faced a new host of challenges for returning Japanese American Buddhists. Given the extent and varied locations for resettlement, the establishment of emergency hostels emerged through a patchwork of initiatives driven by the WRA and resettlers committees comprising liberal civic and religious leaders in cities throughout the United States, as well as through the initiative of Buddhist priests and laypersons themselves. In some cases, priests led the initiative to open a hostel, and in other instances, members themselves led the initiative. In still other cases, local progressive civic and religious leaders initiated plans for a hostel. In all cases, planning of hostels went hand in hand with the reinstitution of local churches and temples. While still incarcerated, members of the Fresno Betsuin gathered at the Gila River War Relocation Center for a meeting planned in conjunction with a visit by their minister, Reverend Itsuzo Kyogoku. Members decided to reopen the Betsuin and establish the hostel. Members then approached Reverend Kakumin Fujinaga, who agreed to travel to Fresno to establish the hostel.[55]

After passing through security screenings, Buddhist priests and lay leaders from camps were released by the WRA in advance of the remaining numbers of the incarcerated; the WRA provided limited financial support to some of those approved leaders who were willing to establish a hostel. Former internees returned to Buddhist churches and temples that were in varied condition. Some, like the Buddhist Church of San Francisco or the Hompa Honganji Buddhist temple in Los Angeles, had been left in trust of European American Buddhist ministers. Others had been locked and left for the duration of the war. Some temples were relatively untouched, while others suffered significant damage from vandalism. Still others, such as the Oakland and San Diego Buddhist Churches, had been occupied by the US government.[56]

Given the hasty conditions under which the temples and churches had been left and the neglect that even relatively well-kept churches and temples suffered, those who returned to establish them as hostels worked for weeks and even months to prepare them for those released from the camps. In Fresno, Reverend Kakumin Fujinaga worked with laypersons Mr. and Mrs. Gunichi Takata for a month to clean and prepare the hostel. Preparation for the return of Buddhist religious services was also made when the *obutsudan* altar was transferred from the Lisle Funeral Home that had agreed to store it to the Betsuin.[57] In San Francisco, Takeo Yamamoto's first memories of returning to the Buddhist church involved gratitude that it was still there. Yamamoto recalled working for a few months with the BCSF minister to prepare the hostel for habitation "because things were broken [and] some things were stolen."[58]

While the temples and churches provided a sense of place and connection with the prewar lives of Nikkei Buddhists, hostels met the immediate needs of those seeking temporary housing, storage, and services to aid resettlers in locating permanent housing and employment. Those incarcerated had utilized the churches and temples for storage, and witness accounts from during and following the

Figure 2.3. Mrs. Chiyo Okamoto pushing Ryo Imamura, Reverend Kanmo Imamura, and Arthur Takemoto, Buddhist Hostel, 1336 W. 36th Place, Los Angeles, 1945. Reproduced courtesy of the War Relocation Authority Photographs of Japanese-American Evacuation and Resettlement, Bancroft Library, Online Archive of California (OAC).

period describe luggage and personal items stacked to the ceilings. Locating housing was a particular challenge for Japanese American resettlers, as there was a national housing shortage driven by the wartime economy. Reverend Kanmo Imamura, his wife Jane Imamura, and Arthur Takemoto, who had recently arrived from Chicago, ran a Buddhist hostel in Los Angeles that opened its doors in April of 1945.[59]

Funded not by the WRA but by private religious organizations, the hostel welcomed all resettlers regardless of religious background for an unlimited period of time. They charged one dollar per day for lodging and three dollars per day for meals. From one week to ten days after arrival, or for those securing employment, the lodging rate was raised to $1.50. The Los Angeles hostel provided separate areas for families and dormitories for individuals, and also provided other services for residents.[60] Art Takemoto remembered, putting "ads in the paper and [making] phone calls to seek jobs for them." He noted, that "if they were an Issei, we would make arrangements so they could get their automobile driver's license."[61]

Beyond basic needs, hostels provided a relatively safe space where returnees could congregate. Art Takemoto explained that the hostel was important because it met people's need for a gathering place. He recalled, "Where else can they gather together as a unit? What area can you be in, where you can intermingle freely with other racial groups? They were right fresh out of camp, and there was still a great deal of fear. So where else but to gather in a temple?"[62]

Hostels emerged during a period when Buddhists were targets of racial animus and continued acts of vandalism and racial violence. In Watsonville, unidentified persons attempted to set fire to the Buddhist temple, which was being used as a hostel in September of 1945.[63] Shinobu Matsuura described the hostel at the Guadalupe Buddhist temple as critical in a small town where race relations between whites and Nikkei remained tense. She found the refusal of the small number of shopkeepers—including those who had been friendly in the prewar years—to sell or even speak to the Japanese "exasperating," though, "among them, some showed kindness, and brought us vegetables and fish." Even more worrisome was a time when "someone shot into a room where many of us were sleeping." Matsuura concluded, "The important thing was that among the returnees, everyone was under the same stressful condition together so everyone became united, helping one another. The hostel evolved into one big family."[64]

Issei Ministers and the BCA Americanization Program

By 1946, most of the hostels had closed. While significant numbers of Nikkei Buddhists had returned to the West Coast, many more remained in new communities and homes throughout the Midwest and eastern United States. Established Young Buddhist Associations, Buddhist churches, and temples reemerged, joined by new organizations and congregations. Meanwhile, the fledgling Nisei leadership of the Buddhist Churches of America began the arduous process of reconnecting and organizing affiliated local organizations, churches, and temples. The hastily organized 1943 emergency conferences pushed Nisei into the spotlight of Nikkei Buddhist leadership. The terms of the BCA Americanization program and its ratification by Young Buddhist Association leaders represented more than a simple endorsement. It reflected changing expectations about leadership and the direction of BCA, shaped by the war and incarceration. The program foresaw the permanent transference of Nisei into key positions as leaders and cultural ambassadors on behalf of Nikkei Buddhist communities. BCA's new programs and Nisei leadership were designed with the intention of maintaining Shin Buddhism while also introducing Buddhism and Buddhists to the general American public. Yet, even in the realm of Shin Buddhist practice, many Nisei and some

Issei also envisioned a future in which services and activities would increasingly be directed toward the priorities of the Nisei, rekindling an idea that emerged alongside the growth of the Nisei population in the 1920s and 1930s.

BCA's new leadership faced logistical and political challenges in its efforts to facilitate the reconstitution and coordination of local Buddhist temples and churches, and in centralizing leadership and administration. Key among these challenges would be the designation of the organizational roles of Issei priests and laypersons in these organizations. Issei Buddhist priests remained an important link to the prewar religious authority of Nishi Honganji. In this sense, they would continue to play an important role as advocates for Shin Buddhist tradition as well as an important symbolic role as living repositories of that tradition.

At the same time, BCA's official severing of institutional ties with Nishi Honganji in Kyoto directly correlated with a loss of influence for Issei priests. Because they were banned from becoming naturalized citizens of the United States until 1952, the legal status of Issei after the war remained as Japanese citizens and alien residents. Despite the fact that most had spent more than two decades of their lives in the United States, many in families that included children who were American-born citizens, their options were either to return to war-torn Japan or remain as alien residents. While some Issei priests and their families had been residents of the United States for decades, others had arrived more recently, some as late as 1941, because both a priest and his family qualified as "Non-Quota Immigrants" under the terms of the 1924 Immigration Act.[65] Journeying to the United States with the intention of serving Japanese American Buddhist communities for a limited period, many of these recent arrivals planned to return to Japan. Furthermore, because they were traveling on R-1 and R-2 religious visas sponsored by the BMNA, their legal status in the United States was contingent on the support of that organization in coordination with Nishi Honganji.

In the aftermath of war, many priests who wished to stay in America did so with the approval of the US government and the sponsorship of BCA for their visas. This placed a great deal of pressure on ministers to maintain good relations with the newly formed BCA organization and its Nisei leadership. At the same time, Issei leaders continued to hold informal influence among Japanese Americans. They were respected because of their age and prior political standing in the community. Many also continued to be important sponsors of local Buddhist temples.

BCA also continued to struggle with shifting demographics among Nikkei Buddhist communities shaped by WRA resettlement policies of assimilation and dispersal. In a 1947 report, the WRA estimated that, of the 106,925 evacuees known to have resettled, between 28,000 and 30,000 remained east of the

Missouri River; 10,000 to 12,000 were in the Great Plains and Intermountain states; and the remainder had returned to the three West Coast states. The WRA estimated that the percentage of Japanese Americans who had lived in Washington, Oregon, and California had dropped from 88.5 percent in 1940 to 55 percent by 1947. Despite these early estimates, many would return to the West Coast. By 1950, more than two-thirds of the Nikkei population of the prewar population had returned.[66]

Thus, while a majority of Buddhist temples and churches remained located on the West Coast of the United States, WRA policies of resettlement and dispersal of Japanese Americans to the Midwest and East Coast of the United States led to the postwar emergence of Buddhist communities and temples in Chicago, Cleveland, Detroit, and Minnesota; and in Washington, DC, and Seabrook, New Jersey; and also led to the growth of new branches in the west, including in Idaho, Oregon, Washington, and throughout California.[67]

Finally, the legacy of the WRA resettlement would have a significant impact on the reconstitution of Buddhist communities along lines that would continue to lead to Nisei ascendance in the Buddhist Churches of America. WRA's assimilationist policies urged Nikkei to blend into white Christian middle-class society and actively discouraged social behavior and external signifiers of Japanese culture that might draw unwanted negative media attention or scrutiny. One of the major strategies that BCA would develop in challenging the very roots of cultural assimilationist programs emerged in its efforts to create public memorials to honor Nisei Buddhist veterans and to present an ethnic-national form of Buddhism.

CHAPTER THREE

Memorialization and Ethnic American Buddhism

In May 1948, the *Los Angeles Times* reported on the funeral of Private First Class George Gushiken, a member of the 442nd Regimental Combat Team (RCT) who had been killed in action in France four years earlier. Born in Baldwin Park, California, in 1916, Gushiken traveled with family to Okinawa at the age of three. He returned to the United States twelve years later, attended high school for two years, and enrolled in a US military intelligence language-training program in 1941. Gushiken was released from the top class in the program in October 1942 for "security reasons" that were likely related to his background as both a Buddhist and a Kibei. After being forcibly incarcerated with his family in a WRA camp, he volunteered to serve in the 442nd RCT where he fought in Italy and then France where he was killed in action in November of 1944.[1] Los Angeles Mayor Fletcher Bowron and army officials, including Colonel Neville Grow and Sergeant Hideto Tanaka, joined a crowd of four hundred who attended his funeral ceremony.[2] The *Times* celebrated Gushiken as a war hero whose sacrifice for the nation bridged cultural divisions, noting that "East met West yesterday at a hero's grave." The *Times* also sought to underscore the role that Gushiken and his Issei parents' sacrifices had played in transforming Issei Buddhist ritual into ethnic American religion. It continued,

> The East was there—expressed in the mystic ritual of the ages old Buddhist faith, framed in the panoplied splendor of the Nishi Hongwanji Temple at 1st Street and Central Ave. The West was there. It was high officers of the Army of the United States. It was mayor Bowron. It was the precision of the military guard of honor. It was most of all, in the fierce pride and loyalty that marked the hero's parents, Mr. and Mrs. Tom Gushiken, 413 E. 7th Street.[3]

The report was accompanied by a photograph of Buddhist priests leading chants, while Buddhist lay leaders and a color guard from the 442nd stood beside the casket draped in the American flag. Addressing those in attendance, Mayor Bowron, who had endorsed the forced incarceration of Nikkei during the war, stated, "Through him and his fellow heroes with their records of glorious and inspiring valor, the Japanese place in Los Angeles has been established, never to be questioned again."[4] In contrast to the *Times* story, which included Buddhist images and description in its coverage, national coverage of the funeral was limited to a photograph of Gushiken's grieving mother pictured beside her son's casket, draped with an American flag. However, no media coverage mentioned that Mrs. Gushiken was a widow and that the family had been incarcerated during the war. Nevertheless, like the *Los Angeles Times* article, most news coverage presented a narrative of familial and religious redemption through the sacrifice of a Nisei war hero.

Beginning in the late 1940s, funeral ceremonies and memorials for war veterans like George Gushiken emerged as key occasions for defining Buddhism and

AGES-OLD RITUAL — Priests chant beside casket of Pfc. George Gushiken, who died in action in France in 1944. Funeral was conducted in Nishi Hongwanji Temple.

Figure 3.1. *Los Angeles Times* coverage of funeral ceremony for Private First Class George Gushiken, 1948. Reproduced from "Tribute Paid to Nisei at Hero's Last Rites," *Los Angeles Times*, May 2, 1948.

Buddhists in relation to the US nation. The reinterment of Nisei who had died on World War II battlefronts overseas offered an opportunity for Nisei leaders of the newly created Buddhist Churches of America to promote ethnic *and religious* inclusion as the reward for Nisei Buddhist wartime service and sacrifice. This strategy of promoting ethnic American Buddhism emerged as a central pillar of Nisei Buddhism. By elevating Nisei war veterans as figures representing Buddhists in America, Nisei Buddhists challenged both the virulent wartime racism that had conflated Nikkei, and Buddhism, with an enemy race and the prescriptions for cultural assimilation by the WRA and US military brass. Working with veterans' groups and civic organizations like the Japanese American Citizens League, Nisei Buddhist leaders presented Buddhists and Buddhism as part of a racially and religiously diverse American nation. In doing so, Nisei Buddhists not only advocated for their own inclusion but, by extension, that of Issei Buddhists as well.

Efforts by Nisei Buddhists to challenge the cultural assimilationist framework of the US government by advocating for the recognition of Buddhists in the armed forces began during the war with campaigns to support the recruitment of Buddhist chaplains. These campaigns continued into the postwar period alongside efforts to memorialize Nisei Buddhist war dead. By the mid-to-late 1940s, these efforts had begun to gain traction with veterans' organizations and military and civic leaders who acknowledged the shared sacrifice of Nisei veterans and the importance of improving understanding between Americans and Asians. For US diplomats and military brass, Nisei soldiers were increasingly recognized as vital to intercultural understanding between the US and Japan, as the latter emerged as a key Cold War ally in Asia.[5] Meanwhile, local civic and business leaders, particularly from West Coast cities actively engaged in situating themselves within an emerging Pacific Rim economy, took greater interest in their city's Asian ethnic character.[6] Within the Buddhist Churches of America, highlighting Buddhism as an ethnic American religious tradition served to consolidate the rise of Nisei leadership, as the figure of the Nisei Buddhist war hero became an important resource not only in advocating for Nisei inclusion but also in reversing discriminatory laws that had denied Issei and other Asian immigrants from becoming naturalized citizens.

Racial Liberalism and Nisei in the Armed Forces

Given the virulent racist sentiment toward Nikkei that existed in the armed forces at the onset of World War II, Nisei wartime service was not a foregone conclusion. The shift toward a policy guided by racial liberalism was driven by a combination of advocacy on the part of a segment of Nisei and the evolving demands for total mobilization, as well as wartime propaganda campaigns of the US government.[7] Like the WRA's release policy, plans for the creation and promotion of Nisei in wartime service reflected policies premised on Nisei cultural assimilation to white middle-class Christian norms. These policies would eventually be challenged by Nisei Buddhist leaders.

In the days following Japan's attack on Pearl Harbor and the US declaration of war, Nisei in Hawai'i and on the West Coast of the United States were subjected to significantly different local political situations but would eventually join together in the formation of the combined 100th Infantry Battalion/442nd Regimental Combat Team. In Hawai'i and in Washington, DC, racial prejudice created initial resistance to the formation of the 100th Battalion, despite earlier precedents of Issei and Nisei in the American armed forces. Seven Issei were among the 268 killed on the USS *Maine* in 1898. Japanese Americans also served in World War I, when Japan was an ally of the United States. An all-Japanese ethnic company was formed in Hawai'i during World War I. Just prior to the US entry into World War II, between October and November 1941, four instructors and fifty-eight Nisei, including Gushiken, out of a total of sixty students were recruited for a covert US Military Intelligence Division Japanese language-school program held at the Presidio of San Francisco.[8]

Despite its initial hesitation regarding Nisei soldiers, the federal government began to consider their inclusion after key military leaders, the FBI, and local business leaders in Hawai'i (including representatives of the "big five" families in Hawai'i) and ethnic leaders expressed support for the Nisei.[9] A majority of those Nisei who volunteered for service had been part of the Varsity Victory Volunteers and were Buddhists, gaining the nickname "Buddhaheads"—a reference to their Buddhist background and also a pun for the Japanese word *buta*, which translated as "pig."[10] Despite this, as will be shown, the Buddhist background of both the 100th Battalion and the 442nd Regimental Combat Team, with which the 100th Battalion would be merged, would be purposely obscured by the US government during the war.

Meanwhile, on the mainland, the Japanese American Citizens League proposed the idea of an all-Nisei battalion in the weeks following America's entry into World War II. Desperately seeking to avoid the mass incarceration of Nisei, JACL's executive secretary, Mike Masaoka, made the extreme recommendation to government officials that an all-Nisei suicide battalion be created and deployed against Japan and that Issei parents be held as hostages. Government and military leaders rejected the wording of the proposal even as they were developing plans for the forced mass removal and incarceration of all those of Japanese ancestry.[11] By the fall of 1942, at the urging of the WRA and JACL, some key members of the military and war department, in particular Assistant Secretary of War John McCloy, began to express support for the creation of an all-Nisei unit. With the endorsement of Secretary of War Henry L. Stimson and General George Marshall, President Roosevelt laid plans for the formation of what would become the 442nd Regimental Combat Team, which was announced to the public by Stimson on January 28, 1943.[12]

Roosevelt's decision to support the creation of the 442nd despite resistance from key leaders such as Lieutenant General John Dewitt, head of Western Defense Command, was primarily motivated by a desire to utilize the visibility of Nisei soldiers in American propaganda efforts. Roosevelt and his advisers believed that its main import was to counter Japanese propaganda in Asia.[13] Office of War Information director Elmer Davis, a leading advocate in support of the creation of the 442nd, stated, "I believe the propaganda value of such a step would be great . . . and I believe that they would make great troops."[14]

WRA and military officials also emphasized the role that Nisei service in the armed forces could play in building support and sympathy for the release and resettlement of Nikkei. WRA officials also hoped that positive press coverage of Nisei soldiers along with the segregation of "disloyal" internees might also subdue growing antigovernment sentiment and divisiveness among Japanese Americans in the internment camps as they entered their second year of forced incarceration.[15] As discussed in chapter 2, many Nisei and Issei who otherwise might have been willing to serve in the US armed forces pointed to the contradiction inherent in "volunteer" service while being forcibly imprisoned without due process of law. Others argued that a segregated unit was contrary to the ideals of a democratic country. Roosevelt and his advisers ignored these concerns and pressed on for an all-Nisei unit.[16]

On February 1, 1943, Roosevelt officially announced the creation of the segregated Nisei 442nd Regimental Combat Team. Roosevelt's speech concluded with a slogan that underscored the government's shift from early wartime portrayals of Nikkei as an unassimilable race apart to a racial liberal policy that emphasized cultural assimilation. A key passage from his speech that would be much quoted proclaimed, "Americanism is a matter of the mind and not of the heart; Americanism is not, and never was, a matter of race or ancestry."[17] Significantly, Roosevelt's speech made no mention of freedom of worship, despite it being one of the "four freedoms" that he repeatedly claimed as a fundamental freedom for countries around the world, beginning with his State of the Union Address in January of 1941. Moreover, with Roosevelt's support, policies of the US Army brass toward Buddhists would reveal themselves to be consistent with the WRA's cultural assimilationist release programs.

The combined wartime record of the 100th Battalion and 442nd Regimental Combat Team has been well documented both during World War II and in the decades that followed. Even today, the regiment remains the most decorated unit for its size in the history of American warfare. In total, about fourteen thousand men served. Excluded from fighting in the Pacific, the 100th/442nd fought primarily in Southern Italy and France, collectively earning 9,486 Purple Hearts and eight Presidential Unit Citations. Those who have chronicled the history of the 100th/442nd, including scholars, journalists, and soldiers themselves, have sought to explain the particularly dangerous assignments given to the unit and the distinguished actions of the troops that together resulted in both the disproportionate number of casualties relative to the size of the unit and the unit's distinction and honoring. Interpretations that emphasize the agency of Nisei soldiers highlight the voluntary nature of the unit (though after January 1944 most replacement troops were drafted), and soldiers' eagerness and even pride in taking on difficult assignments.[18] Interpretations that emphasize Nisei soldiers as victims of circumstance, or of the choices of the government and Allied forces, view the dangerous assignments as a sign of the relatively lower value placed on the lives of Nisei soldiers. The rescue in October 1944 of the "Lost Battalion," the 1st Battalion, 141st Infantry from Texas, in the Vosges Mountains of France—where the 442nd suffered more than eight hundred casualties in rescuing 211 members—has raised questions by soldiers and scholars alike as to whether the army valued Nisei lives as highly as other troops and whether they were being used as "cannon fodder."[19] Others have critiqued the coercive designs of a nation-state that conferred patriotism and loyalty contingent on the wartime sacrifices of Nisei soldiers.[20]

Media publicity for the 442nd unit was consistent with government efforts to portray Nisei as culturally assimilated Americans whose voluntarism were shaped in a climate of political liberty that had been threatened by Imperial Japan. Coverage of the 442nd first emerged with recruitment and basic training at Camp Shelby, Mississippi beginning in May 1943. The OWI, working with the War Department, took statements from recently inducted Nisei volunteers in preparation for shortwave transmission to the Pacific. In one such statement, Private Robert T. Mizukami, a Nisei from Tacoma, Washington, who, together with his brother Bill, had volunteered for service, proclaimed that he was "proud to say that I am a member of the armed forces of the United States." Mizukami noted that prior to the Pearl Harbor attack, he had enjoyed "the liberties of a free people, educated in free public schools, doing what we wanted to do, saying what we wanted to say." However, "because of such an unthinking and cowardly attack, by the Japanese war crazy lords, we have gone through undue hardships. For this reason, my brother and I and a few thousand other liberty loving Nisei have volunteered our services to prevent future hardships for the future generation and that never again in the history of the world may such barbarism exist."[21] Mizukami and his brother Bill Mizukami would fight in Italy, where Bill was killed in action. Robert Mizukami later earned a Purple Heart in France.[22]

Public relations for the 442nd at Camp Shelby was initially directed by Major Oland D. Russell, who had served as editor and columnist for the *New York World-Telegram* in the prewar years. Russell's staff of four included one lieutenant and three enlisted Nisei, one of whom was private Mike Masaoka. Raised in a Christian household in Utah, Masaoka joined the Church of Jesus Christ of Latter-Day Saints.[23] As former executive secretary of the JACL, Masaoka was a prominent voice in support of the government's racial liberal programs, yet he would also prove to be an important advocate for Buddhists. Masaoka was in regular direct communication with government officials, including WRA director Dillon Myer, Assistant Director of War John McCloy, and his assistant, Colonel William Scobey, and was instrumental in helping coordinate the formation of the 442nd. After volunteering for the 442nd, Masaoka had been assigned to the PR team by his commanding officer, Colonel Charles W. Pence, but directions had come from Washington. While still in basic training, Masaoka was given a directive by a representative of Assistant Secretary of War McCoy to prioritize PR work. When Russell was transferred to the Pacific and the two enlisted men were moved out of the department, Masaoka became the primary producer of public relations for the 442nd.[24]

Masaoka wrote press releases that profiled members of the unit and underscored the sacrifices that they had made in joining the 442nd. He also served as liaison between the press and soldiers and recalled "steering [the press] toward the more articulate volunteers in an effort to get as much newspaper space as possible."[25] Masaoka was also careful to support the government's aims in defining Americanism as antiracist while infusing the message with a narrative of Nisei redemption.[26]

As a result of the coordinated efforts of the State Department, army leadership and public relations, and the media, the actions and sacrifices of the 100th and 442nd were covered extensively by the American press. When the 100th was attached to the 34th Division and sent to Salerno, Italy, in preparation for its first combat mission on September 22, 1943, the press was there to greet them. Journalists and war correspondents spent the next two days interviewing Nisei troops and publishing their work in newspapers including the *New York Times* and *Washington Post*.[27] The 100th's first combat engagement began one week after their arrival and was announced by Secretary of War Stimson and praised by General Mark Clark, commander of the 5th Army.[28]

Despite the US government's efforts to promote Nisei soldiers as culturally assimilated, press coverage also drew on cultural stereotypes used to portray enemy Japanese soldiers. As Masayo Duus has noted, much of the early coverage of the 442nd deferred to stereotypes of Japanese fanaticism and collective behavior. Some stories utilized racial stereotypes to argue for the expulsion of those of Japanese ancestry, including Americans, from the western United States. Yet, Duus found that other stories drew from stereotypes to affirm the diversity of America's soldiers. Comparisons of Nisei to the Japanese Imperial Army were used to explain the determination and esprit de corps among members of the 442nd.[29] Toward the end of the war, caricatures involving Buddhist imagery were also used to highlight Nisei martial patriotism. Reporting on the return of the 100th/442nd to Italy after battling in France in April 1945, *New York Times* reporter Milton Bracker noted, "Somehow it is still incredible to see these dark, slight soldiers, who so uncomfortably suggest our Pacific enemy." He concluded however by commenting on the "polyglot nature of both the Allied armies in Italy" stating, "Nothing could possibly emphasize it more than to see one member of the 100th Battalion sitting as cross-legged as a Buddha as he poured over a map and discussed with grave satisfaction the sinking of the battleship Yamato."[30]

"I Am a Buddhist": Campaigns for Religious Recognition in the US Armed Forces

As a result of the racial liberal policies at the heart of US military recruitment of Nisei, Buddhists faced similar presumptions of un-Americanness in recruitment and active engagement in the United States military as they did in the WRA camps. As had been true in the camps, efforts to promote ethnic American Buddhism emerged as a response to unequal treatment based on religion.

As the government sought to recruit them into the 442nd, Nisei Buddhists requested that the government also recruit Buddhist chaplains for the unit, viewing the issue as one involving religious freedom and equality. Internees raised the issue of Buddhist chaplaincy as part of discussions held in the WRA camps with military recruiters in February of 1943. At Gila River, chief recruiter Captain Norman Thompson reported the request to Lieutenant John M. Hall, who endorsed the idea of Buddhist chaplaincy and forwarded the issue to his supervisor, Colonel William P. Scobey, general staff executive to Assistant Secretary of War McCloy.[31]

Significantly, there was division among officials in the Roosevelt administration and military brass over the issue. As Scobey pushed for the recruitment of a Buddhist chaplain, he ran into resistance from Army Chief of Chaplains William Richard Arnold. Writing to the 442nd's commander Colonel Charles W. Pence on April 24, Scobey noted that Arnold told him that "there were not sufficient Buddhists in the combat team to warrant the commissioning and detailing of a Buddhist chaplain to the unit."[32] Scobey did not know where Arnold had gotten that information and requested that a survey be conducted. He suggested that Pence conduct such a survey and forward the information to either the adjutant general or the assistant secretary of war's office. Scobey concluded, "Should you discover that fifteen or twenty percent are Buddhist, a Buddhist chaplain will be provided."[33] Yet, as Mike Masaoka later recalled, Scobey's own boss John McCloy had some reservations about a Buddhist chaplain. In Masaoka's recounting, McCloy "suggested that since there was widespread suspicion of, as well as ignorance about Asian religions, it would be better public relations to approve only Christian chaplains for the 442nd."[34]

According to historian Ronit Stahl, a survey of the religious background of the 442nd was never made, but Arnold did attempt to locate a Buddhist chaplain. Arnold contacted Bishop Matsukage, who forwarded Reverend Kenryo Kumata's name. Both Kumata and Reverend Newton Ishiura wrote to John McCloy to offer their services. Kumata applied for service but failed the army physical because of poor vision. According to Arnold, Matsukage was not able to furnish him with another suitable candidate. When Ishiura wrote a month later charging discrimination against Buddhist priests, Arnold's office again countered that most of the unit was Christian and that there were an insufficient number of Buddhists to warrant a Buddhist chaplain, this despite any formal census being taken. Stahl concluded that "the inadequate supply of ready-to-endorse Buddhist clergy combined with resistance to placing a Buddhist in the corps enabled Arnold to dismiss Buddhism as unnecessary to the chaplaincy."[35]

Secretary McCloy's deep ambivalence and Arnold's resistance on the Buddhist chaplain issue were consistent with broader government efforts to present Nisei in the armed forces as culturally assimilated citizens. In this regard, Roosevelt's public pronouncement that "Americanism is a matter of the mind and not of the heart," while intended as an endorsement of racial and ethnic tolerance and diversity, was consistent with the government's view of Buddhism as a foreign religion and of Buddhists as less than ideal representatives of Americanism. Moreover, the inclusion of purportedly assimilated Nisei Christian chaplains and the endorsement of Buddhist exclusion by a Nisei Christian minister was used to avert charges of discrimination. While serving as the first Catholic army chief of chaplains since the position was created in 1920, Arnold nevertheless demonstrated antipathy toward Buddhists. In making the appearance of being antiracist, Arnold could evidence opposition to the recruitment of a Buddhist chaplain by the 442nd's two Nisei Christian chaplains, as well as a Nisei Christian minister from outside the military who described the Buddhists as a major impediment to Americanization.[36]

Resistance to recognition of Buddhism in the armed forces persisted into the postwar period but, under increased pressure from local and territorial officials, began to show some signs of change. Three years after the end of the war, in the fall of 1948, Nisei again raised the issue of Buddhist chaplaincy, along with the recognition of the option of Buddhist designation on GI identification tags. Buddhist leaders petitioned the United States Army for Buddhist chaplains in the US Army and for the creation of an option for a "B" designation on GI identification tags, or "dog tags." Standard issue at the time were tags with three choices of religious affiliation, which spoke to the Judeo-Christian imagining of American national religious traditions: "P" for Protestant, "C" for Catholic, or "H" for Hebrew.[37]

The "B for Buddhism" campaign reflected a new urgency in efforts to push for greater visibility in the US military and to promote ethnic American Buddhism among the general public. With Nikkei resettlement well under way, and during a period when Nisei war dead were being reinterred and memorialized, Nisei working through Young Buddhist Associations in California and Hawai'i organized a campaign drive to pressure the federal government to recognize and support Buddhists in the US military.

Tad Hirota, who with Reverend Kumata played a key role in navigating BCA through WRA release programs, now took the lead in the "B for Buddhism" campaign. Hirota promoted the campaign at Young Buddhist Conventions, whose members circulated and collected petitions for the campaign from Buddhist churches and temples and then forwarded them to US Secretary of Defense James Forrestal.[38] In November, 1948, for example, Hirota addressed the Central California Young Buddhist Association (CCYBA) and recruited CCYBA members to work in the petition drive and to write letters on behalf of the campaign to their local, state, and, in the case of Hawai'i, territorial government representatives.[39]

As a result of their efforts, Nisei Buddhists leaders began to identify and recruit sympathetic politicians. Ryo Munekata, Elso Ito, and Grace Harada led the Los Angeles petition drive and gained the endorsement of the LA County Board of Supervisors for the "B for Buddhist" measure.[40] Meanwhile, YBA members in Hawai'i convinced a territorial representative, Republican Joseph R. Farrington, to personally contact Major General Luther C. Miller, the US Army's chief chaplain.[41]

Highlighting the continued resistance to the recognition of Buddhism in the armed forces, Miller failed to appoint a Buddhist chaplain, and one would not be appointed until 2008.[42] However on the issue of GI identification tags, Miller proposed a compromise. Rather than a "B," an "X" designation for any religious affiliation that did not fit the Protestant, Catholic, or Hebrew categories could be adopted. Those with "X" designations were also allowed to wear an additional metal identification tag issued by their church.[43] Tad Hirota accepted Miller's offer and noted that the Hawaii Young Buddhist Association had already designed and crafted plastic prototypes of the secondary GI identification tags with the printed words "I am a Buddhist" or "Buddhist."[44]

The "B for Buddhism" campaign promoted ethnic national Buddhism but also exposed the impact of racial liberalism in limiting the rights of Buddhists to enjoy their constitutionally guaranteed protection of freedom of religion even as other ethnic-religious minorities were gaining greater acceptance. As Matthew Jacobson has argued, American Jews and Catholics, particularly the children of Eastern and Southern European immigrants, began to experience greater religious acceptance that paralleled the broadening of the racial definition of whiteness to include "Caucasians."[45] Miller's rejection of Buddhist chaplains and his refusal to fully acknowledge Buddhists on GI identification tags reproduced notions of exclusion from the American national imaginary, particularly when contrasted with the official production and recognition of tags for Protestants, Catholics, and Jews by the United States government.

Despite this, the compromise on GI identification tags was celebrated by Nisei Buddhists as a small victory in a longer battle for religious recognition. Moreover, it underscored to participants the importance of the political mobilization of Buddhists toward that longer struggle. Recalling the work that went into the "B for Buddhism" campaign, the Hawaiʻi Young Buddhist Association Federation reflected, "From the wild scramble for petition signatures, and the rush to the Board of Supervisors of each county and territory, and other government, civic and private groups for their endorsements . . . [thinking back] now, it is like a nightmare." Yet despite the struggles, Hawaiʻi YBA members described the "long drawn out negotiation," as a "satisfactory decision."[46]

Wartime and postwar efforts for the recognition of Nisei Buddhists in the armed forces sought to challenge racial liberalism beyond the parameters set by government-sanctioned cultural assimilation and Japanese cultural stereotypes portrayed by wartime media coverage of the 442nd. Working in partnership with the Japanese American Citizens League, veterans' organizations, and the federal government, Nisei Buddhist leaders would continue to battle discrimination to the grave as they sought to honor and memorialize the efforts and sacrifices of

Nisei Buddhists in the postwar years. As had been true with struggles to make Buddhism visible in the armed services, postwar memorial campaigns aimed to more fully integrate Buddhism and Nikkei Buddhists into American society and the American national imaginary.

Memorial Services for Buddhist Nisei War Veterans

Funerary and other memorial services for Nisei Buddhist war veterans between the late 1940s and early 1950s, played a crucial role in promoting ethnic American Buddhism both within Buddhist communities and among the general American public. The pairing of Buddhist priests and services with US government and military officials and veterans organizations at memorial services infused ceremonies with new symbolic meaning during a period when Asia was emerging as a focal point in the Cold War. Funeral services for Nisei Shin Buddhist war dead appeared in local and national newspapers in the spring and summer of 1948 as the bodies of deceased Nisei Buddhist soldiers began to return in large numbers from overseas for reburial in the United States. Services for twenty-five-year-old Private First Class Kazuo Mitani, who was killed in action while serving with the 442nd in France, were held in his hometown of Salt Lake City in May 1948. Reverend Chonen H. Terakawa officiated a Tuesday evening service at the Salt Lake Buddhist Church.[47] This was followed on Wednesday afternoon with military honors directed by Glen Thompson, commander of the VFW Atomic Post 4355, and John B. Sergakis, commander of the VFW Sugarhouse Post 3586. Meanwhile, members of the West High School ROTC served as pallbearers, on the firing squad, and as buglers for the graveside services.[48]

For Nikkei Buddhist communities, memorial services served as a balm that could address generational divisions that had been exacerbated by the crisis of war. For many Nisei, postwar funerary services infused rituals from their youth with new emotional, spiritual, and ideological meaning. Despite the introduction of programs designed for Nisei, such as Sunday School and Japanese-language school, the Japanese language often remained a barrier to understanding aspects of Shin Buddhist teaching and practice. Through the early 1950s, few Shin Buddhist texts were translated into English. A small number of works on general Buddhism were available in English, such as translations of select Buddhist sutras, commentaries on Buddhist sutras, and, more often, summaries of Buddhism's history published by European and American scholars or convert Buddhist laypersons. The small number of Nisei Buddhists who did encounter these texts drew few connections between what they read and the practices associated with Shin Buddhism.

Figure 3.2. Buddhist funeral service for Nisei soldier, Tacoma Buddhist Church, 1949. Reproduced courtesy of the Seattle Nisei Veterans Committee, Densho Digital Repository.

This did not mean that Shin Buddhist practices, including services and teachings, were devoid of meaning. Nisei grew up attending services with the chanting of the *nembutsu*, the striking of bells, the burning of incense, the repetition of sutras, the presentation of flowers before home (*butsudan*), and church altars enshrining the image of the Amida Buddha. For many postwar exiles returning to the West Coast or dispersed across the Midwest and East Coast of the United States, memories of prewar temple services had come to represent the familiar. Even for those who struggled to understand the teachings and the meaning of the rituals, imagery, and communal gatherings, these elements represented an integral part of their familial, ethnic, and religious upbringing. Thus, as they planned and held services for Nisei war dead, the Issei Shin Buddhist rituals of their youth resonated with new meaning.

Following Shin Buddhist tradition, memorial services (*hoji*) for the deceased began with a bedside service (*makura-gyo*). Although the bedside service was traditionally followed by a wake service (*otsuya*) held one day prior to the funeral service (*soshiki*), some families began to transfer the deceased to the mortuary in order to prepare the body for the funeral service. During the funeral service, the deceased was presented with a posthumous Buddhist name (*homyo juyo*) if they had not previously received one either through ordination rites for priests or during confirmation rites (*kikyoshiki*) performed by the abbot.[49] One copy of the Buddhist name was placed in the casket by the officiating priest and one was given to the family of the deceased to be placed in their home altar (*butsudan*). Following the funeral service, memorial services for the deceased were held in series on the seventh, fourteenth, twenty-first, twenty-eighth, thirty-fifth, and forty-ninth days following their death. This was followed by services on the one-hundredth day and the first, third, seventh, thirteenth, seventeenth, twenty-fifth, thirty-third, and fiftieth yearly anniversaries of the passing of the deceased.[50]

For Nikkei families and communities, Buddhist memorial services offered opportunities for collective remembrance of their loved ones through an affirmation of Shin Buddhist teachings. A 1955 BCA publication described memorial services as "remembrances and observances for the encouragement of those left behind in remembering the deceased; they also afford comfort and solace to the sorrowful heart." Reflecting on the significance of the Shin Buddhist practice of the *nembutsu*, the publication concluded that memorial services "also afford inspiration for the further strengthening of Faith, consolation, and a way of expressing love and appreciation for the departed."[51]

Even as they served the needs of Nikkei Buddhist communities, funerary services also provided BCA's Nisei leadership with a powerful counterpoint to US government policies that had deemed their constituency unassimilated and less American at a moment when a growing number of American civic and political leaders were increasingly sensitive to international public opinion regarding race and religious diversity both at home and overseas. The inclusion of representatives of veterans' organizations and US military and government officials in funerary services elevated Nisei Buddhist sacrifices for the nation while also introducing non-Buddhist participants to a religious worldview that many Americans continued to view as foreign.

The ability of Nisei Buddhist leaders to develop alliances with the JACL, veterans' organizations, and national, state, and local politicians was critical in shaping the iconographic representation of ethnic American Buddhism at public funerals and memorials. The JACL's Mike Masaoka led the campaign for the postwar memorialization of Nisei war dead.[52] By 1946, Masaoka was working as the JACL's Washington, DC, lobbyist when he was appointed to serve on President Harry Truman's Commission on Civil Rights. As Jane Hong has shown, for Masaoka, the presentation of martial patriotism proved central in recruiting political allies among federal lawmakers.[53] Given the centrality of martial patriotism for JACL, it is not surprising, then, that the organization took the lead in advocating for public ceremonies for returning Nisei war veterans and later for the internment of Nisei at Arlington National Cemetery.

Despite JACL's historical emphasis on cultural assimilation, the league's relations with Buddhists was more complicated than has often been portrayed. While some members continued to adhere to a view of Buddhists as foreign or suspect after the war, others were more sympathetic, particularly to Nisei who served in the armed forces. During the war, Masaoka had supported the failed wartime efforts to create Buddhist chaplaincy positions. Years after the campaign, he recalled, "I have always regretted we lost on the Buddhist issue. In a nation based on freedom of worship, men of the 442nd brought up as Buddhist certainly were entitled to a chaplain of their faith."[54]

Moreover, some of BCA's most prominent national and local Nisei Buddhist leaders involved in the planning of Nisei Buddhist memorials were active JACL members. Tad Hirota, who had become president of the Western Young Buddhist League and would serve as the future director of the National Young Buddhist Coordinating Council was active in JACL as was Dr. Ryo Munekata, vice president of the Los Angeles Young Buddhist Association, who led the mainland "B for Buddhism" campaign and would serve as a future BCA president.[55] In addition to his leadership in the Young Buddhist movement, Munekata served as second vice president of the newly established Southwest Los Angeles JACL in 1948. Like other Nisei Buddhists who served a Nikkei clientele, Munekata placed a regular ad for his dental practice in the JACL's *Pacific Citizen*.[56]

Nisei Buddhists also turned to the JACL's publication, *Pacific Citizen,* in addressing racial and religious discrimination and for sympathetic coverage of Nisei Buddhist memorial services. Harold Y. Shimizu, a leading Nisei Buddhist in the small coastal town of Guadalupe, California, took out a full-page advertisement in October 1947. Accompanied by an illustration of a family of four gathered together, crouching in fear as they faced a hand with a finger pointed toward them, Shimizu's ad read, "Guilty of Being Different."

> You who read this have been found GUILTY—by self-appointed "judges."
> You're guilty of being born—if you're different from your "judges." You're
> guilty of praying to your own God—if your "judges" don't like your religion. You're guilty of having a mother and father whose characteristics or
> color your "judges" find displeasing. You're guilty of seeking security for
> your family—something you must not do your "judges" say, if they don't
> like your race, creed, or national origin.

Shimizu concluded that in sowing the seeds of racial and religious division, the activity of these "judges" was "treasonable to our democracy" and that those who stopped them were "defending the American Way of Life."[57]

In addition to the JACL, Nisei Buddhist leaders also coordinated with veterans' organizations in planning and presenting memorials. Two Nisei branches of the American Legion, the San Francisco–based Townsend Harris Post 438 and the Los Angeles–based Commodore Perry Post, played prominent roles in a number of memorials. Nisei Buddhist leaders also reached out to mainline veterans' organizations for support. The participation of non-Japanese American veterans' organizations in Nisei Buddhist funerals highlighted the dramatic shift that had taken place among many veterans since the pre–World War II days as a result of shared combat and the publicity surrounding the 442nd.

West Coast posts of the American Legion were active in the anti-Japanese movement beginning in the 1920s. Yet, beginning with the deployment of the 100th Infantry Battalion to Europe and the announcement of the formation of the 442nd, Legionnaires began to express support for Nisei soldiers and to view discrimination against Nisei as un-American. In the October 1943 issue of the *American Legion Magazine,* Claude N. Settles, a World War I veteran and California Legionnaire, responded to an anti-Japanese American article, "The Japs in Our Yard," published in the June 1943 issue of *American Legion.* In it, the author advocated resettling all those of Japanese ancestry with the exception of American soldiers or veterans to islands in the Pacific. Settles concluded, "The Legion through the publication of *Japs in Our Yard* almost proved itself to be what it has so frequently been called—the 'un-American Legion.' Like the Northfield (Minnesota) Post, I do vigorously protest against our national magazine being used to foster race hatred in violation of our constitution and the Constitution of the United States."[58] *American Legion* editor Alexander Gardiner described Settles' letter as "typical of many that we have received protesting against Dr. Murray's statements."[59]

The willingness of US civic leaders to participate in the commemoration of Nisei Buddhist war dead reflected both a change of heart affected by the wartime heroism and sacrifices of the 442nd and growing Cold War tensions and aspirations for American empire across the Pacific to Asia. President Harry Truman's view that religion could play an important role in the Cold War helped to open space for Nisei Buddhist memorialization. In a widely reported public ceremony of returning members of the 442nd, Truman reviewed the unit in Washington, DC, on July 15, 1946, before a crowd of five thousand. Prior to their review, the five hundred members of the 442nd marched from the Capitol Building, down Constitution Avenue, before a crowd of approximately ten thousand who applauded them. At the review, Truman shook hands with members of the combat team and invoked FDR's adage about Americanism, but modified it to include an explicit reference to religious belief. He stated,

> You are to be congratulated on what you have done for this great country of ours. I think it was my predecessor who said that Americanism is not a matter of race or *creed*, it is a matter of the heart. . . . You are now on your way home. You fought not only the enemy, but you fought prejudice and you have won. Keep up that fight and we will continue to win—to make this great republic stand for just what the constitution says it stands for: the welfare of all the people all the time.[60]

Truman's use of "creed," in place of "ancestry" from Roosevelt's earlier speech, was consistent with his view of the importance of religious tolerance in the aftermath of reports of the extent of Nazi atrocities against Jews in the concentration and death camps. Moreover, as Cold War tensions grew, Truman's definition of Americanism as representing religious tolerance along with racial tolerance was consistent with his increasing conviction that Christianity and other world religions were of central importance in fighting communism abroad.[61]

Truman's actions were echoed by West Coast local and state officials, particularly from cities or regions well positioned to benefit from expanded access to markets in Japan and Asia more generally.[62] Los Angeles mayor Fletcher Bowron, who had endorsed the mass incarceration of Nikkei but later apologized to returnees, credited the actions of the 442nd for his change of heart. At the same time, during his tenure, which ended in 1953, Bowron would go on to successfully integrate Los Angeles into a key hub in an emerging transpacific economy. Like mayors of other major West Coast port cities, Bowron was a visible presence in memorials for Nisei Buddhists.[63] Addressing the Los Angeles Young Buddhist League in a letter published in October 1946 in the league's *Sangha* newsletter, Bowron sent greetings and words of support for their memorial to Nisei Buddhist soldiers, noting their "tribute to the Japanese Americans who fought with the armed forces of our country in the cause of democracy, and are returning to take up their lives interrupted by the war."[64]

Motivated by a complex array of factors, from Cold War geopolitics and economic development to a change of heart shaped by guilt or a sense of justice, the decoration of living members of the 442nd by a growing number of federal, state, and local politicians throughout the country highlighted a narrative of redemption for those of Japanese ancestry through the sacrifices of the Japanese Americans in the 100th/442nd, and, at the same time, the redemption of America from its wartime practices of discrimination. As has been well discussed by scholars, "American redemption" was a repeated trope in the Cold War civil rights discourse professed by the federal government as it sought to appeal to a global audience and, in particular, to an emerging group of third world nations.[65]

Ethnic American Buddhism was on display in both local and ethnic press coverage of the funerals of Nisei Buddhists. George Gushiken's funeral service was performed by Reverend Daitetsu Hayashima at the Hompa Hongwanji Temple in Los Angeles.[66] Most services opened with the Kansho or "calling bell." Buddhist priests led sutra chanting before the altar, during which time family, friends, and other guests offered incense. During the service, Gushiken was given a *homyo juyo* (dharma name), with one copy written in Japanese script placed inside the casket and a second given to his family to keep in their *butsudan* (family home altar).[67] Gushiken's casket was draped in the American flag and carried by pallbearers representing a 442nd Honor Guard. His casket was then placed at the front of twelve wreaths.[68] Eulogies were presented, and invited guest Mayor Fletcher Bowron also addressed the four hundred in attendance.[69] Next, Gushiken's body was accompanied by the family and honor guard to Evergreen Cemetery in Boyle Heights, where military services including a three-volley salute, the performing of taps, and the presentation of the colors to Gushiken's mother, Mrs. Tom (Ushi Iha) Gushiken was planned and conducted by the Nisei Veterans Association.[70]

National press coverage of funerary and memorial services for Nisei Buddhist war dead was rare and demonstrated the limits of presenting ethnic American Buddhism. Gushiken's story circulated as a human-interest story through International Soundphoto, appearing in the *New York Herald* as well as small newspapers across the country, which ignored any mention or presentation of the Buddhist elements, highlighting instead a racial liberal story of the Gushiken family's assimilation to America. Titled, "An American Boy Comes Home," the article included a photograph of Gushiken's mother overcome with grief as she reached out to Gushiken's casket, which was sitting on the bed of a truck while a neighbor tried to comfort her. The International Soundphoto caption read,

> **All THE PAIN AND SORROW** of motherhood is etched on the face of Mrs. Tom Gushiken as she touches the flag-bedecked casket of her son, Pfc. George Gushiken, the first American of Japanese descent to be returned to Los Angeles. The boy died of a sniper's bullet in France. Mrs. Gushiken is being comforted by a neighbor.[71]

In national coverage, Gushiken's mother's foreignness, represented by her Japanese body, was redeemed by her son's sacrifice. Represented as a mourning mother of a dead American war hero, her gesture of grasping her son's flag-draped casket transferred Gushiken's sacrifice to his Issei parents, who were themselves redeemed. Reproducing the cultural assimilation narrative produced during the war by the WRA and armed forces, coverage of the funeral neglected to pair any elements of Buddhism with Gushiken or his mother's sacrifice.

In contrast to coverage for most Buddhist funerals for Nisei war dead, which were largely confined to local and ethnic press, efforts by BCA leadership to have their dead recognized and remembered as American soldiers of the Buddhist faith at national memorials, including Arlington National Cemetery, would have a significant and lasting impact in broadening the national imaginary to include Buddhists. Memorial services at national cemeteries mirrored the pairing of Buddhist ritual and symbols with those of the US government at funerals and interment for Nisei Buddhist war dead at local cemeteries. At a memorial service held in Golden Gate National Cemetery in San Bruno, California, in August, 1948, as part of a celebration of the fiftieth anniversary of the establishment of the Buddhist Churches of America, ethnic American Buddhism was on full display. Fifty-five Nisei war dead were honored along with fellow American war dead. A solemn crowd of four hundred witnessed the mixture of Buddhist ceremony with American military honors. The *o-chigo* procession of forty Japanese American girls and boys accompanying twenty Buddhist priests proceeded to the podium as the Bay District Young Buddhist Association choir, led by Mrs. Jane Imamura, sang Buddhist *gathas*.[72] Memorial service chair Dick Seiki and his committee invited representatives from the US armed forces, veterans' organizations, and Japanese American civic organizations. Serving as memorial chairman, Tad Hirota introduced guest speakers Lieutenant Colonel Charles d'Orsa, who represented General Mark Clark; Sam Bauers, president of the United Veterans Council and vice chairman of the Jewish War Veterans; and William Enomoto, vice chairman of the JACL's Northern California District. In the poignant conclusion to the service, Matt Shigio, Yajiro Okamoto, Shizuo Namba, and Norman Nakano, four members of the all-Nisei Townsend Harris Post 438 of the American Legion, stood at attention as taps and a rifle salute were performed by soldiers from the 6th Army Headquarters in San Francisco.[73]

One month later, in September of 1948, Corporal "Jimmie" Toshio Kokubu was interred at Arlington National Cemetery, becoming the third Nisei and first Buddhist to be laid to rest at the site. Killed in action in France in October of 1944 at the age of twenty-five, Kokubu had been raised in the Shingon Buddhist tradition.[74] His body was laid to rest just a few hundred feet from the graves of Private First Class Fumitake Nagato and Private First Class Saburo Tanamachi, two Nisei associated with the 442nd's rescue of the Lost Battalion who had been interred four months earlier.[75] Nagato and Tanamachi's funeral included high-ranking members of the military and members of Congress. Designated honorary pallbearers included Major General Jacob Devers, who commanded the 6th Army Group, in which the 442nd served in France; four other generals; Colonel Virgil Miller and Colonel Charles W. Pence, each of whom commanded the 442nd; Colonel Charles Owen of the 141st Infantry Regiment, to which the Lost Battalion was attached; and two other colonels with relations to the 442nd.[76] Following standard practice, each received a nonsectarian service performed by First Army Chief of Chaplains Major General Luther Miller, performed with full military honors, followed by a brief civilian Protestant service conducted by the Reverend Andrew Kuroda, associate minister of the First Evangelical and Reformed Church, Washington, DC.[77]

By the 1920s Arlington National Cemetery, created during the Civil War, had come to reflect a powerful vision of the imagined community of the American nation. At the heart of this vision was the juxtaposition of rows of white headstones in proximity with the Tomb of the Unknown Soldier. In her analysis of the 1921 inaugural funeral service and coverage of services for the Unknown Soldier, Micki McElya noted the extensive efforts that went into the maintenance of the anonymity of the soldier, a key that McElya attributes to efforts to underscore the body's universality. Yet McElya noted that these efforts were accompanied by speeches and press coverage that presumed both the whiteness and Protestant Christian background of the dead soldier.[78]

Indeed, the presumed universality of white citizenry in the national imaginary was reinforced by the long history of racial segregation of the dead at Arlington. Significantly, the universality of Protestant Christianity captured in the inaugural service for the unknown soldier was both qualified and reinforced by the introduction, following World War I, of acceptance of two religious emblems on headstones. Headstones for soldiers of the Christian faith could receive a Latin cross, while those of the Jewish faith could receive a Star of David.[79] The particularization of Jewish veterans' headstones through their visibility both qualified and reinforced the unknown soldier's universal racial and religious identification. Still, the development marked an important recognition of religious diversity for the first time in Arlington's history.

Efforts to encourage and support public services for honoring Nisei war dead at Arlington and other American national cemeteries complemented the cultural-assimilation approach toward overcoming racial discrimination. As McElya argued, "Arlington literally and symbolically provided the grounds for authorizing this particular constellation of postwar Japanese American citizenship claims."[80] In 1947, JACL joined a host of other organizations at Arlington National Cemetery on

Armistice Day. In the morning, they laid a wreath at the Tomb of the Unknown Soldier; President Truman also offered a wreath and participated in a moment of silence and prayers before a crowd of 2,500.[81] In the afternoon, JACL and other groups conducted individual services.[82]

Kokubu's 1948 funeral service at Arlington mirrored the army's compromise policy in the "B for Buddhism" campaigns: officially acknowledging without explicitly recognizing Buddhism. As the Nisei newspaper *Northwest Times* noted, a private Buddhist service was conducted off-site "at the conclusion of separate Jewish, Catholic and Protestant services for the war dead conducted by Army chaplains." In order to conduct the service, JACL had requested special permission from the army to release the casket for the service, which included Kokubu's parents, his two sisters and their spouses, and members of the JACL and the Japanese American Society.[83] JACL's Mike Masaoka viewed the lack of visibility of Buddhist ritual and symbols at Kokubu's interment as a missed opportunity to memorialize Buddhism. Contacting Tad Hirota and Nisei Buddhist leaders shortly after Kokubu's ceremony, Masaoka wrote, "As the first Buddhist ever to be interred at Arlington, I believe a special program could have been worked out for Corporal Kokubu with the Army, which would have received favorable nation-wide publicity."[84]

Masaoka recommended that Nisei Buddhist leaders petition the federal government to include Buddhist symbols on government cemetery headstone markers. Noting that "at the present time, I understand that the government provides standard markers bearing a cross for Christians and a Star of David for Jews," Masaoka concluded that not only was it "fitting and proper" for Buddhists to be acknowledged, but also that recognition "would serve to persuade many that Buddhism is not strictly a foreign religion and that members of the Buddhist faith gave their lives for the defense of the United States."[85] In response to Masaoka, National Young Buddhist Coordinating Council (NYBCC) chair Tad Hirota noted that "the marker matter has been discussed with BCA officials and a recommendation is expected shortly."[86]

Meeting in San Francisco in January 1949, the NYBCC resolved to initiate a campaign to propose the recognition of Buddhist markers in military cemeteries. Joined by members of the Hawaii Federation of YBAs, Buddhists gathered signatures for petitions that would be sent to Secretary of Defense Louis Johnson.[87] During the same period, the Hawaii Federation of Young Buddhist Associations went a step further in planting the seeds of Nisei Buddhism. The association formally requested that the Pacific National Cemetery Committee reserve an area of the cemetery for the planting of eight bodhi trees in honor of four hundred Nisei Buddhist soldiers who died during World War II.[88]

Representing the culmination of Nisei Buddhist efforts to recognize Buddhism in the armed services that had begun with efforts to request Buddhist chaplains, the petition campaign played an important role in shifting government policy on the recognition of Buddhism. On September 3, 1949, the *Pacific Citizen* reported that the United States Army officially agreed to recognize the "Buddhist emblem" for the "permanent grave markers of American soldiers of the Buddhist faith."[89] Despite the Hawai'i announcement, the ability to select a Buddhist marker for all military headstones would not be officially approved by the secretary of the army until February 1951.[90] Significantly, the dharma chakra, or wheel of dharma, a symbol shared by Buddhists across denominations and sects, was selected and continues to be used to mark the gravestones of many Buddhist war dead today.[91]

Through campaigns to memorialize Buddhist war dead, Nisei Buddhists gained on-the-ground training experience in community advocacy, public relations, and political networking. As they did so, they also accrued greater credibility and recognition as rising leaders within the Buddhist Churches of America. Yet, as they increasingly immersed themselves in Buddhist institutional leadership, Nisei faced new challenges shaped by competing visions for the future direction of the BCA, which in turn were influenced by shifting Cold War geopolitics and, in particular, evolving relations between the United States and Japan.

Institutional Politics, Ministerial Training, and the Ascendance of Nisei Buddhism

During the BCA annual meeting of ministers and lay representatives in February of 1948, Bishop Ryotai Matsukage became seriously ill. One month later, the bishop traveled to Los Angeles to undergo surgery at the Japanese Hospital in Boyle Heights. Never fully recovering, he remained there for three months before passing away on June 21 at the age of 58.[1] BCA members held an *otsuya* (wake) service in Los Angeles and a second service, along with the *soshiki* (funeral) service, one week later in San Francisco. Forty-three of BCA's priests from across the country participated in rites for the bishop's funeral. Eight Nisei members from BCA's national board of directors served as pallbearers.[2] At Matsukage's request, his ashes were combined with those of his wife Isao and divided into three urns, with one interred at Matsukage's family temple in the prefecture of Hiroshima; one in Kyoto, home to the Hompa Honganji head temple; and a third at the Cypress Cemetery in Colma near San Francisco, where he and his wife had worked tirelessly in support of Buddhism in America.[3]

Tributes were paid and a memorial constructed in honor of Bishop Matsukage. Two months following his death, a Golden Jubilee Festival celebrating the fifty-year anniversary of BCA's founding was dedicated to the bishop, who was memorialized as a pioneer for Issei Buddhism and for *bukkyō tōzen*.[4] The following year, a BCA pamphlet published on the occasion of Matsukage's first memorial ceremony included a poem composed by the late bishop on the occasion of his death.

Waga hone wo America no
Chi ni usumete zo
Toa ni minori no
Iyasaka won en zu.
Bury my ashes
In the soil of America,
And into Eternity
May the Dharma prosper.[5]

BCA's lay representatives also approved the construction of a monument in honor of Bishop Matsukage in February 1949. Standing ten feet high, the natural rock monument was dedicated two years later, on February 18, 1951. The Shin Buddhist "Namu Amida Butsu" was inscribed on the front of the monument in Japanese script, written by Chief Abbot Kosho Ohtani, spiritual leader of the Nishi Honganji head temple in Kyoto.[6]

Appointed by the Nishi Honganji in the 1930s, Matsukage had until his death remained the last vestige of institutional and cultural authority sanctioned by Shin Buddhism's head temple. His willingness to work on behalf of BMNA with US government authorities and Nisei lay leaders during and following the war had been central in smoothing over the wartime transfer of formal control of the Issei-led BMNA institution to shared governance between an Issei-led minister's association, and a Nisei-led national board of directors in BCA. Now, with the bishop's untimely death, plans to reconstitute BCA's institutional relationship with affiliated temples and churches and for the future transmission of Buddhist teachings was thrown into disarray. Efforts by Issei and Nisei lay leaders and ministers to reconstitute BCA led to fundamental questions about the form that *bukkyō tōzen* would take in postwar America: To what degree would BCA continue to be defined by Shin Buddhism and the prewar traditions established by Issei Buddhists? How could BCA serve and remain relevant to its growing Nisei and Sansei (third-generation) population? What contribution could Buddhist teachings make to the broader US society and culture? These were difficult questions for the fledgling organization as it transitioned from the postwar to early Cold War years.

This chapter examines the institutional and cultural politics that ushered in the early transition from Issei Buddhism to Nisei Buddhism within the Buddhist Churches of America from the late 1940s through the 1950s. In the aftermath of Bishop Matsukage's passing, competing visions of the future direction of the Buddhist Churches of America emerged among Nisei leaders. Building on efforts initiated at the wartime emergency meetings, a younger cohort of YBA leaders, with fewer ties to Issei leadership, envisioned a Nisei-led, English-speaking, nonsectarian Buddhist institution that would serve Nikkei communities as well as cultivate a broader appreciation of Buddhism among the general public. The younger cohort founded the short-lived nonsectarian National Young Buddhist Coordinating Council (NYBCC) in 1948 during an ambitious ten-day Golden Jubilee Festival planned to formally and symbolically usher in the transition from Issei to Nisei leadership.

By 1952, NYBCC had been subsumed by BCA, as an older cohort of Nisei and Kibei with closer political and cultural ties to BCA's Issei ministers and lay leaders sought to remake BCA into a Shin sectarian Buddhist institution that primarily served Nikkei communities. Members of this group played a key role as administrative intermediaries across generations and between ministers and laypersons. Their rise to leadership and the narrower sectarian orientation of the organization was greatly facilitated by a shift in US occupation policy in Japan that reopened channels of communication among BCA, Nishi Honganji, and its spiritual leader, Chief Abbot Kosho Ohtani.

In the aftermath of this shift, the younger cohort of leaders redirected their energies toward the formation of Buddhist study groups and the training of English-speaking ministers, programs that could serve Nisei and the growing Sansei generation, while also spreading awareness of Buddhism and Buddhist teachings to the general American public. Despite the varied views and approaches of the older and younger cohorts of Nisei, together, their efforts would prove central in facilitating BCA's transition from a prewar Issei Buddhist to postwar Nisei Buddhist institution and in establishing outreach beyond Nikkei communities, to those Americans interested in Buddhism

The National Young Buddhist Coordinating Council

Following the death of Bishop Matsukage, a group of Nisei lay leaders proceeded with plans already under way to launch a new trans-sectarian Buddhist organization that they envisioned playing a significant role in both transforming the BCA and in promoting Buddhism in America. The National Young Buddhist Coordinating Council would comprise five regional Buddhist Leagues stretching across the continental United States. NYBCC emerged from the prewar YBA organizations that had been elevated to leadership positions during the WRA-endorsed emergency meetings during World War II, and its proponents envisioned an organization that would serve as a critical link between BCA headquarters and affiliated local Buddhist temples and churches, as well as an important vehicle for the promotion of Buddhism among the general American public.[7]

The proposal for a Nisei-led, trans-sectarian council by Nisei, a majority of whom identified as Shin Buddhists, was shaped in part in response to the wartime and early postwar cultural assimilation policies of the US government. As discussed in previous chapters, US government policies toward Nikkei Buddhists remained ambivalent at best, reflecting a tension between a persistent belief among government officials in Buddhism's foreignness and a recognition of the domestic and international propaganda value in promoting Buddhists as part of a racially and religiously diverse nation.

During the wartime incarceration, Nisei Buddhist leaders responded to this ambivalence by emphasizing Buddhism as a world religion, with teachings and values that were compatible with American democracy. The emphasis on general Buddhism and on Buddhism as a world religion by Nisei ministers and lay members continued into the postwar period. In *Bliss of Nirvana,* a 1946 publication of the New York Young Buddhist Association, Buddhism was defined as a democratic, universal, and global religious tradition. When referenced, "Amidaism" and Shin Buddhism were discussed as a stage in Buddhism's longer global history. The founding of Buddhism in Japan and the establishment of the Jōdo, Zen, Shin, and Nichiren sects—along with a short essay penned by the editor, the Nisei Reverend Newton Ishiura, discussing the development of Shin Buddhist teachings from Honen to Shinran—were covered in a little more than three pages. In contrast, the longer history and teachings of Buddhism was addressed in twelve pages. The publication included a map titled "The Spread of Buddhism," which highlighted Buddhism as a world religion with origins in India. While supporting aspects of the Japanese Buddhist conception of *bukkyō tōzen,* by showing Buddhism's "eastward" progression through China and Japan, followed by Hawai'i and North America, the map also highlighted northward and westward paths taken as Buddhism migrated to Tibet and England, thus underscoring Buddhism as a world religion.[8]

NYBCC also formed in relation to shifting Nikkei Buddhist institutional politics shaped by US policies during its occupation of Japan between 1945 and 1952. The rise of a Nisei-led, trans-sectarian council was facilitated by the weakened position of BCA's Issei bishop and ministers which resulted from the uncertainty surrounding the future of the Nishi Honganji home temple and the Chief Abbot Kosho Ohtani. A direct descendent of Shinran and spiritual leader of the Shin sect, Ohtani was elevated to the position of chief abbot in 1933 and was responsible for all official religious ceremonies, including ordination of priests, which included those sent to the United States until the onset of World War II.[9] Under the US occupation, Abbot Ohtani was banned from public service and was prohibited from engaging in some of his administrative duties until at least August 1948 as a result of his wartime association with the Imperial Rule Assistant Association. Meanwhile, feeling both internal pressure from some ministers and lay members and pressure from the Supreme Commander for Allied Powers (SCAP), Nishi Honganji reformed the hierarchical structure of its organization, opening its administrative and legislative body to include an equal representation of ministers and lay leaders.[10]

The emergence of NYBCC as a Nisei-led, BCA-affiliated organization that explicitly defined itself as nonsectarian represented a significant challenge to the fragile balance of BCA's leadership and administration that had been maintained across generations and between ministers and lay leaders during the wartime

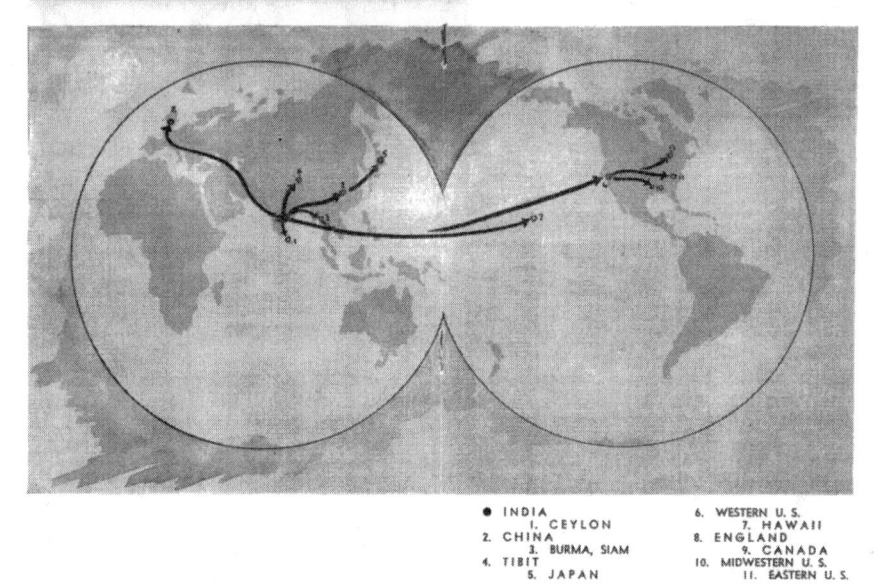

• THE SPREAD OF BUDDHISM

● INDIA
   1. CEYLON
2. CHINA
   3. BURMA, SIAM
4. TIBIT
   5. JAPAN

6. WESTERN U. S.
   7. HAWAII
8. ENGLAND
   9. CANADA
10. MIDWESTERN U. S.
   11. EASTERN U. S.

Figure 4.1. "The Spread of Buddhism." Reprinted from the New York Young Buddhist Association, *Bliss of Nirvana*, 1946.

emergency meetings. NYBCC was created by a younger cohort of Bussei men and women who ranged from their early twenties to their early thirties. They tended to be active members of the Young Buddhist Associations and were a more diverse lot than the older Bussei cohort. Among them were Nisei and Kibei, women and men, students, professionals and laborers, army veterans and those who did not serve in the war, married couples and single individuals. Some of NYBCC's key organizers, including Tad Hirota, Mike Maruyama, Michi Nakamoto, and Manabu Fukuda, had been active in the prewar YBA movement.[11]

In contrast to NYBCC, the composition of BCA's national board of directors during this period was dominated by an older group of Nisei and Kibei professionals in their late thirties to early forties who tended to be bilingual, married, and well-established as businessmen or farmers with strong ties to the prewar Issei Shin Buddhist communities. A few of these leaders such as Masao Murata and Dr. Kikuo Taira had been leaders in the early YBA movement of the

1930s.[12] As they entered the ranks of the BCA's board of directors, these older Bussei played a critical role in bridging divisions and tensions that would emerge between Issei and Nisei and between ministers and board members. Hideo Ito exemplified the role that this older group played in navigating institutional politics. Ito had a prior track record of being able to work with both Bussei and Issei during the tense period of wartime incarceration. At the Rohwer relocation center in Arkansas, Ito was appointed to an organization committee for an "older Bussei group" and was among a group of six Nisei and Kibei who were appointed to serve on Rohwer's nonprofit cooperative committee, where they were tasked with the appointment of Issei to the co-op's advisory board of trustees.[13] In 1946, when he was elected BCA's first Bussei president of the national board of directors, Ito was thirty-six years old, married, and a resident of Monterey, California, where he ran a successful fish market.[14] Praised for his leadership and fundraising skills, and his ability to bridge generational divisions, Ito went on to serve until 1959, the longest term in the history of both BMNA and BCA.[15]

The younger cohort of Nisei lay leaders understood that defining NYBCC as nonsectarian and elevating it to a prominent position with autonomy from BCA would likely be controversial and face some resistance, particularly from those Issei ministers and lay leaders most dedicated to the maintenance of Shin Buddhist teachings and established prewar Issei Buddhist tradition. The Chicago-based *Nisei Vue* magazine noted that as "an independent and all-sectarian" organization, NYBCC was "new and perhaps revolutionary," concluding that, "in the 50 years of [BCA's] existence, this was looked upon as the first public announcement which endeavored to unite the various sects of Buddhists in America."[16] Indeed, these Nisei envisioned the broader role that their organization could play in the transmission of Buddhism in America, one that included but was not limited to local Nikkei Shin Buddhist communities. As such, they hoped that the celebration of BCA's upcoming fifty-year anniversary could serve to both elevate NYBCC's profile and its new mission of uniting Buddhists and spread Buddhist teachings more broadly in America.

NYBCC was formally launched as the culminating event of an ambitious ten-day Golden Jubilee Festival set in San Francisco, California, in August of 1948. The festival was designed to initiate the transfer of obligation and struggle across generations by showcasing the NYBCC convention and paying homage to Issei Buddhism. Attended by an estimated crowd of more than five thousand BCA members, including three hundred charter NYBCC delegates from across the country, along with Buddhists from the territory of Hawai'i, the festival was reported in Japanese American newspapers and magazines and garnered coverage in *LIFE* magazine.[17] In supporting the elevation of NYBCC, the festival adopted the slogan "Carry On Bussei," which had been introduced during the wartime emergency YBA meetings.[18] Golden Jubilee general chairman and national board of directors member Toshio Yoshida proclaimed,

> GOLDEN JUBILEE! Commemoration of 50 years, since our parents first brought Buddhism into this country. Only by their undying interest and effort was it able to survive these hard and long years. To those who have departed and cannot see and enjoy the fruits of their toil, we bow our heads in deep reverence. To those still with us, we express our sincerest appreciation for carrying the torch for us. But we cannot expect them to carry it on forever.[19]

While paying tribute to Issei sacrifices, Yoshida and the organizing committee posited the centrality of NYBCC in continuing the work of *bukkyō tōzen*. Yoshida continued, "Therefore, we the committee for the Golden Jubilee Celebration have planned our program with the following two objectives in mind":

(1) We feel that a Young Adult Group is essential at this time to take over all the church activities.
(2) We wish that this celebration will be a goodwill demonstration towards our Caucasian Friends.[20]

In pursuit of these two objectives, the Golden Jubilee Festival, showcased NYBCC's activation and honored Issei Buddhists and prewar Issei Buddhist traditions.

Figure 4.2. 1948 Golden Jubilee Festival photo. Reproduced courtesy of the Conventions Collection, Seattle Betsuin Buddhist Temple Archives, Densho Digital Repository.

NYBCC Activation at the Golden Jubilee Festival

The Golden Jubilee opened with a three-day conference of delegates with representatives from regional organizations representing the eastern, intermountain, northwest, and western regions of the United States, together with the Hawaii Federation of YBAs.[21] Nearly three hundred delegates gathered to discuss the current state of the YBA movement and the role that NYBCC should play in the Buddhist Churches of America organization.[22] The death of Bishop Matsukage, just two months prior to the Golden Jubilee Festival, had raised the stakes of these issues. Significantly, the next bishop, Enryo Shigefuji, was elected by a council of BCA's priests. Shigefuji's election and appointment represented a break from the long-standing precedent of appointment by the Chief Abbot Ohtani.[23]

Young Adult Convention delegates joined other Golden Jubilee attendants in an opening religious service held at the Buddhist Church of San Francisco. The service was led by the new Bishop Shigefuji and chaired by Reverend Shintatsu Kyozan Sanada. Attendants viewed an *o-chigo* procession of children dressed in Japanese ceremonial clothing from the Heian era followed by a line of Buddhist priests. Delegates listened to a guest talk by Reverend Shinjo Nagatomi of the Gardena Buddhist Church and joined in singing Buddhist *gathas* with a San Francisco Bay Area choir under the direction of Mrs. Jane Imamura, a Nisei leader and wife of one of the few Nisei ministers, Reverend Kanmo Imamura, who had been assigned to the Berkeley Buddhist Church. Following the service, delegates spent the remainder of the day attending representative and general meetings and a panel discussion before participating in a Golden Jubilee opening ceremony.[24]

The following day, participants joined BCA members in a memorial service for Bussei soldiers killed in action, along with fellow American war dead.[25] As discussed in chapter 3, the demonstration of ethnic American Buddhism served to challenge characterizations of Buddhism as a foreign religion by highlighting the sacrifices of Nisei Buddhists for the US nation. However, reading Nisei Buddhist memorials in relation to the activation of NYBCC provides another lens for consideration of the significance of these memorials. Among Nikkei Buddhists, wartime sacrifice was highlighted as justification for the elevation of Nisei leadership within BCA. Many argued that, given their sacrifices, not only would Nisei serve as better cultural ambassadors on behalf of Buddhism in America, but also that they had earned the right to serve in leadership positions.[26]

The Golden Jubilee Festival provided opportunities for Nisei to highlight the political networks—particularly ties with supportive allies outside the ethnic community—that they had developed through their cultural ambassador work. At a Golden Jubilee banquet held at Club Shanghai in San Francisco's Chinatown,

NYBCC delegates, together with BCA's national board members and ministers' association, were joined by invited guests that included San Francisco Board of Supervisors member George Christopher, representatives of the American Friends Service Committee, and the International Institute, a progressive San Francisco–based immigrants' rights organization.[27]

The keynote speaker for the banquet was Edward Howden, executive secretary of the San Francisco Council for Civic Unity. Addressing a packed crowd of nearly three hundred, Howden discussed the challenges faced by Bussei and how these challenges compared with those of the larger Japanese American community and other minority groups. Citing discriminatory practices that shaped all minorities, Howden noted that it was necessary to "always fight to combat discriminatory laws which prevent them from obtaining proper housing and good employment." He encouraged Nisei to not limit their perspective on discrimination to their particular challenges but to consider racial problems on a broader scale.[28]

After a week of meetings, social events, public ceremonies, and talks, organizers closed the festival with a weekend full of community and public events that nostalgically celebrated Issei Buddhism, while elevating Nisei Buddhism to the fore. On the final Saturday of the festival, Young Buddhist Convention delegates participated in an afternoon ceremony that activated the NYBCC.[29] Delegates supported a motion to activate the National Young Buddhist Coordinating Council as a nonsectarian organization and to place that language in the organization's constitution.[30] NYBCC was to comprise five major regional delegates, each with two representatives. Tad Hirota was elected to serve as executive director. Cabinet officers included Manabu Fukuda as president; Mike Maruyama, vice president; Michi Mayemura as secretary; Mike Iwatsubo, treasurer; and Noby Yamakoshi as auditor. As a nondenominational organization, NYBCC would aim to coordinate the activities of all Buddhists in the United States. In addition to Jōdo Shinshū, NYBCC sought to include other Japanese Buddhists from the Nichiren, Zen, Jōdo, and Koyosan sects. It also sought to connect with, and to include, new non-Japanese "convert" Buddhist organizations.[31]

Memorializing *Bukkyō Tōzen:* Issei Pioneers at the Golden Jubilee Festival

The nostalgic portrayal of Issei Buddhist priests and laypersons as "pioneers" who had dedicated and sacrificed their lives to establish Buddhism in America was a key theme repeatedly invoked by Bussei during the Golden Jubilee Festival. This portrayal aimed to both revere Issei Buddhism and promote the transition from

Issei to Bussei leadership by inculcating a sense of mutual obligation through reference to a shared history of racial and religious struggle in America. When paired with efforts to elevate the nonsectarian NYBCC and secure Nisei positions of leadership within BCA, the festival's honoring of prewar Issei Buddhists and Issei Buddhism at the festival can be viewed as driven by mixed motives. On the one hand, Nisei organizers proceeded with a mixture of feelings, gestures, and proclamations that conveyed humility, deference, compassion, sadness, a sense of obligation, and, most of all, gratitude toward the Issei generation. At the same time, tributes to Issei sought to assuage pockets of anticipated resistance, particularly from Issei Shin ministers, that a nonsectarian orientation would provoke. This was compounded by the inexperience and limited economic resources and cultural capital of American-born, predominantly English-speaking laypersons. From the perspective of the broader Nikkei Buddhist community, many Nisei lacked the credentials that had come to define leadership in the Issei-dominated prewar communities.

The Issei Buddhist pioneer symbolism challenged but also reified racial and gendered presuppositions attached to both the figure of the pioneer and the notion of the frontier invoked by the pioneer symbol. Historian Frederick Jackson Turner famously defined the American frontier as a process wherein "civilization" met "savagery," set within the context of westward American expansion across the continental United States. As a number of scholars have shown, the frontier was a highly racialized and gendered concept. As they met and overcame nature and the indigenous peoples that they encountered, European immigrants were allegedly transformed into "Americans." As Americans turned their gaze farther west across the Pacific toward Asia during the late nineteenth century, they adapted earlier ideas about conquest and civilizing missions in interpretations of encounters with Pacific Islanders and Asians. Racial difference and distance from the US nation was also constructed through religion. Christian missionary efforts to convert native American "savages" were quickly applied to Asians both in Asia and among Pacific Islander and immigrant populations across the Pacific and in the United States.[32]

In contrast to Turner's pioneer figure, the Issei pioneer emerged at the confluence of two imperial discourses. As Eiichiro Azuma has shown, the Issei pioneer figure was first developed among immigrant intellectuals and disseminated through the Japanese American ethnic press beginning in the 1920s. Arguments and narratives about Issei pioneers grew out of dominant Anglo-American frontier discourse and Japanese discourses on overseas development in efforts to craft a cultural narrative for Issei elites during a period of growing hostility, especially after the passage of the Johnson-Reed Immigration Act of 1924. As Duncan

Williams and Tomoe Moriya have noted, a Buddhist variation of the Issei pioneer figure was also developed by Issei Buddhist ministers in America who fused the concept of *bukkyō tōzen,* or the eastward expansion of Buddhism, with efforts to cultivate Buddhist communities and proselytize to the general American public.[33]

The honoring of the late Bishop Ryotai Matsukage underscored the role that the narrative and the figure of the pioneer could play in both venerating and laying claim to the legacy of Issei Shin Buddhism for Nisei Buddhists. The Golden Jubilee Festival committee formally dedicated the festival to the memory of the late bishop. Committee member Arthur Takemoto wrote Matsukage's dedication for the festival program. Takemoto, a future Nisei Buddhist priest, had studied under Matsukage at the Topaz War Relocation Center.[34] In his dedication, he recalled the late bishop's commitment to the continuation of Buddhism, noting, "To his dying days, his one concern was for the improvement of the headquarters movement (BCA) and for greater Buddhism in America." Takemoto continued: "Let us recount the wishes of the Bishop Matsukage; let us take a few solemn moments to review the past and all the hardships of the pioneers who struggled to bring Buddhism to this land, so that you and I too, can enjoy the teachings of the *Nembutsu.*" With the sacrifices of Issei pioneers in mind, Takemoto urged festival participants to "rededicate [their] lives with greater vim and vigor in treading the path towards greater understand[ing] of our own religion" and urged participants to "relive Buddhism by practicing its ideals," something that was "surely the dream-come-true of the Bishop Matsukage to whom we dedicate the Golden Jubilee."[35]

While Takemoto's tribute to Matsukage fittingly referenced Shin Buddhist doctrine, other Nisei tributes to pioneers framed Issei as pioneers for general Buddhism. In the opening verses of a poem dedicated to the Issei, and included in the opening pages of the Golden Jubilee Festival Program, Ruth Kodama, a Nisei from San Diego, California, wrote,

> Across the forbidden blue Pacific
> Some fifty years ago
> Traversed pioneers into a strange land
> With Buddhism in their hearts and souls
> To spread the Exalted Lord's Teachings
> Was the common aim
> Strange language did not daunt them
> They taught countless just the same
> Barriers, obstacles, stones on the road
> Did not slacken their courageous mission

From parents to children, neighbor to friend
Mere one of many ways of transmission
Two great wars could not
Weaken this great religion
Through discrimination and bigotry
Was built a mightier legion
Within the fifty short years
The pioneers blazed the hidden trail
That we might continue their mission
Into more unknown land without fail.[36]

An expression of gratitude to the Issei, Kodama's poem charted the course of Buddhism from its arrival in a "strange land," to its transmission across generations and communities, and its survival despite war and discrimination. Rather than reference Shin Buddhist teachings, Kodama's poem noted the "Exalted Lord's Teachings," referring to the historical Buddha, complementing NYBCC's identification as a nonsectarian organization. Kodama's poem concluded with a reinforcement of the theme of generational transfer of leadership by noting that the Nisei would carry on "into more unknown land without fail."[37]

The celebration of Issei pioneers at the 1948 Golden Jubilee Festival represented Bussei efforts to express their deep gratitude to Issei for the sacrifices that they made for Bussei and Buddhism in America. The figure of the Issei pioneer drew from earlier figures invoked by Issei themselves in the face of religious and racial hostility. Yet, in representations at the Golden Jubilee, the Issei pioneer was a historical figure whose days were ending. The Golden Jubilee theme, "Carry On Bussei," and the goal of creating a young Buddhist group to take over, highlighted the role that the Bussei were to play as the progenitors of *bukkyō tōzen*.

Cold War Diplomacy and the Reinstitution of Ties with Nishi Honganji

Following the Golden Jubilee Festival, NYBCC leaders set about pursuing the twin aims of coordinating the five (Shin) Young Buddhist Leagues with "other Buddhist organizations and leagues irrespective of denomination" and "to propagate Buddhism."[38] Toward these ends, NYBCC sought to establish itself as a central resource center for information about Buddhism and Buddhists in America by collecting information about organizational histories of affiliated Buddhist "chapters, districts, leagues, church organizations and national organizations," "church and Buddhist materials," and updated information on Buddhist teaching centers, including the recently established American Buddhist Academy in New York. NYBCC leaders requested publications from its affiliated leagues, districts, and chapters; produced a directory of its affiliated chapters, officers, districts, and leagues; and charged NYBCC director Tad Hirota with compiling a "national file of all Buddhist organizations" in the United States.[39]

NYBCC and its member organizations also sought to raise awareness of Buddhism among the general public through a range of activities, from public relations campaigns for the national recognition of Buddhism, such as the previously discussed campaigns for the recognition of Buddhists in the armed forces to the sponsorship of English-speaking ministers' national tours.[40] Beginning in 1948, NYBCC's Eastern Young Buddhist League (EYBL), which included organizations stretching from the Midwest to the East Coast, sponsored a ministerial speaking tour. In a 1949 news release, EYBL announced the visit and talk by Reverend Noboru Tsunoda at the Sunday Young People's Service of the New York Buddhist Church. One of BCA's few Nisei ministers, Reverend Tsunoda was supportive of NYBCC, offering his assistance to the council.[41] The news release described Reverend Tsunoda as in high demand thanks to his ability to discuss Buddhism "in understandable English." It described his talk, which coincided with a Nisei War Memorial Service, as "one of the largest turn-outs of the year," with an audience that included members of Columbia University's Buddhist Study Society and International House, as well as members of the Broadway Tabernacle (Broadway United Church of Christ).[42]

NYBCC's broader vision of promoting projects and programs that served younger Nisei and Sansei as well as the general American public would persist; however, the creation of an independent nonsectarian organization proved to be ill-timed, and the council itself was short-lived. By February, 1952, facing criticism and under increasing pressure from BCA's leadership, NYBCC board members resolved to rename their organization the National Young Buddhist Association, to affiliate directly with the Buddhist Churches of America and to identify themselves exclusively with the Shin Buddhist sect.[43] What had changed in the short span of four years since the successful staging of the Golden Jubilee Festival? NYBCC's demise was not simply the product of internal disagreements within BCA but was also shaped by larger historical forces that would lead to the reestablishment of contact between BCA and Nishi Honganji's Chief Abbot Kosho Ohtani, who visited each of BCA's churches and temples and toured the United States, for the first time, from November of 1951 to February, 1952.[44]

The chief abbot's first visit to America was the result of a BCA request made to the Supreme Commander for Allied Powers, to grant him a travel visa, during a period when US occupation policy was pivoting. Driven by domestic Japanese and international fears of communism amid the Cold War, SCAP policy shifted from a "democratic revolution from above" to a "reverse course," beginning around 1947 and 1948, and continuing through the end of occupation in 1952.[45] The shift in policy opened the possibility of renewed contact between BCA and Nishi Honganji, a central priority for those advocates of the revitalization of BCA as a Shin Buddhist organization. At the same time, it provided the chief abbot and Nishi Honganji with an opportunity to present themselves as being in line with American democratic values and as anticommunist.

Bishop Enryo Shigefuji requested the assistance of Teruo Mukoyama and Tameji Eto in representing them while in Japan. Mukoyama had traveled to Japan in the fall of 1948 to deliver relief aid on behalf of the Chicago Committee for the Relief of Displaced People in Japan, a joint effort that included contributions from the BCA-affiliated Midwest Buddhist Church. While in Japan, Mukoyama met with General Douglas MacArthur and was granted a fifty-minute audience with Emperor Hirohito as a result of his publicized involvement in Japanese civilian relief.[46]

In May of 1949, Shigefuji wrote to Mukoyama offering his "deepest appreciation for the kind services you have rendered our congregation in the past." Shigefuji then asked Mukoyama if he could "contact the proper authority" and request that the Chief Abbot Ohtani and one escort be permitted to visit the United States for a period of two months, with all expenses to be covered by BCA. Shigefuji also asked Mukoyama to meet with Tamaji Eto, an Issei Buddhist leader from San Luis Obispo, California, who also happened to be in Japan and to "contact General McArthur's [sic] Office and the American Consulate to submit our request." Shigefuji concluded, "It is our wish to have the Chief Abbot Ohtani see the present conditions of the churches in America, extend any encouragement whenever and wherever he can as well as speak before his congregation."[47] BCA turned to its membership to sponsor Ohtani's visit, including raising $30,000 from members, resulting in the first postwar visit of Abbot Ohtani and Lady Yoshiko Ohtani to the United States, from November 1951 to February 1952.[48]

Both the Abbot and BCA understood the extent to which the American public continued to scrutinize Japanese Buddhism as a foreign religion associated with a former enemy. BCA press releases emphasized the important role that Abbot Ohtani played as a Cold War cultural ambassador between Japan and the United States. They did so in ways that engaged and contributed to American government and popular discourses emphasizing Japan as an underdeveloped potential democracy.[49] Toward this end, both the Abbot and BCA highlighted the role that American Shin Buddhist institutions could play as models for democratic change in Japan. One BCA press release described the purpose of the chief abbot's visit as "establishing a closer relation with the Buddhists in America and to bring goodwill to the people of the West from the people of the East." The press release noted that Ohtani was interested in reviewing "techniques and policies of administration and teaching of Buddhism in America . . . that could be advantageously adopted in Japan."[50] Interviewed by the *San Francisco Chronicle,* Ohtani also sought to convey his role as a Cold War cultural ambassador, noting the important role that Buddhism could play, within the climate of religious liberty, as a bastion against communism. Jack Morrison, the writer who interviewed Ohtani for the *Chronicle,* distinguished between Buddhism and state-sponsored Shinto, both during the 1930s and in the present. He noted that Japan as a nation was making progress in the area of freedom of religion, a contrast with the 1930s, when "Shinto was forced on the people as a national religion." Ignoring his own role, and that of Nishi Honganji, in supporting the military state, Ohtani stated that, even during the 1930s, "Buddhists held to their beliefs, . . . and now they and other religious groups are free to propagate their religion." He noted that the major challenges facing Japan were the "building of foreign trade and preparing to resist a possible communist attempt to subvert the government."[51]

While engaging with the American media, Ohtani spent the majority of his first postwar trip working to reestablish contact with BCA's members. The abbot and Lady Ohtani visited all of BCA's churches and temples. The Ohtani's three-month tour traced the path laid out over the past fifty years by Issei Buddhists. Much of their tour took place across the western United States, where they met with numbers ranging from small congregations in rural agricultural towns to large groups of more than a thousand in urban centers. In California's Central Valley and coastal regions, until the forced wartime incarceration, a generation of Issei men and women worked as agricultural laborers, tenant farmers, and independent produce farmers. In Fresno, the Ohtanis dined with approximately one hundred lay leaders from the town and surrounding area.[52] In San Francisco, Ohtani conducted religious services at both the Golden Gate National Cemetery and the Japanese Cemetery in Colma to honor American soldiers who had lost their lives during World War II.[53] In Los Altos, California, the Ohtanis visited a nursery owned by Tom Furuichi, described by the local paper as a "member of a pioneer Los Altos family." Furuichi's Issei parents, both deceased, had founded the local Buddhist Sunday School.[54]

The Ohtanis next traveled to Salt Lake City, which, as discussed earlier, had emerged during the war as an important new center for BCA activities. Fifty local members of the Intermountain Buddhist Church greeted them at the Salt Lake City airport. While in Salt Lake City, they visited the nearby town of Ogden to conduct services, followed by a reception to honor Ogden Buddhist lay members.[55]

The tour of BCA's churches also provided opportunities to meet with other American religious organizations and local politicians. In Tacoma, Washington, the abbot was welcomed by the mayor, John H. Anderson.[56] En route to visit congregations in the Midwest and on the East Coast, Ohtani visited Asian studies scholars at the University of Wisconsin and Harvard University before traveling on to Washington, DC, to meet with American politicians.[57]

During the tour, the abbot conducted Kikyoshiki (confirmation) services, enabling thousands of BCA members to reaffirm their commitment to Shin Buddhism and to receive *homyo juyo* (dharma names).[58] Notices that accompanied application forms for the Kikyoshiki confirmation at the Sacramento Buddhist Church described the ceremony as

> the most significant rites to the Buddhist. This rite is performed only by the Abbot, and thus bestows on the person receiving a Buddhist Name and Omyogo (Namu Amida Butsu—scroll in His personal Handwriting), and is symbolic of a blessing to enter the Buddhist Brotherhood. . . . People from far and wide travel to Kyoto for this sacred ceremony, and we are very fortunate to be able to receive it at our local church. It is an opportunity that comes once in a lifetime.[59]

Participants made small donations to their local Buddhist churches. In Salinas, California, Ohtani attended a welcome banquet, visited the local Japanese cemetery, and held Kikyoshiki services for seventy-five local church members before conducting a Buddhist service that was open to the general public.[60] Those who received confirmation made donations ranging from as little as one dollar, for Sansei children, to up to five dollars for Issei.[61] When the abbot conducted Kikyoshiki services for two hundred members in Salt Lake City, Utah, the *Ogden City-Examiner* noted the symbolic use of a "golden razor," which was touched to the head of each recipient. Reverend Kenryo Kumata was quoted as stating that the razor symbolized the "old custom of shaving the heads of all who joined the Buddhist faith." In an effort to relate the ceremony to the broader American public, Kumata likened the ceremony to a Christian baptism.[62]

The abbot's tour was impactful in shifting support away from NYBCC's emphasis on trans-sectarianism and back toward Shin sectarianism. He attended six major Buddhist conferences, including meetings with BCA ministers and board of directors members, as well as with members of regional Young Buddhist Associations.[63] With the abbot in attendance at the annual meeting of the Western Young Buddhist League (WYBL), the largest and most influential of the regional leagues, delegates passed a resolution defining YBA's affiliating with NYBCC as "belong[ing] to the Shin sect" and proposing that NYBCC "be directly affiliated with the Buddhist Churches of America and reorganize as the National Young Buddhist Association." At the same time, WYBL persisted in advocating for projects and programs relevant to the Nisei and Sansei, as well programs facilitating the promotion of Buddhism among the general public. These included development of an official English-language publication; support for a ministerial training program, particularly geared toward "sons of ministers and other who [were] interested in becoming English-speaking priests"; and development of a Buddhist study center.[64] Though BCA would maintain its institutional autonomy from Nishi Honganji, Abbot Ohtani's tour reinitiated ties between the two organizations. The shift toward the consolidation of leadership of BCA's Nisei board members, together with its Issei bishop and ministers, took place concurrently with BCA's affiliation with Nishi Honganji and its reaffirmation as a Shin Buddhist organization.

Buddhist Study Groups and Early Ministerial Training in Japan

With the demise of NYBCC in 1952, Nisei Young Buddhist Association leaders reassessed the ambitious twin goals set during the 1948 Golden Jubilee Festival. While it was clear that a trans-sectarian Nisei-led organization like the council would no longer "take over" BCA activities, a number of younger YBA leaders would continue to push for what they viewed as a broader, more dynamic vision of BCA that could appeal to younger Nisei and the general American public. They began to be elected to positions of administration and leadership within BCA, and working with the national YBA movement, continued to press for the priorities of developing English-language-oriented projects and programs that would support the needs of both Nisei and Sansei, as well as aid in the promotion of Buddhism among the general public through the development of study groups, publications, and public outreach programs. Toward these ends, they continued to be driven by the view that Buddhism and its transmission in America could extend beyond Nikkei communities in ways that could profoundly transform American society and culture.

At its final meeting, NYBCC delegates passed a series of resolutions that highlighted these priorities. One resolution called for the development of an official English-language publication to "represent the Buddhist Churches of America as an instrument of official announcements, policies, public relations; and coordinating of various activities of the affiliated organizations throughout the country." The resolution would eventually result in the creation of the BCA's

American Buddhist.[65] Nisei leaders also pressed BCA for two resolutions that would support the training of an English-speaking Buddhist ministry. The first resolution called for the establishment of a ministerial training center in the United States rather than Japan. This was followed by a second resolution to establish a Buddhist study center in Berkeley, California, where efforts to identify and recruit Nisei ministerial candidates was already under way. In advocating for the study center resolution, YBA leaders noted that the recent visit of Chief Abbot Ohtani had "truly been an inspiration to our Buddhist movement in America" and that the abbot "ha[d] repeatedly expressed that Buddhism in this country should be spread through English." Reminding fellow delegates of Nisei sacrifices and Issei pioneers, YBA leaders proclaimed that the study center should serve as "a living memorial to the Bussei who were killed in action and to the ministers who have passed on while giving their untiring efforts [on] behalf of Buddhism in America."[66]

YBA leader calls to develop ministerial training programs and a Buddhist study center in the United States aimed to bolster initial efforts already under way to recruit Nisei and other English speakers for the ministry and to increase institutional support for their training. In 1949, the BCA Bishop Enryo Shigefuji, assisted by Reverend Kanmo Imamura, the Nisei minister assigned to the Berkeley Buddhist Church, together with his wife, Mrs. Jane Imamura, formed a Buddhist study group in Berkeley, California. The Imamuras maintained the study group for the next decade. The early study group was also supported by Mrs. Shinobu Matsuura, Jane's mother, who, as wife of Reverend Issei Matsuura, had been a prominent participant in early Issei study group circles. After returning to Guadalupe, Shinobu Matsuura had moved to Berkeley, near three of her children, including oldest daughter Jane and Jane's family.[67]

While steeped in Shin tradition, Reverend Imamura, who would go on to play a key role in the establishment of an American ministerial training center, shared the NYBCC vision of Buddhism's importance among Nikkei communities as well as among the general American public. Like his father Yemyo Imamura, who served as the first Shin Buddhist Bishop to Hawaiʻi, Kanmo Imamura believed that Buddhism could play a critical role in bridging cultural divisions between East and West and create a path toward a more peaceful world.[68] This could be accomplished only through the development of "subtle" changes in BCA's programs. He noted in a 1953 *Berkeley Bussei* editorial, titled "Panorama," that if "Buddhism [was] to become the envoy for peace, the bridge of East-West that our parents have started must be completed." For Imamura, completing what the Issei had started required a shift in perspective and attitude. He added, "The next half century must be of introspection as well as of altruism. A subtle change is needed in the systems of the Buddhist Churches." Imamura concluded that "study classes, services and good publications must become the criteria of activities."[69]

Efforts to recruit ministerial students through the Berkeley Buddhist Study Group[70] were aided significantly by proximity to the University of California. Unlike at most branch churches and temples, college students accounted for a significant majority of the membership at Berkeley. In 1951, for example, college students made up 72 percent (84) of the church's 116 members.[71] In addition to providing students, the University of California also served as a resource for post-war experts in the emerging field of East Asian studies, beginning with the founding of the Institute of East Asiatic Studies in 1949.[72] Reverend Imamura had established contacts with faculty in both the anthropology and Oriental studies departments after taking a staff position at the university's Museum of Anthropology to supplement his modest income as a BCA minister.[73] As a result, Shigefuji and the Imamuras were convinced that Berkeley would become an important resource for recruiting and developing future Bussei ministers and lay leaders.

Shigefuji and Reverend Seimoku Kosaka led the first study group meeting at the home of Jane Imamura's mother, Mrs. Shinobu Matsuura on October 29, 1949. They were joined by the Imamuras and a group of enthusiastic young Nisei. Jane Imamura noted, "Bishop Shigefuji gave official confirmation to this important work. And, although there was as yet no financial foundation, the Berkeley Study Center, nurtured by the members of the Berkeley Buddhist Temple, was set into motion with high energy."[74] A second meeting, which included fifteen students, was held a month later. Bishop Shigefuji invited participants to a Chinese garden restaurant, followed by study group discussion held at Mrs. Matsuura's home. From the outset, the study group introduced participants to both general and Shin Buddhist teachings, contrasting them with Christian concepts and teachings. Shigefuji and the Imamuras recognized that most Bussei had grown up in a society with an official tradition of religious liberty but also where Christianity was viewed as normative. Discussion topics at the first study group meeting such as "Questions in regard to karma and transmigration, no-soul theory, the cause of life, Amida Buddha as contrasted to [the] Christian God, and fatalism," introduced Buddhist concepts while also addressing common criticisms of Buddhism by Christian theologians.[75]

By December, the study group had managed to recruit a core group of regular participants, including a number whose parents were ministers and Berkeley students. These included two of Jane Imamura's sisters, Lily and Mary Matsuura, as well as Sei Shohara, Hitoshi Tsufura, Taitetsu Unno and Kimi Yonemura.[76] Participants discussed the question, "What does Buddhism consider as Right?" The *Berkeley Bussei* reported that "the group disbanded with the realization that there is an amazing depth to Buddhist philosophy."[77] As Taitetsu Unno recalled, early study group meetings were conducted in Japanese, despite varying Japanese-language abilities of Bussei, because of the limited English-language ability of Bishop Shigefuji and concerns that Buddhist teachings lost some of their "flavor" in translation. To aid Bussei, the Imamuras and Nisei priest Art Takemoto translated terms and concepts into English.[78] News about the study group meetings spread through YBA publications and informally by word of mouth. Isao Fujimoto, a pre-med student at the University of California, learned about the study group while attending a service at the Berkeley Buddhist Church.[79] Despite the efforts of the bishop, together with Mrs. Matsuura and the Imamuras, progress in recruitment and in developing a program to support English-language ministerial training candidates in the early 1950s was slow.

The Buddhist study group began to influence Berkeley YBA members, as evidenced in its publication *Berkeley Bussei*. Beginning with its first postwar issue in 1950 and continuing through the decade, the publication would distinguish itself among YBA publications through its inclusion of lay Buddhist perspectives from Berkeley's YBA members, together with articles penned by BCA's Shin Buddhist ministers as well as academics from US and Japanese universities. Many of the early articles represented extensions of conversations initiated at Buddhist study group meetings, some of which challenged Nisei to not accept traditional Shin Buddhist teachings at face value but to explore them further. In response to study group interest in the doctrine of karma and rebirth, *Berkeley Bussei* included two reprinted articles, by M. G. Mori and B. L. Broughton. Both articles had contributed to growing debates between literalist and contextualist interpretations by Shin Buddhist theologians and scholars in the 1920s.[80] While Broughton, a leader in the early Mahabodhi society, addressed karma in more general terms, Mori's article, which focused on Amida's Western Paradise, tried to reconcile the two views while maintaining the significance of the new modern interpretation. In introducing Mori's article, Taitetsu Unno and Kimi Yonemura, the two religious editors, challenged fellow Nisei Buddhists to critically examine the basic teachings in which they had been raised rather than accept them out of habit or in deference to BCA leadership. As they noted, the Mori article was offered "as a true stimulation to the minds of our fellow Shinshu Bussei. True faith, we believe, must come from a careful consideration of the tenets expounded by the church. Nothing is too sacred in our search for the truth. The spirit of inquiry must be hampered neither by tradition nor authority. Such a quest is the Buddhist way."[81]

The early activities of the study group culminated, in August 1952, with a three-day Buddhist seminar organized by former NYBCC director Tad Hirota and former NYBCC representative and study group member Hitoshi Tsufura and attended by at least four additional former NYBCC leaders, including Dr. Ryo Munekata, June Tokuyama, Jiro Nakaso, and Mike Maruyama.[82] The seminar exemplified the trans-sectarian vision that Nisei YBA leaders had tried to pursue in creating NYBCC four years earlier.

The seminar drew a registered audience of some 250 people, including Bishop Shigefuji, BCA ministers, and laypersons, together with "50 non-Japanese" that included an international group of scholars, students, and religious practitioners. Thubten Norbu, brother of the Dalai Lama, attended together with Dilowa Hutuktu, the spiritual leader of Mongolia. Also present were Ferdinand Lessing, a Chinese and Central Asian expert at the University of California, and Dr. Haridas Chaudhuri, Tokan Tada, and Alan Watts, three faculty at the recently founded American Academy of Asian Studies.[83]

On the first day of the seminar, attendees listened to lectures that presented Shin Buddhism within the broader context of Buddhism as a world religion. Reverend Kumata's opening lecture on "general Buddhism" took the long view of its development. As one observer noted, Kumata's discussion included "the development of religion in the history of mankind from naturalism and animism to the more rational thinking of analyzing the non-existence of atman and the acme of the existence of Sunyata" from the Pratītyasamutpāda doctrine.[84] This was followed by a lecture on Shin Buddhism by the Nisei Reverend Takashi Tsuji, whose talk focused on the development of central Shin concepts within the context of Shinran's historical struggles. Dr. Chaudhuri's talk examined the six Hindu philosophical systems in relation to Buddhism, and Alan Watts' concluding talk addressed Buddhism and philosophy, taking, as one observer noted, "a Zen intuitive approach" which the observer found as "refreshing as it was diverse."[85]

Tsufura recounted mixed responses, including critical ones, likely from within BCA's membership, over the issue of the trans-sectarian and trans-religious format of the seminar. He noted, "The seminar proved to be highly successful despite biased reports to the contrary."[86] Tsufura concluded by again invoking NYBCC's broader vision of the role that Buddhists could play in American society: "It is the general opinion that the invoking of the Seminar herald a new phase of Buddhism in the United States—a phase which will not yield to traditions and orthodoxy, but which will possibly transform Buddhism to fit the needs of an evanescent society."[87] Another observer took a more neutral position, noting, "Whether the Seminar served as an improvement or hindrance to our Shin Buddhist movement remains to be seen. However, . . . one thing was clearly visible in the reaction of those who attended, . . . the feeling of oneness in this search

Figure 4.3. The 1952 Buddhist Seminar, Berkeley, California. Reprinted from the Buddhist Churches of America Collection, Japanese American National Museum.

for mature thinking. All barriers of sect, race and even the name of religion was overcome in this search." The observer concluded, "The atmosphere that prevailed in those three days was of reverence and deep stimulation that was never felt before at any young Buddhist gathering."[88] Given the success of the seminar, organizers created an annual seminar. First held at the Buddhist Church of San Francisco and the Los Angeles Hompa Hongwanji temple, the annual conference, renamed the "Pacific Seminar," would be hosted for decades at the Asilomar Hotel and Conference Grounds in Pacific Grove, California.[89]

The inspired climate of shared exploration of Buddhist concepts and thought among Nisei that had resulted in the BCA Study Group and the BCA Seminar likewise cultivated in some early Nisei graduate students (and future ministerial candidates) an openness and proclivity toward exploring Buddhism more broadly and comparatively than they might have had as ministerial candidates in the prewar years. Some of the first Nisei Shin Buddhists to depart for Japan during the same period, to study Buddhism at the graduate level, included BCA study group member and editor of the *Berkeley Bussei,* Taitetsu Unno, and LaVerne Sasaki, a former YBA member who had served as a speaker at the first Buddhist Seminar.[90]

With little formal institutional support, these students relied on themselves and their personal contacts in navigating the challenges revolving around the pursuit of study abroad. Born into Issei Shin Buddhist priestly families, these early students shared with NYBCC's Nisei leaders an interest in the study of Buddhism beyond a strictly Shin sectarian orientation. Taitetsu Unno was the first bilingual and bicultural student to journey to postwar Japan to pursue graduate studies in Buddhism at Tokyo University. Born in Japan, and thus technically an Issei, Unno arrived in the United States at a very early age and was raised for most of his life in the United States. The son of Issei minister Reverend Enryo Unno, Taitetsu Unno had already begun to distinguish himself as a leading young Buddhist thinker when he left for Japan to begin his studies in 1951.[91]

Unno's decision to pursue advanced study of Buddhism at Tokyo University rather than at Ryukoku University, a Shin University where a majority of BMNA's ministers had been trained, was influenced by Daisetz Teitaro (D. T.) Suzuki. Unno met Suzuki when the noted scholar of Zen Buddhism presented a series of lectures over three days held at the Buddhist Church of San Francisco as part of a nationwide lecture tour in 1950. Unno recalled that Suzuki, whose work he had read, "talked about Shin Buddhism and I thought, 'wow, this is really interesting,' an entirely different world opened up." Suzuki encouraged the undergraduate to study Buddhism with Professor Shoson Miyamoto, at Tokyo University, and wrote a letter of introduction to Miyamoto on Unno's behalf. After being accepted as a special student in 1951, Unno enrolled in coursework for two years before passing an entrance exam to enter the MA program in Indian philosophy, to study Buddhism.[92]

Rather than ministerial study, Unno's early interest in the study of Buddhism in Japan was shaped by his own quest for spiritual meaning, something that he believed that Suzuki shared. As he later recollected, because Suzuki had recommended Tokyo University, he thought that he would be studying with "five or six D. T. Suzuki types." To Unno's disappointment, he didn't find anyone like Suzuki because his instructors were purely academics. "D. T. Suzuki was in his own way an academic," he recalled, "but he was also a seeker and there was a spiritual quality, and that's what I was looking for, but I never found it."[93]

Like NYBCC's leaders, Unno expressed frustration with the narrow focus of BCA's leadership, including the bishop's office and national board of directors. In an article penned for *Berkeley Bussei* prior to his departure, Unno noted that BCA's leadership was "doing their best," but he was nevertheless critical of their "think(ing) in terms of their own small world." Unno predicted that "a day will come when a man will rise among us to lead the epoch-making introduction of organized Buddhism into the West" who "will think in terms of society in the broadest sense and take into consideration the whole of history—past, present, and future."[94]

Lacking former institutional support from BCA, Unno had little assistance in acclimating to a postwar Japan still recovering from the aftermath of war. Among the challenges that he faced were the divergent legacies of war, which he witnessed compared to his own recent experience of wartime forced incarceration. Unno recalled his impressions upon first arriving in Tokyo.

> Japan is still trying to restore a shattered economy. Tokyo is just devastated, the bombing just razed the whole city. And so, I hadn't gone through the suffering of the people and here I am from the outside. And when I met people my age, I couldn't talk to them like I could talk to a Nisei or even a Caucasian here [in the US] in the same way. . . . And also, the camp experience had affected me. It was already six years since I got out of camp, but that was I think a deep psychological scar. I can talk about it now but then I wasn't even aware of it. So that was also a deep discomfort.[95]

Unno also recalled the challenges presented by the Japanese language. He recalled that "the students [were] really top notch students and they are keeping up with the class, and my Japanese was pretty good because I studied Japanese at Berkeley but still there was a huge gap." Despite these challenges, Unno earned an MA in Buddhist studies in 1953. After returning to the United States to serve as a BCA minister, Unno enrolled in further graduate study at Tokyo University, completing a PhD in Buddhist studies in 1968. He would go on to work at UCLA before a long and illustrious career as a professor of religion at Smith College.[96]

Like Unno, LaVerne Senyo Sasaki also came from a Shin Issei Buddhist priestly family. Sasaki descended from twenty-five generations of Shin Buddhist ministers, including his grandfather, Senju Sasaki, the first Shin Buddhist minister to Canada, and his father, Sensho Sasaki, who served BMNA and then BCA.[97] Yet Sasaki's path toward the ministry was a gradual one, beginning with assisting his father in translating Buddhist sermons. Sasaki recalled, "I felt sorry for him during Sunday Services, when he struggled with the English language. . . . As I translated, I became interested in the Buddhist religion and ministry."[98] Like Unno, Sasaki studied at Tokyo University rather than Ryukoku. Significantly, despite his own family history and training as a Shin Buddhist minister, Sasaki's father Sensho encouraged him to study at Tokyo University.[99]

Upon his arrival in Tokyo in 1953, Sasaki, like Unno, was struck by the physical and economic devastation that war had wrought. He recalled students who were so malnourished that they "resembled TB patients." Some graduate students had so little money that they "would occasionally even sell blood to buy books, which could cost 3,000 yen per month [less than $10]." The facilities at the elite Tokyo University were equally poor. Sasaki recalled that "we often listened to the lectures in our overcoats, scarves, and gloves" because the steam radiators did not work." Students cut the tips off their gloves in order to turn pages.[100]

Sasaki's Japanese-language skills, outgoing personality, and social networks facilitated his transition to life and study in Japan. Professor Reverend Gido Uno, a friend of Sasaki's uncle and a private tutor to Abbot Kosho Ohtani, was Sasaki's private tutor. Sasaki recalled, "I once looked at a piece of calligraphy and asked [Uno], 'What does that mean?'—not realizing the answer was being covered during his talk. I got hell for not paying attention to what he was emphasizing. Despite missteps like this, I was learning a lot."[101] Sasaki studied under Dr. Shinso Hanayama, head of the Indian Philosophy Department at Tokyo and became close friends with Hanayama's son and fellow classmate Shoyo Hanayama. Sasaki and Shoyo would review Buddhist lecture notes and Sasaki would give him English conversation lessons regularly from midnight to 3 a.m. Sasaki also recalled how the Hanayama family "adopted" him during his five-year stay in Japan. He and Shoyo rode the train every Friday to the Hanayama home for "dinner, study and an overnight stay."[102] Following Sasaki's graduation, the Hanayama family were there to bid him farewell in June 1958, not realizing at the time that they would meet again in San Francisco the following year, when Shinso Hanayama would be appointed bishop of the BCA.

In contrast to Unno, Sasaki's primary interest in pursuing graduate studies was for the purposes of ministerial training. Initially interested in pursuing studies on commentaries by Shotoku Taishi (574–622 CE) on the *Vimalakīrti Sūtra,* Sasaki was encouraged by one of his professors to focus his graduate thesis on the work of Tendai scholar Genshin (942–1017 CE), who was much revered by Shinran.[103] Despite the narrowing of his interest in serving as a BCA minister and the narrowing of his thesis toward a more sectarian-focused topic, Sasaki's graduate experience, like Unno's, would lead him to seek out experiences and contacts with Buddhists beyond strictly sectarian ones (as discussed in chapter 5).

From the BCA Study Center to the Institute of Buddhist Studies

Between the mid-1950s and 1960s, BCA developed the first accredited Shin Buddhist graduate institution outside of Japan. The process unfolded slowly, in incremental stages, as the result of experimentation and negotiation among BCA's bishops, ministers, and lay leaders and between BCA and the Chief Abbot Ohtani, and administrators at Nishi Honganji and Ryukoku University.

As late as 1953, BCA had still not formally addressed the issue of ministerial training. Instead, its primary focus remained identifying and connecting its dispersed membership through the compilation of a member directory and a one dollar membership drive to raise funds and identify its membership.[104] Support among BCA leadership for the development of a ministerial training program in the United States grew with the gradual inclusion of younger Nisei, including some of NYBCC's key leaders in the ranks of BCA's leadership and efforts by lay leaders to raise funding in support for such a program.

Following the success of the Buddhist Seminar, Hitoshi Tsufura was appointed by BCA's board of directors to serve as executive assistant to Bishop Shigefuji in 1953.[105] From 1955 to 1958, BCA's board of directors included two former NYBCC representatives, Dr. Ryo Munekata and former director Tad Hirota, as well as four members of the Golden Jubilee organizing staff (including Hirota). At the same time, a number of Issei ministers, most of whom were trained at Ryukoku University, also served on the board. Five of six Issei ministers on the board had studied at Ryukoku, as did Reverend Kumata, the sole Nisei minister. BCA's bishop was also advised by five older Issei ministers who made up the Sanyokai (Advisory Council), four of whom were educated at Ryukoku. Many of these ministers were likely to disapprove of ministerial training in the United States.[106]

In 1956, BCA's board members endorsed a proposal by Fred Nitta calling for the division of governance between a "religious affairs division," led by the Bishop, and a "secular affairs division," under the direction of the board of directors, a predominantly lay organization. The proposal also called for the creation of the Special Projects Fund (SPF), with the goal of raising $500,000 for a number of major projects, including the further development of English-language ministerial training programs. Fred Nitta was appointed chair of the SPF Committee, which consisted of Bishop Shigefuji and eighteen board members, a majority of whom represented the older cohort of Nisei.[107] Largely relying on volunteer donations, SPF raised approximately $10,000 in 1956. In 1957, the SPF Committee set a $50,000 goal for the year and directly appealed to its Nisei membership. In a SPF pamphlet titled, "An Urgent Appeal to You," Bishop Shigefuji argued that the time had come for Nisei to join the Issei in providing substantial financial support for BCA, noting, "when we consider the future of Buddhism in America, the present shortage of English-speaking ministers leaves one with a sense of uneasiness." The brochure also highlighted how SPF funds would be distributed: $22,000 would cover funding for a ministerial training program in Japan; another $8,500 would support funding for scholarships and study in the United States; $10,000 would go to a minister's retirement fund; and the remaining $9,500 would be used for Sunday School teacher training, BCA's publication *Horin,* and other administrative expenses.[108] Gaining the support of the BCA Ministers Association, Young Buddhist Associations, and Fujinkai Leagues, the SPF

Committee met its 1957 goal. Between 1956 and 1964, the Special Projects Fund raised a total of $285,458.[109]

Supported by the growing resources of the SPF, a compromise was reached over where to develop ministerial training, as BCA developed a pre-ministerial training center in the United States and sponsored a new Ministerial Training Center in Kyoto. Pre-ministerial training was launched in Berkeley, California, at the newly created BCA Study Center and library in 1956. The study center had been created as part of a larger project to build a new chapel and student dormitory for the Berkeley Buddhist Church. When Berkeley Buddhist Church members agreed to raise $50,000 to build two new buildings, Bishop Shigefuji convinced its membership to include space for a Buddhist study center. This in turn led to a national fundraising campaign in support of the study center from BCA membership.[110] Groundbreaking ceremonies were held in 1954, and the project was completed at a cost of $80,000 in 1955. A year later, the bishop allocated additional funds to support a library located in the study center.[111]

The BCA Study Center and library was strategically planned as a multiuse space that would be welcoming to Nisei and Sansei students. Having established the SPF, BCA initiated efforts to recruit ministerial candidates from among Nisei by offering scholarships to high school graduates, college students, and college graduates. To qualify for scholarships, applicants needed the recommendation of a local minister, had to express an interest in studying for the ministry and serving the Buddhist Churches of America, and had to be willing to complete their training in Japan.[112] In 1956, the study center accepted its first class of pre-ministerial students. With Reverend Imamura serving as director, Reverend Taitetsu Unno, recently returned from his own graduate training, served as instructor for the first cohort of six students. Four among them—Haruo Yamaoka, William Masuda, Leslie Kawamura, and John Doami—would go on to study at Ryukoku University and become ordained Shin Buddhist ministers.[113]

Meanwhile, BCA also worked to establish an "overseas" ministerial training center (MTC) in Kyoto for students at Ryukoku University. In developing this program, BCA worked with Ryukoku University president Kenju Masuyama, who had served as BMNA bishop in the 1930s and had long advocated for the development of training programs for Nisei and other English-speaking Shin Buddhist ministers. BCA board members established a committee to address support for English-speaking ministerial training in Japan. After researching the issue over the course of 1956, the committee made the proposal to BCA's General Conference, and the conference approved the establishment of the BCA MTC, whose goal was to annually provide five students from Ryukoku Buddhist University with intensive English-language training.[114] Coordinating with English-language ministerial training in Japan was greatly facilitated by the donation of Shinshinji, a temple in Kyoto that was leased without fee by Seiichi Hirose, a wealthy Japanese industrialist and patron of Buddhist institutions in America. BCA MTC, informally called "Shinshinji," served as both training center for Japanese ministerial students and a dorm for students from the United States, some of whom also served as instructors.[115]

While officially endorsed by the abbot and Nishi Honganji, Shinshinji's budget was supported primarily by BCA's Special Projects Fund. BCA was also charged with hiring and supporting Shinshinji's staff, which in 1957 included the director and instructors.[116] In addition to intensive English-language courses, MTC students were introduced to courses such as "Propagation of Buddhism in America," "Buddhist Texts in English," "Anjji Rondai" (Subjects in Faith), "Service Procedures," and "English Conversation," designed to acclimate the Shin Buddhist ministry in America.[117]

The program began in April 1957, with funding for five ministerial students from Ryukoku to enter the intensive English-language training program. BCA appointed Reverend Gyoyu Hirabayashi of the Oakland Buddhist Church as MTC director. Faculty included William G. Flygare, a linguist and ordained Shin Buddhist minister, and three Nisei students, Yuri Kyogoku, Sus Ikuta, and Tetsuo Unno, who attended Ryukoku (and was brother of Taitetsu Unno), along with Will Peterson, an instructor at Kyoto Women's College who had been an active member of the Buddhist study group in Berkeley.[118]

In addition to preparing Japanese ministerial students for work in the United States, Shinshinji would also support Nisei ministerial candidates enrolled in courses at Ryukoku. By February 1958, the BCA Board of Directors had awarded scholarships to six Nisei, including John Doami, Haruo Yamaoka, Leslie Kawamura, William Masuda, George Shibata, and Henry Yamada. Four of the scholarship recipients began attending Japanese-language classes and lectures on Buddhism at the BCA Study Center in preparation for training in Kyoto.[119]

Challenges related to maintaining the MTC led to efforts to move the center onto the Ryukoku campus. On July 15, 1958, during a phone conversation between Bishop Shigefuji and President Masuyama, Shigefuji discussed such a move. Shigefuji's recommendation led to a number of meetings between MTC's director Reverend Hirabayashi, Masuyama, and a Reverend Miyaji. Masuyama proposed the addition of a one- to two-month intensive training course for recent graduates prior to their being sent to the United States. In addition to English language study, training would include topics such as "preparation for ministerial etiquette and other pertinent matters in regards to the ministry." To support the training program, Ryukoku would offer a room within the university library.[120] However,

Figure 4.4. BCA Study Center Pre-Ministerial Training Scholarship recipients, 1958. Reprinted from the Buddhist Churches of America Collection, Japanese American National Museum.

with the move on campus, Masuyama wanted the MTC to support not only ministerial training for BCA members but also for those being sent to Hawai'i, Canada, Mexico, and Brazil. Additionally, he expected BCA to continue to provide "some financial aid from the United States."[121] One month later Bishop Shigefuji passed away suddenly from a cerebral brain hemorrhage, leaving the future of the MTC uncertain.[122] Meanwhile, both Nisei and Japanese ministerial students continued their studies at Ryukoku University.

Translation and Transformation: Nisei Ministerial Students at Ryukoku University

From the late 1950s to the mid-1960s a small number of Nisei who had completed pre-ministerial training at the BCA Study Center journeyed to Kyoto to continue their training at the BCA Ministerial Training Center at Ryukoku University. Like Unno and Sasaki, all those recruited for the program were college graduates, a requirement for all potential ministers. While some were bilingual (the sons of overseas Buddhist ministers in the United States and Canada), others had little Japanese-language ability and limited background knowledge about Shin Buddhist doctrine. Nisei students were accepted to the graduate program contingent on the completion of a year of courses for foreign students. While enrolled in the program, they resided in the BCA MTC dorm.[123] Like Sasaki and Unno, these students met and befriended Japanese students who, together with faculty members, mentored the US students.

Prior to earning a BCA scholarship, John Doami had demonstrated a long-standing interest in Buddhism. He had been an active member of the San Francisco Junior YBA and recalled attending informal Buddhist study classes organized by older Bussei at the San Francisco Buddhist Church. He also borrowed books from BCSF's library, including Junjiro Takakusu's *Essentials of Buddhist Philosophy* and the work of D. T. Suzuki. After graduating from the University of California, Berkeley, in 1957, where he majored in social psychology, Doami, who grew up in a bilingual house but had never had formal training in Japanese, began taking language courses at the BCA Study Center. He recalled traveling weekly from San Francisco to Berkeley on Saturdays to study Japanese language for two to three hours. Through contacts established by the Reverend Taitetsu Unno, Doami was also able to study Sanskrit under the direction of a scholar in San Francisco before he left for Japan.[124]

Doami found the transition as a student at Ryukoku University to be "very difficult, especially since nearly all the classes were in Japanese." The exceptions were courses in Sanskrit and Tibetan, which were taught in English. Doami and the other students from the United States, Canada, and Hawai'i enrolled in general Buddhism courses, while Japanese students training for the ministry enrolled primarily in Shin Buddhist courses. A breakthrough in Doami's training came when Kenju Masuyama, president of Ryukoku University, created the Ryukoku University Translation Center to translate Shin Buddhist texts into English. Masuyama recruited Nisei, including Doami, Haruo Yamaoka, Leslie Kawamura, and others, to work with Ryukoku's instructors and other graduate students. Not only did the center benefit from the English-language skills of Nisei, but participation in the center helped Nisei vastly improve their Japanese-language skills. Doami recalled, "We'd meet on a weekly basis. About a dozen of us, which would have included four or five professors who would be the ones that would say that our translation was good or no good." These included professors Yoshifumi Ueda, Daien Fugen, Mitsuyuki Ishida, and a student and future scholar named Hisao Inagaki. During Doami's time at Ryukoku, the translation center published between three and four translated texts.[125] Doami would eventually complete his MA in 1961. He went on to enroll in doctoral course work and continued his translation work at Ryukoku before returning to the United States in 1965, when he began ministering to BCA communities.[126]

Like Doami, Haruo Yamaoka, the son of a farming family in West Fresno, California, found himself pushed toward the ministry by family and community leaders despite early efforts to purge himself of things Japanese after his family returned from the Jerome and Gila River internment camps. As Yamaoka recalled, "When I came out of camp, the discrimination was so bad. . . . I was always getting picked on, so in order to stop getting picked on, I had to fight and because of that I started to hate anything Japanese. I didn't want to go to Japanese language school, I didn't want to go to Buddhist services because it was all [in] Japanese."[127] Basketball drew Yamaoka back to the West Fresno Buddhist Temple. Once he returned, he was pressured by his mother to support the YBA, and then by Mrs. Wada, a YBA adviser, to get involved with teaching Sunday School. A cousin who was going through a difficult period in her life and whom Yamaoka counseled was the first to suggest that he consider the ministry.[128]

Yamaoka joined Doami, William Masuda, and Leslie Kawamura at the BCA Study Center in Berkeley as the first cohort enrolled in courses in preparation for transfer to the BCA MTC center and Ryukoku University. Yamaoka stayed at the Berkeley dormitory for six months. Because he was not the son of a Buddhist priest and because he came from a small rural town, Yamaoka approached the BSC program with some apprehension. He recalled, "I felt inferior because they were ministers' children but the nurturing nature of the Imamuras was that anyone who wanted to be [a minister], they would take in [and] took care of everything."[129] The four BSC students took courses in Japanese and a course taught by Taitetsu Unno on general Buddhism. Yamaoka recalled that there was not much Shin Buddhist instruction, due to a lack of reading material. The Imamuras' support and encouragement of Yamaoka raised his self-confidence in pursuing the ministry, particularly after they asked him to give a presentation to a group of Berkeley YBA students.[130]

After completing preparation courses at BSC, Yamaoka traveled to Kyoto, enrolled in courses, and attempted to acclimate to life in Japan. In his first year, he struggled to adapt and found himself homesick and depressed. He described his first year as "horrendous," noting, "I couldn't stand the food, I couldn't speak the language, I couldn't do anything. I wanted to come home." Yamaoka eventually adapted to the local diet, and his confidence and spirit were improved after a Japanese ministerial student and karate instructor, Masanori Ohata, befriended him and introduced him and Doami to karate instruction.[131]

Given his limited initial Japanese-language ability, Yamaoka found the first year immersion classes particularly challenging. He remembered sometimes falling asleep in class:

> I took this Japanese history [course] and the teacher was a short guy, I think he was in the military, he would come in marching then bow very deeply and then we all said *ohayo gozaimasu* and then he would start, "*kakuno gotuku . . .*," and then just go on and on and I would try to listen and I couldn't understand, I'd try to listen and listen, I'd get so tired, I'd fall asleep in class. That was the extent of the classes for me because I didn't understand it.[132]

Yamaoka and the other foreign students would write short English reports for the tests and recalled "we would get by and pass all the initial courses." Yamaoka also struggled with reading works on the history of Buddhism and on Shin Buddhist doctrine, which were all in Japanese.[133]

Once he had completed course work for foreign students, Yamaoka and the other students had to decide whether they were going to pursue a master's degree in Shin studies or Buddhist studies. He and Leslie Kawamura applied and were accepted into the program in Shinshu studies. He found the general courses to be even more challenging; however, as was the case for other Nisei ministerial students, he was able not only to adapt but, eventually, to flourish in courses with the assistance of Japanese faculty mentors and students. Yamaoka was sponsored by Reverend Ryogen Fujimoto, who helped with translation of his courses. For a year, Toshio Murakami, a student and future bishop of the Buddhist Churches of Canada, would regularly come to his dorm room to help him translate an abbreviated version of Shinran's *Kyōgyōshinshō* (Teaching, Practice, Faith, and Enlightenment).[134] This served as Yamaoka's first introduction to the Japanese language, and of how to read *kanbun,* a rendition of Classical Chinese text into Japanese, and of Shin Buddhist thought.[135]

As had been the case for Doami, being recruited to work at the Ryukoku University Translation Center vastly improved Yamaoka's language skills and knowledge of Shin Buddhist texts. He was assigned to work with Professor Daien Fugen and fellow student Ryoji Oka and developed good relations with both. Yamaoka remembered Fugen as "very instrumental in [his] whole educational thinking." Yamaoka described Oka as "a really good friend [who] would go into classes with me if I didn't understand and he would protect me in classes trying to explain things to me simply." Thinking back to this time, Yamaoka recalled these gestures of friendship, self-sacrifice, and generosity as being as important as course work in understanding what Shin Buddhism "meant." The work of the translation center was instrumental in helping him learn about Shin Buddhist doctrine. Yamaoka recalled that their work included background study of histories on the texts as well as the *romaji* and *kanji,* and the English translation of the texts. He concluded, "This was how we got really close to the text itself.... This helped us to understand Shinshu. Up until this time, we had no idea what Shinshu was."[136]

Yamaoka completed his master's degree in 1961 and enrolled in doctoral course work, during which time he met with Fugen to study Shin Buddhist doctrine. He noted, "It was in the last three years of study that my teacher Dr. Daien Fugen said to me, 'you have to come into my office once a week and I'll teach you doctrine. Because without doctrine, your ministry is not going to be anything.' So he taught me doctrine for three years."[137] Following this period of intensive study, Fugen instructed Yamaoka that, when he returned to America, he should "set the doctrine aside and listen to what the people are asking and wanting to know. You have to work with *their* situation. You can't bring in your doctrine and hope that they will understand. You have to get to know *them first,* where they're at and then begin to relate the doctrine.... Because you're in the West now and people are different."[138] Yamaoka returned to the United States in 1964. He would go on to minister to communities in Oakland, serve as BCA's bishop in the 1980s, and earn his DLitt in Shinshu studies from Ryukoku University.[139]

From Kyoto to Berkeley: The Founding of the Institute of Buddhist Studies

Between the end of World War II and 1972, BCA, in coordination with Nishi Honganji and Ryukoku University, trained approximately eighteen of the twenty-six Nisei ministers who would return to serve Shin Buddhist communities in the United States.[140] The successful training of this cohort of Nisei ministers resulted from transpacific cooperation among Shin Buddhists. This included the dedication of BCA ministers and lay leaders in the United States who supported funding and the development of ministerial training programs; the students who studied at the BCA Study Center and then journeyed to Japan to engage in graduate studies; and those Japanese instructors and students who provided mentoring and linguistic, cultural, and emotional support to the American students.

Yet, programs established to support ministerial training in Japan for Nisei and other American ministerial candidates were expensive, and even with long-term fundraising campaigns to support these programs, difficult to sustain. As was discussed earlier, prior to his untimely death, in 1958, BCA Bishop Shigefuji had explored the idea of moving the MTC onto the Ryukoku campus. As it entered its third year of funding ministerial training in Japan in 1959, BCA began to revisit proposals to develop a Buddhist studies graduate program in the United States. BCA struggled in efforts to raise donations for its Special Projects Fund between 1959 and 1962, which was the main source of funding for the MTC. Advocating for continued donations for long-term BCA projects, SPF chairman Ben Sato acknowledged in his 1962 report to the BCA Board of Directors, "it is true that 'annual drives' become very tiresome and less glamourous as time goes on, but that does not mean that the work is becoming less important."[141]

In working to transform the BCA Study Center in Berkeley into an accredited graduate program that could be endorsed by Nishi Honganji, the BCA benefited from the background and contacts of their new bishop, Dr. Shinso Hanayama (1898–1995). Nominated by Nishi Honganji as one among three candidates to serve as BCA's next bishop, Hanayama was selected by BCA's ministers associations. Hanayama's name was then forwarded to the BCA Board of Directors, who approved of the selection in 1959.[142] Like many of BCA's former bishops, Hanayama was both an ordained Shin Buddhist minister and a highly respected scholar of Japanese Buddhism. As a former professor at Tokyo University, Hanayama had also served as instructor and adviser to some of BCA's early ministerial candidates. One of Hanayama's first acts was to host Professor Ryosetsu Fujiwara as a visiting scholar at the study center for three years. A professor at Ryukoku University, Fujiwara was affiliated with the Ryukoku Translation Center. During his time in Berkeley, Fujiwara published short essays on Shin Buddhism for lay leaders, presented guest lectures to BCA members, instructed pre-ministerial candidates at BSC, and visited BCA's temples and churches. Fujiwara would go on to play a critical role in helping to establish a permanent ministerial training program in the United States.[143]

By 1964, BCA's ministers and lay leaders had concluded that the demand for ministers in America had reached a crisis point. Given the costs and challenges associated with funding the training of English-speaking ministers overseas, leadership believed that the best course would be to develop the BCA Study Center in Berkeley into an accredited Shin Buddhist graduate program. This complicated endeavor would require the coordinated efforts of three different groups, including BCA's bishop and ministers who, as spiritual authorities, had oversight of ministerial training procedures; academics affiliated with BCA and Ryukoku University; and BCA's board of directors, who would be responsible for raising funds and supporting the project.

The BCA Study Center established the groundwork for its accreditation in 1960 when Bishop Hanayama and BSC director and Berkeley Buddhist temple minister Reverend Masami Fujitani (who had replaced Reverend Imamura in 1958) and Professor Ryosetsu Fujiwara submitted a proposed curriculum for the center's pre-ministerial training and the training of lay leaders to the Hongwanji Education Department in Kyoto. A year later, courses "compiled by the BCA Study Curriculum Committee and in reference to the Hongwanji Gakuin Seminary Curricula" included "History of Japanese Buddhism" taught by Dr. Shinso Hanayama; four courses taught by Professor Fujiwara, including "Outline of Jodo Shinshu," "History of Shinshu," "Problem of Faith," and "Shoshinge"; and "Buddhist Languages," including Sanskrit and Buddhist Japanese, taught by Reverend Masami Fujitani.[144]

When Nishi Honganji's director Reverend Jokatsu Yukawa traveled to San Francisco in August of 1962, he was approached with a request from Bishop Hanayama to consider developing BSC into an auxiliary of Ryukoku University. Yukawa was reported to be supportive but also noted "that there might be difficulties as [Ryukoku University] must receive the approval of the Japanese Ministry of Education." Nevertheless, he was reported to have stated that "Hongwanji will recognize the pre-ministerial training of the Study Center and will grant full ordination (*tokudo* and *kyoshi*) to any ministerial aspirant who has completed this training, upon his arrival at the Hongwanji."[145] Nishi Honganji's leadership sent signals to BCA that it was supportive of the proposal; however, Bishop Junsho Ota was vague about the current plans. Nevertheless, he acknowledged, "We have a moral obligation to spread the teachings of Nembutsu, as demonstrated by Shinran Shonin, far and wide throughout the world for the benefit of mankind."[146] When Reverend Ejitsu Hojo, a member of the BCA Ministerial Research Committee, traveled to Japan toward the end of 1962 to meet with Honganji and Ryukoku University's officials, he confirmed Yukawa's earlier statements.[147]

In 1964, BCA significantly increased its commitment to the development of a full-fledged ministerial training center in the United States. At its annual February meeting, BCA created a Taisaku Iinkkai (Ministerial Development Committee). The ten-person committee—which included Bishop Hanayama, together with five ministers, including two Nisei and five Nisei board members—was charged with developing a plan for BSC, which would be renamed the Institute for Buddhist Studies.[148]

Nishi Honganji's Bishop Jonsho Ota spent a month between November and December 1964 in the United States and Canada attending ministerial and lay-persons conferences. His trip concluded with a meeting with Bishop Hanayama and Hawaii Hongwanji Mission Bishop Shojitsu Ohara, to discuss "future missionaries overseas policies."[149] At the time, Bishop Ota only committed to the "expansion of facilities of the BCA Study Center," pressing for the continued training of ministers at Ryukoku. The three bishops also agreed to the establishment of policy committees to address issues, including those addressing ministerial training. Ota agreed to establish the Office of Overseas Policy Committee, and the two American Bishops agreed to establish missionary policy committee(s). Once these groups had studied the issue of the training of English-speaking ministers and had mutually agreed on a policy, the policy would be put into effect.[150]

During the same year, BCA received a flurry of visits from Nishi Honganji and Ryukoku University. A delegation of sixteen members of the board of directors of the Nishi Honganji, led by Reverend Bumpo Kuwatsuki, chief of the Foreign Department, visited the Berkeley Buddhist Church and nineteen other BCA churches and temples over a two-week period to meet with ministers and lay members.[151] After more than a year of studying the problem, BCA's Taisaku Iinkkai committee recommended to BCA's board of directors that BCA establish a ministerial training center in Berkeley, near the University of California.[152]

When the BCA's Institute of Buddhist Studies received the official endorsement of Nishi Honganji in 1966 as a Shin Buddhist institution for ministerial training and graduate study, it represented the culmination of postwar efforts to establish training for English-speaking ministers and a center for the advanced study of Buddhism in America. Honganji's Bishop Taijun Toyohara noted:

> We look forward in keen anticipation to the success of your ministerial training program, which reflects your foresight when we consider its necessity for the progress of the kyodan (Shin Buddhist sangha). We are deeply concerned with your project when we picture the overall plan of our denomination for the next hundred years. We shall surmount all the difficulties and put forth our efforts for the completion of the institute and its facilities.[153]

While NYBCC's early postwar vision of a Nisei-led, trans-sectarian organization did not come to fruition, its members' efforts to develop Buddhist study groups and English-speaking Shin Buddhist ministerial training remain its most lasting legacy. Yet, the realization of these early efforts, which culminated in the founding, in 1966, of the Institute for Buddhist Studies (IBS), required the combined sustained commitment of BCA's ministers, lay leaders, and members, across generational lines, together with religious administrators at Nishi Honganji and academics from Ryukoku University. Today, IBS is affiliated with the Graduate Theological Union and remains the only Jōdo Shinshū–affiliated seminary and graduate school located outside of Japan.

CHAPTER FIVE

Nisei in the Buddhist World

The Way of the Good Life begins, says the Buddha, when the individual appreciates the fact that he cannot live alone, for himself, by himself, but that he is a member of a community. An individual is like a wave in the ocean, ocean and wave being mutually dependent on each other. This conception of the individual and community as being interdependent also means that there are obligations.

—G. P. Malalasekera, "Message," Berkeley Bussei, 1953

The time has now come for the Nisei and Sansei people to take over and expand [the] life of Nembutsu. . . . When we consider the universal nature of the English language, this will not be limited to propagation of Buddhism in the American continent and Hawaii only, but it will also mean that the door to Buddhism will be opening to all of the nations and races, thus offering an opportunity of spreading Buddhism in the entire world.

—Kosho Ohtani, "A Message to Shin Buddhists in America," Young East, 1953

Beginning in the early 1950s and continuing through the early 1960s, programs associated with Nisei Buddhism were influenced by transnational contact and exchanges with Buddhists in Asia. These exchanges allowed Nisei to envision themselves as part of a sangha that extended beyond the boundaries of the nation-state. Mirroring internal divisions within BCA between sectarianists and trans-sectarianists, Nisei were drawn into two distinct streams of international community. First, they joined in efforts by the World Fellowship of Buddhists (WFB) to create a global Buddhist organization and movement. Founded in Ceylon (Sri Lanka) in 1950, the WFB was initiated by lay Buddhists leaders in South and Southeast Asia. The organization's first president, G. P. Malalasekera, was met with an enthusiastic reception when he appealed directly to Nisei during a tour of the United States in 1953. Yet, even as they became involved in the WFB, Nisei also sought to reestablish ties with Nishi Honganji and Shin Buddhists in Japan. Postwar efforts to reconstitute ties were encouraged by the Chief Abbot Kosho Ohtani, together with BCA's leadership in preparation for the 700th Memorial of Shinran (1173–1262), the founder of the Shin sect of Japanese Buddhism. These efforts culminated in 1961, with a "pilgrimage" of more than one thousand BCA members to Kyoto for memorial services and related tours.

In contrast to members of racial minorities who served as official cultural ambassadors on behalf of the US government, Nisei Buddhists viewed themselves as informal cultural bridges on behalf of Asian Buddhists rather than solely representing America and America's interests in Asia. Despite their relatively small numbers, they were valued by Asian Buddhists for their contacts with the US government, American media, and the public, as well as for what they represented symbolically. Portrayed variously as American Buddhists, "overseas Japanese," and the children of "Issei pioneers," Nisei Buddhists were referenced as evidence of Buddhism's presence and vibrancy in the West. Yet, even as they embraced roles as ambassadors for Buddhism, Nisei also drew inspiration and hope from their transnational contacts, which provided them with a source of affirmation of their Buddhist background and a sense of belonging that stood in contrast to their status as both a racial and religious minority in the United States.

The World Fellowship of Buddhists and a Global Buddhist Perspective

The establishment of the World Fellowship of Buddhists was initiated by lay Buddhists in South and Southeast Asia who sought to develop a global Buddhist organization that could disseminate Buddhist teachings and share a Buddhist perspective in the postwar period. Their efforts were greatly influenced by decolonization, the rise of postcolonial nationalism, and efforts to develop a nonaligned "third world" amid growing Cold War tensions.[1] Ceylon (Sri Lanka) and Burma (Myanmar), were the first two nations with Buddhist majorities to gain independence from European colonial powers after the war. Ceylon gained its independence from Britain in 1947, and Burma followed in 1948. India also gained independence in 1947. Though a majority of the population was not Buddhist, given Buddhism's long historical roots in India, and under the leadership of Jawaharlal Nehru, the country played an important early supporting role in the intensification of postwar Buddhist revival as an important feature of postcolonial nation building in South Asia. Meanwhile, in Thailand, which had maintained its independence from colonial powers, the state had long recognized Buddhism as an important symbol of national unity and international prestige and thus provided substantial economic support for both national and international Buddhist organizations.[2]

In 1950, 129 delegates from twenty-nine countries gathered in Ceylon to participate in an inaugural conference of the World Fellowship of Buddhists.[3] The WFB Conference drew participants from each of the three major Buddhist traditions, underscoring its commitment to building unity across the Buddhist world. Theravada Buddhists made up a majority of the participants: eighty attended from Ceylon, twenty-two from Burma, and eight from Thailand. Smaller numbers of Mahayana Buddhist delegates from Vietnam and Japan attended, and, representing Tibetan Buddhism, Nepal, Tibet, and Mongolia also sent representatives. In addition to delegates from predominantly Buddhist nations, representatives were also invited from the broader Buddhist world: twenty-one delegates journeyed from Malaysia, India sent eighteen representatives, and small numbers journeyed from Pakistan and Dar-es-Salam, Tanganyika (Tanzania). "Convert" Buddhists of European descent from around the world sent a handful of representatives. Two Nisei from Hawai'i, Sunao Miyabara and Tumika Maneki, attended.[4]

The conference provided key political leaders and lay Buddhist organizations with a platform for highlighting the shared historic and doctrinal origins that united Buddhists across Asia and the world.[5] Prime Minister U Nu of Burma celebrated the shared origins that led to the establishment of Buddhism in Ceylon and Burma.[6] Prime Minister Jawaharlal Nehru of India expressed his "homage to the memory of the greatest of the sons of India" and urged delegates to "think of the basic truths that the Buddha taught, not the many dogmatic and other accretions that grow round every truth, but rather that truth itself in all its simplicity and nobility." Lay Buddhist representatives in Thailand declared their historic regard for Ceylon and India as the "cradle of Buddhism" and recalled that Thailand had played an important role in helping restore the ordination of monks in those nations during the mid-eighteenth century.[7]

At the 1950 conference, delegates drafted and approved a constitution for the organization. The WFB constitution expressed delegates' interest in promoting Buddhist values and practice globally to people and governments in the name of world peace. The preamble declared delegates' intention to "observe and practice the teachings of the Buddha that we may be radiant examples of the living faith." It also sought to "make known the sublime doctrine of the Buddha, . . . inspiring peoples of the earth and their governments to lead the Buddhist way of life which is for all ages and times, so that there be peace and harmony amongst men and happiness for all human beings."[8]

In working toward this end, the constitution included provisions designed to support the development of transnational Buddhist networks. Underscoring the important role that South Asia was to play, the constitution established a WFB World Centre Headquarters, initially housed in Colombo, Ceylon. The headquarters would move to Burma in 1958 and later to Thailand, in 1963, which would become its permanent home.[9] Next, the constitution authorized the creation of WFB "regional centers" in countries "with appreciable numbers of Buddhists" or with existing Buddhist organizations.[10] The forty-two initial regional centers underscored the centrality of Asia as a region but also highlighted WFB efforts to develop transnational networks with Buddhists beyond Asia. A majority of the regional centers (twenty-three) were located in Asia, in countries with large numbers of Buddhists.[11] Regional centers were also located in areas with smaller numbers of Buddhists, in regions representing major Cold War powers, including North America, Hawai'i, and Europe (nine), and one in the USSR, as well as one each in Latin America, Africa, and Australia.[12]

The WFB faced major challenges in their efforts to develop WFB as a Buddhist organization across lines of tradition, nation, and race. First, they had to bridge doctrinal and historical divisions among the three major Buddhist traditions: Theravada, Mahayana, and Vajrayana or Tibetan Buddhism. They also faced regional divisions created under European colonialism and had to grapple with intraregional animosities and distrust that resulted from the events of World War II, including the significant role that Japanese Buddhist sects played in Japanese settler colonialism in Taiwan, Korea, and, later, through Japanese imperialism and campaigns to develop a pan-Asian coalition under the Greater East Asia Co-Prosperity Sphere.[13] Buddhists leadership also faced criticism from Asian communists who identified them as representing or closely linked to elites and the bourgeois class. Yet, by the mid-to-late-1950s, socialists and communists also viewed Buddhism as a point of commonality across nations in Asia. Even as the People's Republic of China was engaged in campaigns to close Buddhist monasteries in China and to annex Tibet and reduce the power of its lamas, it also sought to engage in developing relations with other Buddhist nations.[14]

To reinforce unity and understanding across the major divisions of Buddhism, WFB delegates forwarded and approved four motions at the inaugural conference. The first two motions, which were also included in the WFB constitution, were proposed by Nisei Sunao Miyabara, representing the United States and the regional center in Hawai'i. The WFB adopted two universal Buddhist symbols to reinforce unity. The first was a six-colored Buddhist flag that had been used in Ceylon as an "international Buddhist flag." The second was the dharma chakra or eight-spoke wheel of dharma, representing the Buddha's eight-fold path as an "international Buddhist symbol," which, as discussed earlier, was also adopted by Nisei in successful campaigns for the recognition of Buddhist cemetery markers at American national memorials. Inaugural conference participants also resolved to create Vesak or Buddha Day as a public holiday in all countries where Buddhists resided. A third resolution, which sought to build unity by removing titles demarcating two major Buddhist traditions that some found offensive, involved changing "Hinayana" to "Theravada." Hinayana, or "lesser vehicle," was a term that contrasted with Mahayana or "greater vehicle"; Theravada was translated as "doctrine of the elders."[15]

The WFB also sought to promote unity in two additional ways. First, through the circulation of WFB conferences to host nations representing the various traditions of Buddhism. While a majority of the conferences were hosted by Theravada Buddhist nations, the WFB's second conference, in 1952, was hosted by Mahayana Buddhists in Tokyo, Japan, while the fourth conference in 1956 was hosted by Nepalese Buddhists, in Kathmandu, representing Tibetan and Mahayana Buddhism.[16] WFB also sought to draw Buddhists together through shared efforts to restore sacred pilgrimage sites. At the third Buddhist conference, delegates passed a resolution to restore the sacred sites of Lumbini in Nepal, and Kusinārā in India, the sites of the birth and death of Siddhartha Gautama, the historical Buddha. In restoring sacred pilgrimage sites, the WFB was influenced by similar efforts beginning in the late nineteenth century.[17]

In further developing transnational networks among Buddhists throughout Asia and the broader Buddhist world, WFB leadership turned to its regional centers. Beginning in 1951, WFB headquarters, in coordination with WFB regional centers, helped to plan and sponsor visits by WFB presidents to meet with Buddhist organizations, laypersons, and clergy across the world. In April 1951, the WFB executive council sent G. P. Malalasekera on a two-month tour across Southeast Asia that included stops in Singapore, Malaysia, Thailand, Cambodia, Vietnam, and Burma.[18]

WFB coverage of the presidential tour promoted the organization's message of Buddhist unity. Malalasekera filed reports that were published in the WFB's *News Letter.* These reports were later collected and published as *The Buddhist Flag of South Asia,* which was distributed to delegates and observers in attendance at the second World Fellowship of Buddhists Conference held in 1952, in Tokyo, Japan.[19] Readers in regional centers throughout the world learned that Buddhist laypersons, politicians, and dignitaries responded to Malalasekera's tour with much enthusiasm. In Cambodia, Malalasekera presented a WFB Buddhist flag to King Norodom Sihanouk, who issued an official decree to fly it over his palace on

Vesak Day.[20] As Malalasekera visited cities such as Malacca, Bangkok, and Hanoi, he reported viewing prominent displays of the WFB Buddhist flag.[21]

In addition to promoting unity, both political leaders and Buddhists in Asia believed that a Buddhist perspective could also serve as a counterforce to a world increasingly subjected to Cold War politics and the possibility of nuclear warfare. In a message presented to the inaugural congress of the WFB in 1950, India's prime minister Jawaharlal Nehru expressed hope that the efforts of the conference will "lead more people to think [about] the teachings of the Buddha." Nehru concluded that the Buddha's teachings:

> have a value in every age. But no other period in history requires them more than this present one in which we live. We pass from crisis to crisis and think always in terms of violence and coercion, forgetting that these methods have seldom, if ever, yielded any substantial results. The vicious circle goes on and both as individuals and as national communities, we are dragged into it.[22]

Other delegates shared Nehru's concern about violence and were particularly concerned with future wars fought with atomic weapons. Delegates from Japan proposed a seven-point program that included arms reduction and the use of atomic energy for peaceful rather than destructive purposes.[23] Somdej Phra Vajirananavamsa, the supreme patriarch of Thailand, contrasted the efforts of Buddhists from around the world to build unity with the "militant powers" who were "striving hard for world domination to gain their selfish ends through greed, hatred and ignorance."[24] The primary focus of the second WFB Conference, held in Tokyo, Japan, was the promotion of peace amid a world increasingly threatened by nuclear war. During the conference, delegates created and adopted a resolution "on the Establishment of World Peace on the Basis of Buddhist Principles."[25]

As Cold War tensions escalated, a number of Asian Buddhist delegates to the WFB imagined themselves as part of a third space, beyond the world that was in the process of being defined and demarcated by the United States, the Soviets, and their respective allies. Delegates to the inaugural congress sought to respond to the shared need to preserve regional integrity and promote peace. They envisioned the WFB as "an economic, political and cultural federation to stand out as a bastion of peace in East Asia and to lead the world on the path of peace, brotherliness and universal love as indicated by the Great Master." The organization also planned to "appeal to the different Buddhist countries to evolve a machinery on the model of the United Nations Organization for the aforesaid purpose."[26]

The specter of the Cold War escalating into nuclear war was of great concern to Asian lay Buddhists. The opening report of the WFB Conference held in Burma in 1954 began, "The world has no sooner emerged from the most cruel and devastating war ever known in its history, than it is faced with the possibility of another and yet more catastrophic conflict, which threatens mankind and all life on this planet with nothing less than total destruction." In the face of this threat, the report noted that Burma and WFB Buddhist delegates offered the world "the sublime Teaching of the Buddha as the beacon of hope and salvation."[27] During the Burma conference, the All Japan Buddhist Youth Organization proposed that the world's peoples were "standing at the turning point of history." Commenting on the "political antagonism between the free and Communist countries," the organization declared, "Buddhist countries in Asia in general and of Southeast Asia in particular," had a responsibility to "constitute a Third Power of the world" based on their "unique Buddhist qualities such as upholding of the Middle Way, the spirit and concord, and the persevering effort for creating quiet and peace in any environment."[28]

Asian Buddhist lay leaders and other participants in the World Fellowship of Buddhists believed that the spread of Buddhist teachings was both timely and critical in addressing both the legacy of colonialism in Asia and emerging Cold War tensions. For Theravada Buddhists in particular, the timing of the formation of the World Fellowship of Buddhists, amid mass decolonization and postcolonial national independence movements, was auspicious because it coincided with the Buddha Jayanti, the 2,500th anniversary of the Buddha's entry into Parinibbāna, in 2493 BE (1956). In the Theravada tradition, the anniversary was believed to mark a period of "great renewal and resurgence" of Buddhist *dhamma* (teachings).[29] While Theravada and Mahayana Buddhists held a long-standing disagreement on the exact date, in a show of unity, Mahayana Buddhist participants in the WFB recognized the year as significant for Theravada Buddhists. At the WFB Inaugural Conference, delegates across the major Buddhist traditions resolved that their organization's primary purpose was to bring

> closer together the Buddhists of the world, of exchanging news and views about the conditions of Buddhism in different countries and of discussing ways and means whereby Buddhists could make their due contribution towards the attainment of peace and happiness, so that, when the 2,500th year after the Passing Away of the Buddha was reached in 1956 A.C., the whole world would have adopted the Buddhist Way of Life.[30]

It was in preparation for the Jayanti that the All Ceylon Buddhist Congress, a leading group of Sri Lankan laypersons, organized the WFB Inaugural Conference. Burmese Buddhists, under the leadership of U Nu, planned and organized the Chaṭṭha Sangayana (Sixth Buddhist Council)[31] to be held in Burma from 1954 to 1956 in conjunction with the Jayanti.[32]

The creation of the WFB and efforts to foster unity and spread Buddhist teachings and perspectives globally were central tenets supported by the organization's core members in Asia as well as members from around the world. WFB-affiliated centers in the United States, the Soviet Union, and Western Europe were viewed as critical conduits for infusing Buddhist teachings and perspectives into the arena of Cold War politics.

"Bonded by Reverence to the Buddha": Nisei Join the World Fellowship of Buddhists

Participation in the World Fellowship of Buddhists organization opened Nisei to a broader Buddhist world that provided a sense of community, purpose, and a new global lens from which to assess and interpret Cold War politics and international relations. One of the first to become acquainted with Malalasekera was Sunao Miyabara. An active YBA member and Nisei Buddhist war veteran, Miyabara first met Malalasekera at the 1949 East West Philosopher's Conference held in Honolulu, Hawai'i. As Miyabara later recalled, the conference provided him and Malalasekera with "the opportunity to discuss the future of Buddhism." Miyabara described a late-night conversation "burning the midnight oil together with Dr. Malalasekera in a ramshackle wooden building called the Hale Aloha at the University of Hawaii." The conversation led to Miyabara's participation in the WFB Inaugural Conference, where he would play a prominent role on the committee in charge of drafting the WFB's constitution.[33]

Nisei Buddhists from BCA participated as delegates at the second conference of the WFB, held in Tokyo, Japan, in 1952. Two Nisei lay leaders, Dr. Kikuo Taira, who served as the chief American delegate, and Manabu Fukada, along with Mrs. Shinobu Matsuura, joined Arthur Takemoto and Daitetsu Unno, two Nisei enrolled in ministerial training programs in Japan.[34] The visibility of Nisei and their perspectives was accentuated by the fact that the official language of the conference was English. Press coverage in the *Pacific Citizen* noted that Taira had observed some of the "shortcomings" of Buddhism in Japan, including the "dogmatic attitude" of the major Japanese sects.[35]

Many more Nisei were introduced to the WFB when G. P. Malalasekera met with them during an extensive tour of the United States and Europe in 1953.

Addressing a crowd of Nisei Buddhists members of the Western Young Buddhist League during an annual memorial service for Nisei soldiers held in Los Angeles, Malalasekera reflected on another service that he had attended a year earlier in Tokyo during the World Fellowship of Buddhists Conference. "The purpose of the memorial service held in the Gokokuji Temple," he noted, "was to remember with gratitude the great sacrifice made by soldiers of all nations who laid down their lives in the last great world war and to wish that they should find happiness and ultimately attain the peace of Nirvana."[36]

Yet, Malalasekera also cautioned against focusing on such ceremonies at the cost of losing sight of core Buddhist teachings. He noted, "All these other things that we do whether it is ceremonial, or prayer or ritual, whether it be these vast gatherings that we have, . . . the ultimate goal must not be lost sight of. . . . We must find a way out of suffering into happiness, that is salvation." For Malalasekera, a true understanding of suffering could begin only when Nisei began to look beyond themselves to the broader world.[37] He stated,

> We cannot be convinced of the fact of sorrow unless we are aware of what is happening in the world, in our own personalities, and in the affairs of those who live in the world. The awareness must always be there and that awareness can come only when we give up our feeling of smug self-satisfaction, when we forget, or are prepared to forget our own petty business of life and to realize that we are part of the whole universe, that whatever we do and feel and think, that is going to affect the rest of the world and that therefore there is a tremendous responsibility upon all of us.[38]

Malalasekera concluded his talk by discussing the limits of materialist solutions and of reliance on technology and even of knowledge itself in addressing suffering and by emphasizing the role that Nisei could play in sharing Buddhist teachings and a Buddhist understanding of suffering and liberation in the United States. For Malalasekera, the range of materialist approaches, from redistributive policies to modernization theories, did not adequately address the question of suffering and its cause. He noted, "we find that the mere accumulation of wealth, the mere acquisition of various kinds of material comfort does not lead to happiness. The more we try to satisfy our desires we seem to set them aflame, to increase our desire, to increase our needs." He noted that technology and the expansion of knowledge did not of themselves lead to happiness, but instead led to their opposite:

We find that quite often the greatest crimes which bring misery and destruction to the world and unhappiness to men are being committed by those who have a large amount of knowledge at their disposal. The guns and weapons of war, the atom bomb and the hydrogen bomb are the results of discoveries of those who have tremendous knowledge in their heads and that knowledge is being used not in order to bring about happiness but in order to bring about destruction and war and unhappiness as a result.[39]

In sum, Malalasekera urged Nisei to join with fellow Buddhists around the globe in efforts to bring Buddhist teachings and a Buddhist sensibility to American society and culture. He implored them to embrace and introduce core Buddhist ideas about the nature of suffering and interdependence, even as they refuted negative characterizations of Buddhists.

The message of building Buddhist unity and utilizing Buddhist teachings in addressing the world's problems presented at WFB conferences, and during visits from WFB representatives such as Malalasekera, made a lasting impression on some of BCA's key Nisei lay leaders, who sought to share the message of building unity across division and infusing the West in particular with Buddhist ideas and perspectives. Following his return from the second WFB Conference in 1952, Manabu Fukuda, former president of BCA's National Young Buddhist Association, contributed an essay titled, "The Coming Religion," to the 1953 *Berkeley Bussei*. Fukuda emphasized the importance of a living, progressing, socially engaged Buddhism. He proclaimed that "there shall be no faith in a religion and its leaders if they are standing upon the laurels of the past and being complacent about the future of mankind." Echoing the words of WFB leaders, Fukuda argued "religion must not only follow in the footsteps of science, medicine and philosophy, but it must lead them in the right direction." He concluded "the wisdom, courage, and energy of the 20th century must be embodied in Buddhism before it can be of any value to the people who live in these times of grave uncertainty."[40]

Reporting on the second WFB Conference in the *Berkeley Bussei,* Nisei lay leader and future BCA president Dr. Kikuo Taira observed that, "what struck us more deeply than anything else was the friendly nature of the people who assembled there. Within this atmosphere, our anxiety for world peace was quieted to an objective resoluteness." Taira explained that he and fellow delegates "had not realized before that many of these countries were inherently of 'Buddhist' nations with actual cabinet positions, such as Minister of Religious Education, existing within the government systems."[41] Yet, the conference also impressed upon Taira

Buddhism's potential in bridging divisions among human beings. He noted that conference participants, "realized that these delegates from different parts of the world appeared differently, dressed differently and spoke different languages, but underneath these superficial appearances, all were bonded by reverence toward the Buddha and the Truth that Buddha had taught."[42]

Taira also sought to share Buddhist teachings and WFB's perspective with the American public. He regularly gave public talks about the World Fellowship of Buddhists, accompanied by color slides of the 1952 conference, to local Central California civic and social organizations.[43] Taira also shared the WFB's message and perspective on local public radio. In a broadcast to listeners on April 8, "Buddha Day," in California's Central Valley, which was likely presented within a decade of his participation in the 1952 conference, Taira noted that "due to tremendous advance[s] in science, mankind is standing on the threshold of an atomic era whose possibilities and potentials defy our imagination" yet also "is beset with [a] multitude of problems and confrontation[s] of opposing ideologies." Added to this were the issues that advances in science "were primarily with [a] military purpose in mind" and had led to atomic arms buildup." Taira argued that the sources of these problems were that "man [had] failed to keep up his spiritual development with his material progress." Even the "freedom of democracy" had for "many persons meant nothing more than an unbridled license to grab something for himself without any consideration for others whatsoever." Taira concluded that guidance was available from "the sage of India who became a Buddha—the enlightened one."[44]

BCA members who journeyed to WFB-sponsored conferences and activities after 1952 were often joined by other American Buddhists across lines of sect, ethnicity, and race. At the 1954 WFB Conference held in Rangoon, Burma (Yangon, Myanmar), Reverend Kenryo Kumata delivered an address on the floor of the general conference on behalf of the North American delegation that included two Issei ministers, Reverends Ejitus Hojo and Chonen Terekawa; along with LaVerne Sasaki, a Nisei ministerial student in Japan; the Reverend Leslie Lowe, a Chinese American leader of the Universal Buddhist Fellowship in San Francisco; Reverend Bunpo Kuwatsuki of Senshin Buddhist Church, Los Angeles; and Robert Stuart Clifton, a white convert Buddhist with previous ties to the Buddhist Churches of America.[45]

For some Nisei Buddhists, participation in conferences led to broader and deeper engagement with the Buddhist world. LaVerne Sasaki's participation in the 1954 WFB Conference inspired his return to tour the Buddhist world more extensively in 1955. Sasaki visited important historical Buddhist pilgrimage sites in Burma, India, Nepal, and Ceylon and reported on his travels with fellow ministerial student and friend Shoyu Hanayama and Reverend Shojun Bando of the Higashi Honganji Otani University in Kyoto in the Tokyo-based Buddhist publication *Young East*.[46] As it had for Kikuo Taira, Sasaki's participation in the conferences underscored both the unity and diversity of the Buddhist world. He was impressed with the respect shown for Buddhist pilgrims in Ceylon. Upon landing at the airport in Jaffa, Ceylon, Sasaki recalled that "it was during the custom inspection that we learned how much of a Buddhist country Ceylon is." After mentioning to the inspector that they were entering the country as Buddhist pilgrims and planned to visit historical Buddhist sites, the inspector "smiled and calmly stated that our group will not be inspected for customs because it [was] comprised of Buddhists!"[47]

The three visited a number of important religious sites. In Sravasti, India, at the Jetavana monastery, Sasaki recalled that he was "disappointed at the noted spot, for there was hardly any trace of the former grandeur of the original monastery except for some red bricks that obscurely formed what appeared like the base of the temple." Traveling to Sanchi, an ancient ruin, they visited the Great Stupa established by Aśoka (3rd century BCE), which Sasaki noted was discovered by Sir Alexander Cunningham in 1851. Sasaki also described the presence of stone memorials to the sacred relics of two of the Buddha's chief disciples that were housed at the Maha Bodhi Vihara and formally recognized by the government of India. The memorial read, "Namo Buddhaya. Opening of this Vihara and enshrinement of sacred relics of Arahans Sariputta and Maha Mogallana were performed by Jawaharlal Nehru, Prime Minister of India on November 30, 1952."[48] In Ceylon, they visited the Sacred Tooth Relic at Kandy, Sigiriya Rock, and Anuradhapura, which Sasaki referred to as "the most famous of Ceylon's ancient cities."[49]

Sasaki's visit also underscored the role that Buddhism played in bridging emerging divisions among American, Japanese, and other Asians, during a period when Japan's close Cold War partnership with the United States strained relations with nonaligned Asian nations. In India, Sasaki and his Japanese companions met with Sarvepalli Radhakrishnan, vice president (and future president) of India, whom Sasaki characterized as "one of the great thinkers of the world." They met with the vice president for over half an hour at his home. Enjoying tea and sweets, Radhakrishnan "discussed the great significant role that Buddhism had played in Asian history and the need for the West to understand better its profound underlying thought it treasures."[50] Sasaki's fluency in English and Japanese likely facilitated the discussion and clearly revealed Sasaki as an American of Japanese descent to Radhakrishnan, who, like Malalasekera, stressed to the young Nisei and his companions the need to spread the Dharma to the West.

Sasaki was also able to meet G. P. Malalasekera at the University of Ceylon and to reconnect with Mr. Raja Hewavitarne and Mr. Mahiman Amarasuriya, two Ceylonese lay Buddhists from Colombo that he had met at the 1954 Burma conference.[51] Sasaki noted the charitable work of his affluent hosts. They visited the Malikka Home for the aged, which had been founded by Hewavitarne's grandmother, a small orphanage, and one of forty-nine Maha Bodhi schools managed by Hewavitarne. Sasaki was informed that 1,500 students between the ages of three and eighteen were enrolled, and that they learned both English and Singhalese. He described the class as "well disciplined," and was impressed by "the fact that they would worship the Buddha daily before class."[52]

During his travels and encounters with Asian Buddhists, and following his return to Japan and later the United States, Sasaki expressed a self-consciousness about his role as a cultural ambassador. Significantly, he viewed himself as both a bridge between Buddhists in Japan and the rest of Asia and as a bridge between Asia and the West. In the concluding report to the Japan-based *Young East* publication, Sasaki summed up the visit as "a kind of good will mission." He continued, "We hope that, however small it may have been, we had contributed to a better mutual understanding between the southern Buddhist countries and Japan and only wish that the continued warm understanding and mutual assistance prevail between the many Buddhist countries in the world."[53]

Sasaki's participation as a delegate to the WFB Conference and as a participant in a WFB-sponsored cultural exchange program also shaped a view of himself as bridge between Asia and America. After completing studies in Japan, Sasaki returned to the United States to minister to Nikkei Buddhist communities. In the early 1960s, he attended the University of the Pacific in Stockton, California, and wrote a master's thesis in the field of education that was inspired in part by his participation in the 1954 Burma conference and his 1955 participation in the WFB pilgrimage to South Asia. The thesis addressed a proposed plan for a Buddhist curriculum for Japanese American high school seniors.

Sasaki's curriculum revealed the impact that participation in the Buddhist world had made. Among the acknowledgments in his master's thesis, Sasaki thanked Bhikkhu Amritananda, whom he had met in Kathmandu, Nepal. He also thanked his friend Shoyu Hanayama and Reverend Shojun Bundo "for making possible the never-to-be-forgotten Buddhist pilgrimage." Moreover, Sasaki's participation in the WFB's conferences and cultural exchange programs had exposed him to anticolonial attempts to build Buddhist education programs, which in turn had provided him with a model for addressing racial and religious discrimination in the United States. Sasaki's thesis framed the project as one that sought to address tensions revolving around Japanese American Buddhist acculturation. Sasaki concluded that "Buddhism in the United States [was] confronted with a great challenge that any foreign religion faces in a predominantly non-Buddhist country such as problems of comparison and lack of the Buddhist tradition and background."[54] Time spent in Buddhist-majority countries also enabled him to more clearly identify and highlight the Christian-centric biases inherent in defining religion in America, rather than addressing the issue as simply a "minority problem."

Pilgrimage and the Reconstitution of Transpacific Shin Buddhism

Even as small numbers of Nisei joined the WFB and engaged in efforts to spread their message of Buddhist unity, and the spread of Buddhist teachings, across traditions, sects, nations, and races, Nisei were also called upon to serve as cultural ambassadors on behalf of Shin Buddhists in the United States and Japan. The emphasis on Shin sectarianism took on a particular importance for both the Nishi Honganji head temple and Buddhist Churches of America as they prepared for 700th Memorial Services in 1961 for Shinran (1173–1262), the founder of Shin Buddhism. Nisei embraced the role of bridge between BCA and Nishi Honganji even as, for some, their experiences and actions were shaped by more personal efforts to bridge familial connections that had been lost during the war.

Nearly one thousand members of the BCA participated in 700th Memorial Services for Shinran at the Nishi Honganji temple in Kyoto, from February to August of 1961, in what organizers and participants described as a once-in-a-lifetime pilgrimage. The participation of BCA's members, together with another one thousand Nikkei from Brazil, Canada, and Hawai'i, were recognized and celebrated by Shin Buddhist leaders throughout the memorial services as the living embodiment of the spirit of *bukkyō tōzen*. Nishi Honganji was located at Shinran's gravesite and originated as a memorial chapel. Rennyo (1415–1499), the eighth head priest of the Hongwanji, transformed the annual Hōonkō memorial service for Shinran into a mass service.[55] Modern mass pilgrimage in relation to travel for the 700th Memorial for Shinran likely had roots in earlier efforts by Nishi Honganji to present Buddhism and the Shin sect as in step with adaptations made by Christians and other religious traditions. From the nineteenth to early twentieth centuries, narratives of pilgrimage to Bodh Gayā, the site of Sākyamuni, the historical Buddha's enlightenment, were utilized to underscore successful modernization by Shin Buddhists. Historian Michihiro Ama noted similar efforts to commemorate Shinran by Nishi Honganji after the return of Shimaji Mokurai and Akamatsu Renjo from a religious studies tour of Europe in the 1870s. Shinran was further elevated when both branches of Honganji (Nishi and Higashi) mobilized large numbers of regional followers to travel by train to the head temples for Shinran's 650th Memorial Service in Kyoto in 1911.[56] According to Imre Galambos, two million people attended this memorial.[57] In 1922, another 550,000 laypersons, together with 1,500 priests, commemorated the seven-hundredth anniversary of the publication of Shinran's *Kyōgyō Shinshō* in 1922.[58]

Much was at stake for Nishi Honganji and BCA as the 700th Memorial approached in 1961. The United States and Japan were in the midst of consolidating a transformed relationship as Cold War partners, and religious institutions in Japan were grappling with the transformed social and political landscape. As discussed earlier, the end of the Pacific War and the early postwar years had left Nishi Honganji's future uncertain, with declining moral authority and membership.[59] Scholars have pointed to a number of factors driving instability and decline. Honganji's commitment to the Pacific War resulted in challenges to the institution's postwar leadership and moral authority. Established Buddhist institutions like Nishi Honganji were also affected by the US occupation policies of SCAP, particularly those related to land reform and religious institutions. These policies reduced revenues and loosened the hold of institutional authority of headquarters over branches.[60] Longer-term demographic shifts and the growth of new religions as a result of SCAP's policies on freedom of religion, which were adopted in Article 20 of Japan's constitution in 1946, played a significant role in declining Shin Buddhist membership in Japan. Driven by wartime devastation, followed by postwar industrial growth and urban migration of the population— especially young people, beginning in the 1950s—Shin Buddhism's traditional rural power based declined. Meanwhile, established Buddhist institutions faced competition from new Buddhist movements like Soka Gakkai and other religious organizations and movements who successfully recruited a growing demographic of young urbanites.[61]

Given these significant challenges, "overseas Japanese," particularly Nikkei in the United States, provided economic support as well as political and symbolic capital as Abbot Kosho Ohtani and Nishi Honganji sought to reconstitute themselves as Cold War allies and Jōdo Shinshū as a modern world religion. In the years leading up to the 700th Memorial, both Nishi Honganji and BCA leaders solicited membership in support of the memorial. Ohtani expressed a particular interest in the participation of Japanese Americans in memorial services.

Nishi Honganji's inclusion of overseas Japanese in the memorial reflected, in part, earlier patterns developed in late Imperial Japan of commemoration of overseas pioneers. As Eiichiro Azuma has noted, the celebration of overseas pioneers was utilized to legitimize metropolitan institutions and Japanese imperial expansion in Asia.[62] During the postwar years, the pilgrimage of "overseas" Buddhists would evoke nostalgic selective rememberings of *bukkyō tōzen* that elided its imperial aspects. Overseas Japanese Buddhists in the Americas were a reminder of the extent to which Shin Buddhism had already traveled across the Pacific. Yet, unlike those overseas Shin pioneers who had engaged in colonial efforts in East Asia, North America did not carry the same explicit associations with imperial power.[63] Contrary to representations of Japanese Buddhists in places like Taiwan, Korea, and Manchuria, Issei Buddhist communities in North America during memorial related services would characterize Japanese Buddhists as pioneers who brought Buddhism to the West in the face of harsh discrimination.

Two years prior to the memorial in 1959, Abbot Ohtani, together with his wife, returned to the United States for a six-month visit to BCA's temples and churches.[64] During the visit, the abbot stressed the significance of the memorial, not only for Shin Buddhists but also for the revitalization of Shin Buddhism in Japan and globally. When asked by Young Adult Buddhist Association members to explain the significance of the memorial, the abbot noted that the service provided an "opportunity to spread the Jodo Shinshu Teaching in Japan and throughout the world, and to realize the greatness of this Teaching which will help create a harmonious world."[65]

BCA's Nisei leadership shared the view that the memorial provided an opportunity to revitalize Shin Buddhism. For Takashi Tsuji, a Nisei minister and newly appointed director of the BCA's Bureau of Education, the memorial provided an opportunity for Shin Buddhists to engage in liberal humanitarian causes and demonstrate a greater social engagement in the world. He explained that "no occasion will be more opportune than this to appeal to the conscience of mankind for the adoption of humane immigration laws, for international cooperation in effective foreign aid programs, and in essence for the realization of a decent standard of living everywhere." He concluded, "Where ignorance darkly beclouds the minds of men, bring forth the light of compassion and understanding!"[66]

A final request and formal invitation from the abbot to BCA members was published in January 1961, just four months prior to the memorial. The abbot noted that, given the once-in-a-lifetime opportunity, "[we] sincerely hope . . . that as many faithful members as possible setting aside all other business, will make a special effort to join in the pilgrimage to Hongwanji." Ohtani reminded members of the importance of the memorial for Shin Buddhists noting that "here and here alone, will the real meaning of the Nembutsu be discovered—that its saving power lies in this life—and the social destiny of our Faith takes on a higher value."[67]

"A Continuous Flow of Gratitude": Nikkei Participation in 700th Memorial Services

The abbot's appeal to participate in the pilgrimage to the 700th Memorial Services was enthusiastically met by an energized BCA leadership and membership. BCA plans for the memorial and pilgrimage required the coordinated efforts of Bishop Shigefuji (until his death in August 1958) and his successor, Bishop Shinsho Hanayama, together with BCA's ministers and Bussei lay leaders. In 1961, BCA created the Committee for the Buddhist Tour of Japan, comprising Bishop Hanayama; two Issei ministers, Reverend Giko Abiko, chairman of the Ministers Association and Reverend Shozen Naito, executive secretary; and four Nisei, including newly elected BCA president of the board of directors, Albert Kosakura, together with Reverend Takashi Tsuji, Hiroshi Kashiwagi, and Tad Hirota.[68]

Kosakura had been involved in the planning for the pilgrimage since 1959, when he submitted a proposed plan to the BCA Board of Directors. He journeyed to Japan to research and make hotel and travel arrangements and plan the length of the visit for BCA pilgrims.[69] Kosakura's election as president of the board of directors during the later planning phases of the pilgrimage tour was timely. According to Hiroshi Kashiwagi, Kosakura had grown up in the travel business, because his father owned a travel agency. By the time he was planning the pilgrimage, Kosakura possessed extensive experience in the travel industry, having worked as a manager for Pan American Airlines and, prior to that, for the American Shipping Company.[70] Under Kosakura's direction, BCA hired Seiso Tamaru to work part time in assisting with travel arrangements, beginning one year prior to the pilgrimage. A Japanese travel agency, Kinki Nippon Tourist Company, was hired to organize the tours of Japan. BCA members were able to meet with Genji Yamaguchi, director of air and ocean travel, who set up a temporary office at BCA headquarters beginning in December 1960.[71]

BCA leaders set as a goal the participation of one thousand members in the pilgrimage; indeed, nearly one thousand participated in the pilgrimage and memorial.[72] BCA arranged nine different tours, ranging from ten to twenty-one days,[73] that reflected the growth and expansion of transpacific commercial leisure travel after World War II. Many combined travel to cities with visits to cultural and religious sites that were tailored to the anticipated interests of Nikkei Buddhists. BCA members visited a variety of religious, cultural, and commercial sites in Kyoto, Tokyo, Osaka, and surrounding areas. Stops in Kyoto underscored the city's historical, cultural, and religious importance. For example, travelers visited the Imperial Palace, Kinkaku-ji (Golden Pavilion) Temple (Zen), Heian Shrine (Shinto) and Kiyomizu-dera Temple (Hossō Sect). In contrast, stops in Tokyo—including visits to the Imperial Palace Plaza, the National Diet Building, Meiji Shrine, Yusukuni Shrine, Ueno Park, Asakusa Amusement Center, Ginza Street, and a visit to Kabuki-za Theatre—underscored the city's importance as the nation's capital and center of commercial enterprise.[74]

While many BCA members traveled directly to Japan to attend the memorial, others joined BCA-sponsored tours to Buddhist sites in Japan or the broader Buddhist world, reflecting Nikkei interest in the global Buddhist vision promoted by the World Fellowship of Buddhists.[75] Sponsored by BCA's tour committee, the most extensive (and expensive, at $2,550) tour, was a "43-day 'Around the World Buddhist Tour'" organized with the help of a New York travel agency. The tour, led by Reverend Hozen Seki of BCA's American Buddhist Academy in New York, departed on March 1. Travelers visited a number of European cities including London, Paris, Geneva, Milan, Venice, Florence, Rome, and Athens, before traveling to Cairo, en route to South Asia. In India, they visited Bombay (Mumbai), New Delhi, and Calcutta, together with two Buddhist pilgrimage sites at Agra and Benares. The trip concluded with visits to Bangkok and Hong Kong, before arriving in Tokyo.[76]

The culminating event for each of the twenty-three pilgrimage groups, which ranged in size from fifteen to a hundred people, was attendance at the 700th Memorial Services held at Nishi Honganji between March 19 and April 14, 1961.[77] BCA's pilgrims joined hundreds of thousands of Shin Buddhists in formal ceremonies that included the mass chanting of the *nembutsu*. Haruo Yamaoka, a Nisei ministerial student at Ryukoku University, participated in memorial services and was a guest to a number of ceremonies and conferences related to the memorial service. In an article published in BCA's *American Buddhist,* Yamaoka described "what seemed like a million people gathered at Hongwanji, . . . a little lost [and] asking [for] directions here, looking around for lost companions or footwear there," but all gathered "to pay respects to Shinran Shonin on the 700th anniversary of his passing."[78] The morning service began with the procession of the Honganji order and then culminated with the chanting of Shinran's Shōshinge (Hymn of Truth Faith) led by the Abbot Ohtani.[79]

While overseas Japanese might have been easily overlooked in the sea of Shin Buddhists, Nishi Honganji was careful to highlight their presence, suggesting the elevated role that Nikkei played in supporting the representation of Shin Buddhism as a world religion. The 700th *dai-onki* memorial actually comprised a series of memorials held throughout the month of March and April of 1961. To highlight the presence of overseas Buddhists, Nishi Honganji arranged for overseas Buddhists to attend the sixth, tenth, and fourteenth memorial days during April. BCA members, along with other foreign guests, were also invited to related receptions and conferences where they were publicly acknowledged. As Bishop Hanayama recalled,

> It was agreed that the groups from North America, Canada, Hawaii, Brazil, Okinawa, and other overseas places would attend these services. After the services a reception was held with Lord Abbot and Lady Ohtani as the central figures; on rainy days it was held at the Hyakkaen. Pictures were taken on each occasion to commemorate the event.[80]

During an afternoon service that followed the morning *dai-onki* service, Haruo Yamaoka recalled that, "in the afternoon, during the chanting of the *Junirai,* the members offer(ed) incense in the memory of Buddhists who have passed away overseas." Yamaoka and other foreign guests then attended a garden reception hosted by Lady Ohtani.[81]

Nishi Honganji also highlighted the presence of overseas Buddhists by requesting that BCA send an "Overseas Temple Exhibit" to be displayed at Nishi Honganji in conjunction with the memorial. The exhibit included eight-by-ten-inch photographs of church buildings and those of affiliated organizations, along with photos of active members. It also included sixteen-by-twenty-two-inch charts of BCA's church histories, activities, and membership.[82]

Overseas Buddhists were also recognized at memorial-related conferences and ceremonies. BCA members were among the invited honored guests to the twelfth annual All-Japan Young Buddhist conference, held at the Nishi Honganji Kaikan as part of the 700th Memorial.[83] Haruo Yamaoka attended the conference and reported on the proceedings. The Abbot Ohtani addressed the crowd and stressed how the recognition of Shinran's emphasis on faith in Amida's Vow could contribute to greater peace and understanding. The abbot noted that "living in such a world of fierce entanglements man must have true faith." Yamaoka noted that the abbot "urged the young delegates to make the teachings of Amida a dynamic force in their daily lives" and "stressed the importance of intimate communications of the youths of Japan and other parts of the world."[84] In addition to BCA's bishop and Mrs. Hanayama, BCA was represented at the conference by Yamaoka, along with two other Nisei BCA ministerial students, and Dr. Ryo Munekata, who addressed the audience on behalf of BCA's national YBA.[85]

On April 14, the final memorial day attended by overseas Buddhists, a ceremony attended by the Abbot Ohtani, Bishop Hanayama, Reverend Hozen Seki of the American Buddhist Academy of New York, and other ministers and honored guests was held at the Honganji Kaikan. During the ceremony, a formal presentation of an Amida Buddha statue was made to the American Buddhist Academy.[86]

The ceremony also celebrated the transportation and installation of a fifteen-foot, two-and-a-half-ton bronze statue of Shinran that had been transported from Japan and installed in New York City six years earlier, in 1955.[87] The statue of Shinran had survived the Hiroshima bomb blast and was transported from Hiroshima to a courtyard adjourning the BCA's American Buddhist Academy, located on the upper west side of Manhattan. The transportation of the statue had been organized by Reverend Seki and had been made possible thanks to the generous sponsorship of Mr. Seiichi Hirose, a Japanese industrialist and Jōdo Shin layperson, who, as discussed earlier, was a key figure in supporting the ministerial training of Japanese Americans in Kyoto.[88] Three days later, the American Buddhist Academy and Kokushikan University of Tokyo formally agreed to initiate a "sister-university" relationship involving faculty exchange.[89]

At the conclusion of the memorial, Nishi Honganji and BCA's leaders reiterated their hopes that the memorial would revitalize Shin Buddhism, particularly among youth and the general public in Japan and the United States. During the final memorial on April 16, 1961, the Abbot Ohtani made a proclamation that was recounted to BCA leadership by Bishop Hanayama. After expressing gratitude for the successful service and pointing out the importance of gratitude and faith for Shin Buddhists, the Abbot articulated key points of focus for members in Japan and abroad to carry out after the conclusion of events. A prominent focus was to "embrace faith yourself and teach others to embrace faith." The abbot noted that it was particularly important to reach young men and women. Concluding that "if this vision is to materialize, the Hongwanji must make a great decision not to be attached to the past tradition and with strong conviction formulate new policies to meet the needs of our youths" and to do so "both within our country and abroad."[90] Bishop Hanayama echoed the abbot's call to prioritize youth education and let go of attachment to past tradition. Hanayama stressed the importance of "formulat[ing] policies in keeping with the times and striv[ing] to realize the steadfast growth of the Buddhist Churches of America" while also "striv[ing] to spread the way of Nembutsu among the general public."[91]

From the standpoint of BCA's leadership, the 700th Memorial had been a success. They believed that a stronger connection between the Abbot Ohtani, Nishi Honganji, and BCA and its membership had been cultivated as a result of the coordinated efforts to plan the event. Yet, while expressing gratitude for BCA's successful sponsorship of the pilgrimage to the 700th Memorial, Hanayama and BCA's ministers and lay leaders continued to express a sense of urgency concerning the work yet to be done. Hanayama urged ministers and lay leaders to continue in their efforts toward a membership drive, developing youth education

Figure 5.1. Statue of Shinran, New York Buddhist Academy, 2015. Reproduced from Wikimedia, Licensed by Creative Commons.

through Sunday Schools and other programs. Most importantly they sought to develop young ministers from among BCA's membership.[92]

Ordinary Lay Participation and Perspectives of the Memorial and Pilgrimage

Many of BCA's lay members supported efforts to reconstitute ties with the abbot and Nishi Honganji, believing institutional ties to be vital toward the revitalization of Buddhism in America. At the same time, they also held distinct perspectives on the significance of pilgrimage and participation in the memorial that reflected personal, familial, and community histories. Although one thousand of BCA's estimated membership of fifty thousand actually took part in the pilgrimage and memorial services, many more members participated in other ways. BCA organizations, families, and individuals made substantial monetary donations to Honganji in support of the memorial. Publications chronicled memorial activities, BCA temples and churches held local 700th Memorial Services, and laypersons also organized highly publicized memorial-related goodwill tours of Japan.

Fundraising provided a powerful collective means of expressing support for the memorial, both for those who could afford to participate in the pilgrimage and those who could not. BCA members raised $30,000 to support the initial visit of Abbot and Lady Ohtani during 1952 and 1953, and initiated fundraising campaigns in support of missionary work related to the memorial in the aftermath of their visit. By 1955, members had raised and donated $3,500 to the Hompa Honganji, which was used to purchase a "Missionary promotional car" with a modern public address system for the memorial. That same year, the BCA's national Fujinkai raised $5,542 for the purchase of two trucks, which Lady Ohtani named Tsubame (Swallow) and Hiun. The cars were to be used for "missionary purposes" during the 700th Memorial Services.[93] Following a visit by the abbot in 1959, BCA created a Memorial Fund Committee. The committee initially decided that, rather than appealing for donations for the memorial, BCA would simply accept "voluntary free offerings" from the membership.[94] The new BCA bishop, Hanayama, took a more proactive position toward solicitation of funds by spending twenty-three days visiting district representatives, local church board meetings, and advisers on the West Coast, urging members to support the memorial with donations.[95] By 1960, members had donated $44,005, with an additional $5,954 sent directly to Honganji from the Seattle Betsuin, Pasadena, and Senshin Buddhist Church, for a total of $49,960.[96] By 1961, just two months prior to

700th Memorial Services, BCA reported that a total of $130,000, more than double BCA's annual general budget, had been donated to Nishi Honganji.[97]

The most significant donations came from the San Francisco Bay Area and Central California, where churches in cities like San Jose, Fresno, Oakland, and San Francisco, as well as smaller towns like Salinas, Watsonville, Reedley, and Stockton, had been important centers of Issei Buddhism dating back to the prewar years. Significantly, however, churches with more recent Buddhist populations in states such as Idaho, Oregon, and Utah also contributed generous donations. In contrast, in Chicago, Cleveland, New York, and Washington, DC, with new small congregations comprising predominantly Nisei and white convert Buddhists, no donations were made by members. Most of BCA's ministers donated amounts ranging from $100 to as much as $1,000, for a total of $11,740.[98]

While donations signified support from BCA's members, reports by BCA lay members provide some sense of the personal experience and significance of the memorial services and associated pilgrimages. Reporting back to the *American Buddhist* shortly after participating in memorial services, Nisei Haruo Yamaoka recalled,

> What impressed me most of all at these services, wasn't the colorful pageantry, or the solemn ritual but the way the followers recite Nembutsu. Throughout the services, except for the reading of the Shoshinge and the singing of "Ondokusan" or "Shinshu Shuka," there is a virtual hum of voices. Hardly audible at a distance yet close up, the endless flow of Namandabu Namandabu Namandabu ... can be heard. The flow is unhindered like water down a stream. True, the people are old with long religious experiences, but it is not just one nembutsu, nor even three, but a continuous flow of gratitude.

Yamaoka's recounting emphasized the mass chanting of *nembutsu*, which superseded the accompanying "colorful pageantry" and "solemn ritual." Moreover, for Yamaoka, the memorial's energy and force was generated by the followers "virtual hum of voices."[99] Years later, Yamaoka recalled the impression that this "hum of voices," this "continuous flow of gratitude" made on him in greater detail:

> 700th Memorial was an experience that was very interesting to me. When I went into Hondo for that service, [there were] massive [numbers] of people and the ritual part of it is pretty set, marching, chanting but in between those periods, there is Namandabu, Namandabu which keeps flowing, you hear it all over the place but then they are very respectful when

a certain time comes they [stop] but it's a free flowing thing. . . . That's the thing that impressed me so much. . . . When I was there you could see the tears. The first time I went to Hongwanji for the morning service, I went there and it was 6'oclock in the morning and there were all these people "Namandabu, Namandabu" and behind me is this lady going (slowly) "Namandabu." I got upset, because I didn't know what was going on and when I turned around [and saw her] she had tears in her eye chanting, and that kind of thing prevailed at that time, at the 700th, . . . and that's the thing that impressed everybody, how free flowing the *nembutsu* is within the context of the teachings.[100]

Other participants in events related to the memorial stressed the importance of social connections with fellow laypersons and reunions and remembrances with family members both living and deceased. May Nimura, from Oakland, California, chronicled her participation with twenty fellow Nisei from Northern and Central California in the Dana Choir Group on a goodwill tour of Japan associated with the 700th Memorial.[101] Hours after arriving in Tokyo, the group, named for the Buddhist concept of *dana* (charity), visited Asoka Buddhist hospital, including the hospital's day nursery and orphanage, where they sang songs with the children there. Nimura recalled, "Tears came to our eyes as we watched the children facing the *obutsudan* (Buddhist altar) and singing so sincerely."[102] The image of Japanese orphans singing before the Buddhist altar would have been a poignant one for BCA's readership. Japanese Americans carried with them actual and imaginary senses of transpacific connection. The image of orphans in front of the family altar might have triggered memories of lost family and cultural connections, as well as their own experience of loss of connection to the United States and Japan. Choir members met in private and in public events with the Lord Abbot and Lady Ohtani on a number of occasions. They were taken on a guided tour of both the Nishi and Higashi Honganji home temples by the Ohtanis. The group also visited other sites important to Shin Buddhists.[103]

Scheduled on the visit were a number of public performances and meetings that highlighted the presence of overseas Buddhists for the 700th Memorial. The Dana Choir Group performed on radio and television in a number of cities. The most highly publicized event took place on July 17, when the group appeared before a national audience on the television program, *Watashi no Himitsu*—the Japanese version of *I've Got a Secret*. An estimated audience of thirty-six million[104] watched an interview with Mrs. Kikuo (Mary) Taira, and learned that she "represented a group which was working for Buddhism outside of Japan."[105] The group then performed while an image of the Buddha was superimposed onto them.[106] The following day, BCA choir members were honored in a meeting with Tokyo governor Ryotaro Azuma.[107]

Performances included selections of Buddhist *gathas* (songs) accompanied by a selective narrative history of Issei Buddhist pioneers written by Nisei Hiroshi Kashiwagi and translated into Japanese by Reverend Ryumei Iguchi.[108] The historical narrative that accompanied one of the earliest Buddhist *gathas* written in America, "Nori no Miyama," framed the development of Buddhist music within the context of the struggles of Issei Buddhist migrants to America from the perspective of their Bussei children. It opened,

> The history of Buddhist music in America goes back nearly seventy years when many of our parents and grandparents left their native country of Japan and after crossing the Pacific Ocean landed in San Francisco—the City of the Golden Gate. But life in America was not as easy as they had dreamed or hoped; there was much hard work at menial jobs with long hours, and the task of making a living was further complicated by the problems of adjusting to the new customs and getting along with strange peoples who were often unfriendly and even hostile. The threat of danger and violence was not uncommon for our parents in those days, as many Americans tried to make life miserable for them.[109]

Kashiwagi's narrative then turned to the centrality of Buddhism in the lives of Issei:

> In the face of all these hardships, there was, however, one thing which helped them most of all. This was the religion which they had brought over from Japan—their Buddhist religion. Although their families had been identified with Buddhism for centuries past, it was in distant America that, perhaps for the first time, they discovered and appreciated the true meaning of its teachings. Buddhism became a source of great spiritual comfort giving them strength to endure the hardships and to meet the challenges of their pioneering life. Moreover, it gave meaning to their very struggles and efforts.[110]

Kashiwagi's narrative then reflected on how *gathas* like "Tsuki ga deta" allowed Issei to express a shared longing for family and friends in Japan: "Living so far away from their relatives and friends, it was only natural for our parents to become homesick for Japan. Gathering at the temple for services gave them a chance to exchange stories and sing of their happy childhood days."[111] The narrative of the evolution of *gathas* alongside Issei Buddhism continued with a discussion of the birth of children, the growth of families, and the gradual improvement in living and work conditions, as well as illness and death. Kashiwagi noted, "When a loved one passed away relatives and friends gathered to comfort them and a funeral service in the Buddhist tradition was conducted by the priest. Both the sadness of death and the keen awareness of the truth of life are well expressed in the funeral song, 'Mihotoke ni Idakarate.'"[112]

Kashiwagi's introduction to English-language *gathas* like "Nembutsu," penned by Nisei Jim Araki, and the addition of American secular songs like the folk ballad "Go Way From My Window," were discussed as adaptations developed as Nisei Buddhists came of age:

> As the children grew older they began to speak English which they learned in American schools. Despite the efforts of the parents to teach them Japanese at home and in Japanese language schools, English became the dominant language of the Nisei. Before long, it became increasingly necessary to use more and more English in the Sunday Schools. Some priests who foresaw the need for English *gathas* encouraged young people with music ability to write new *gathas* in English.[113]

Significantly, Kashiwagi's narrative made no mention of Nikkei internment, allowing his audience to nostalgically remember the struggles of Issei pioneers while eliding more recent memories of war between the United States and Japan.[114] He concluded with a discussion that evoked Japanese American Buddhists and the development of Buddhists *gathas* in America as the embodiment of *bukkyō tōzen*. He stated, "In tracing the history of Buddhist music in our country we have also tried to suggest the spread of Buddhism in America." Even as he presented a hopeful picture of the growth of BCA and its membership, including "Caucasian Americans who have begun to show a strong interest in Buddhism" and the continued development of Buddhism in America and Buddhist music, Kashiwagi gestured reverently back to Issei Buddhism.[115]

The BCA choir's highly publicized tour and narrated performances were warmly, and at times poignantly, received by Japanese audiences. May Nimura noted that, following their television performance, the Dana Choir group "heard many favorable reports of our reception among the millions of Japanese who watched us on their favorite program."[116] At one performance with the Kyoto Women's University choir in front of an audience that included the Abbot Ohtani, Nimura later recounted, "Many of the old people in our audience had a good cry listening to our narrator Rev. Fujinaga tell of the hardships of the first Issei." She then noted that "After the performance we were thanked by Abbot Ohtani in a beautiful speech in English."[117]

In addition to emotional meetings with orphans, students, and Buddhist lay audiences, the trip also offered Nimura and fellow choir members opportunities to reunite with family and friends. The final stop on the BCA choir's tour was to Hiroshima, where the group arrived for a memorial service at the Hiroshima Memorial Peace Park. Greeted by "many relatives, friends, and newsreel cameramen," they gathered in front of the Cenotaph, "a structure symbolizing the rebirth of Hiroshima after the devastation of the *gembaku* [atomic bomb]." This was followed by a visit to the Atomic Bomb Memorial Mound, the A-Bomb Dome, the Children's Peace Monument, and, finally, the Memorial Museum, where Nimura recalled that they "saw graphic evidence of the horror of the bombing. We can understand why Hiroshima has dedicated herself to the cause of world peace."[118]

Despite their busy schedule, some time was reserved for personal visits and reuniting with family members. In Hiroshima, most of the choir group visited relatives. Nimura visited the grave of her maternal grandmother who had been killed in the bomb blast. She recalled, "The crowded cemetery was in the tiny yard of a shining new Buddhist temple." Following this visit, which she described as "melancholy," Nimura reconnected with her mother's past by visiting Kwannon Temple on Hijiyama. The temple had a restored pagoda and statue, and Nimura recalled climbing "the stone steps that my mother had trod as a girl."[119] When asked about her visit years later, May Nimura (Tomiye Sumner) could not recall most of the details of her pilgrimage and choir tour of Japan. However, she did remember visiting her grandmother's grave. She recalled, "I remember these little grave plots, . . . and you don't usually think of graveyards so crowded. Usually, at least here [in the US] they're vast with lawns and everything but in Hiroshima they were really very crowded looking."[120]

Nimura had never met her grandmother but recalled that when she returned to the United States she made a point of funding a visit to Japan for her mother. She stated, "When I came back . . . I sent her back to Japan to visit. So she was able to visit all the old places and grave and so forth, so she hadn't been back since 1920 or something. So that was gratifying."[121] When asked whether the idea to send her mother back arose during her trip, Nimura (Sumner) responded, "Well, I thought she would love to go back to see all her relatives whom she hadn't seen since 1920 and to visit all the old places especially since they had been bombed and so I thought it was very incumbent upon me to send her."[122] Despite this gesture, Nimura never spoke with her mother about the bombing or what had happened to her grandmother.

Jōdo Shinshū's religious leaders on both sides of the Pacific, and BCA's lay-persons, invested significant time and resources in support of the 700th Memorial of Shinran and the pilgrimage of Nikkei Buddhists for the memorial. The memorial provided an opportunity not only to reestablish institutional ties but also to create a forum for communicating the concerns of religious and secular leaders as well as those of BCA's lay membership. For Shin Buddhist leaders in Japan, a primary concern was the revitalization of their institution through the propagation of Shin teachings directed toward its membership, but also beyond its membership, with a particular concern for youth. While sharing support for the reestablishment of institutional ties, the memorial provided opportunities for BCA's lay members to reestablish personal, familial, and cultural ties and, in the process, retrace and recognize the complexity of prewar Issei Buddhist lives lived across the Pacific, between two empires.

For Nisei, participation in both the World Fellowship of Buddhists and in the 1961 700th Memorial Services offered connection to two distinct transnational Buddhist communities with varying perspectives and goals. Yet, for both the WFB and Nishi Honganji, BCA's members and Nisei Buddhists in particular were viewed as important cultural bridges between Buddhists in Asia and those in America. Nisei embraced their role but also drew from their contacts and exchanges a broader context for considering both Cold War politics abroad and the racial liberal policies that they had faced at home in the United States.

CHAPTER SIX

Domestic Revival and Family Buddhism

A January 1964 article titled "The Buddhist Family" appeared on the front page of the BCA's official newsletter, *American Buddhist*. Proclaiming the Buddhist family as "the cradle of our Buddhist values," the article stated, "we cannot call our family a Buddhist family if we do not live in the Wisdom and Compassion of Amida Buddha. It is no mere accident that we are living together as brothers and sisters, mother and father."[1] Describing the Buddhist home with the family gathered together before the "family shrine" (*butsudan*) to recite the *nembutsu*, the article next highlighted the central role of Buddhist churches and temples in connecting Buddhist families to the sangha (community of Buddhists):

> As the shrine with the image of Amida Buddha is the center of the Buddhist family, so is our church the center of our community. The members of the church make up the Sangha—the brotherhood of Buddhists. We have a responsibility to this Sangha to help it increase its moral influence for the good of the community.[2]

By illustrating a chain of relations, from nuclear families gathering before the *butsudan* to recite the nembutsu, to church service and, ultimately, to the "brotherhood of Buddhists" represented in the sangha, "The Buddhist Family" sought to connect emerging Nisei Buddhist–anchored families back to their local Shin Buddhist churches and temples.

Over the course of the 1950s, and continuing through the early 1960s, BCA's priests and lay leaders responded to changing social and spatial relations among its membership by emphasizing the importance of Buddhist "spirit" and the centrality of the Buddhist family in supporting the sangha, or community of Buddhists. In contrast to other Nisei Buddhist articulations of the sangha, which defined it more broadly and in ways that sometimes crossed sectarian, ethnic, racial, and national lines, programs that emphasized Buddhist spirit or the centrality of the Buddhist family, defined the sangha more narrowly around Nisei-anchored nuclear and extended families who were temple and church members.

The emphasis on Buddhist spirit and focus on family Buddhism was also a response to the emerging Cold War domestic revival and, in particular, domestic containment norms around "proper" gender roles and sexuality. Nisei Buddhists adopted domestic revival and invoked it as a key component of racial liberal discourse. In this regard, they utilized strategies for inclusion shared by other ethnic and racial minorities. As Cindy I-Fen Cheng has shown, stories about Asian American heteronormative nuclear families in middle-class suburban neighborhoods played a key role in narrating their acceptance as assimilable Americans.[3]

Efforts by Nisei lay leaders, together with BCA's ministers, to introduce family Buddhism programs emerged in response to three interrelated issues: first, an acknowledgment of the historical importance of the social role played by Young Buddhist Associations and, at the same time, concerns with declining membership; second, Nisei family formation and the spatial dispersion of Buddhist families across rural, urban, and suburban space, including previously segregated white suburban neighborhoods. Third, family Buddhism was directed toward meeting the needs of an emergent Sansei (third-generation) cohort of youth and concerns about the lack of mentors and spiritual guidance for them.

By the early 1960s, BCA had responded to these three issues by launching a number of new programs that sought to reintroduce Buddhist ritual in the family home, in Buddhist churches and temples, and in the broader community. In doing so, they sought to highlight connections between families and the broader Buddhist sangha. In developing programs for daily *butsudan* (family home shrine) ritual and a Buddhist Life Program that offered mentoring for Sansei youth, as well as Buddhist Boy and Girl Scouts, BCA leaders often reinforced the emerging discourse around domestic revival that emphasized heteronormative nuclear families as "security" in combating the spread of communism. At the same time, family Buddhism programs also sought to highlight the interdependence of emerging Nisei families with the broader sangha of Nikkei Shin Buddhists.

Cold War Domestic Revival

Nisei Buddhist socialization leading to the selection of marriage partners paralleled that of the larger population of Nisei. The shared experience of forced mass incarceration during World War II, together with the persistence of anti-miscegenation laws and pressure from Issei parents, encouraged a majority of Nisei Buddhists to select romantic partnerships from among co-ethnics.[4] During the 1950s, YBAs were the primary vehicle for Nisei socialization and for meeting potential marriage partners. YBAs hosted regular conferences, social outings, Buddhist study groups, and sports leagues, continuing traditions first established in the prewar era.

Regional and national conferences represented the social highlight of the year for many Nisei and drew large numbers of delegates. Attendance grew steadily during the 1950s, attesting to their growing popularity, before dropping in the early 1960s. The Western Young Buddhist League (WYBL), the largest regional association of young Buddhists, saw attendance increase to 1,305 at its 1956 conference, nearly doubling the number of attendees three years earlier.[5]

The twenty-fifth anniversary conference, hosted in December 1959 in Greeley and Denver, Colorado, by the Tri-State YBA, included a program typical of many conferences hosted during the era. Delegates arrived at the local Buddhist Church in Greeley on Thursday evening to register for the conference and then attend an opening devotional service. The service was followed by an evening social mixer where delegates met and were introduced to the four contestants for the Miss Tri-State Bussei beauty contest. The next three days were filled with a range of activities, from a memorial service to delegate meetings and the election of new YBA cabinet officers. Delegates participated in a variety of other social events including a pancake breakfast, bowling tournaments, a variety show, and an oratorical contest. The conference highlight was a formal banquet followed by a coronation ball for the Miss Bussei Queen, featuring the music of Mike Disalle and his orchestra.[6]

Conferences allowed Nisei to reconnect with old friends and to become acquainted with new ones. LaVerne Sasaki remembered attending the 1960 WYBL

Table 6.1. Western Young Buddhist League Conference Attendance

Year	Location	Est. Attendance[a]
1953	Los Angeles	667
1955	San Francisco	900
1956	Sacramento	1,305
1960	Berkeley	1,200
1961	Sacramento	873
1962	San Jose	900
1964	Fresno	800

[a] "Minutes of the Cabinet and Board of Directors' Meeting," WYBL, Oakland, CA, August 8, 1953, 1; "Young Buddhists Meet," *LA Times,* March 26, 1955, 8; BCA 75th Anniversary, 107; *Los Angeles Times,* March 14, 1956, 32; Reverend LaVerne Sasaki, Interview by author, 1997, 1–2; "19th Annual Young Buddhist Conference," *American Buddhist,* April, 1961, 4; "President Harvey Takikawa Installed Other Events at the 20th Annual WYBL Conference," *American Buddhist,* April, 1962, 4.

conference in Berkeley. In considering why the conferences were so popular, Sasaki recalled, "We didn't have television, we didn't even have a black and white TV, we had no competition. Plus, I think the Japanese Americans were closer within the community. There was a distinct Japanese community area in Sacramento."[7] While ostensibly a religious conference, the social dimension remained equally important to young Buddhist men and women. When asked about his impressions of the conference, Sasaki recalled, "Well, there were a lot of girls, I think the main motivation was to meet members of the opposite sex. That's a very clear, very honest, very truthful [response]."[8]

During the 1950s, Nisei Buddhist beauty pageants held in conjunction with annual conferences emerged as key sites in which Nisei demonstrated aspirations for assimilation. "Miss Bussei" contests and corresponding coronation balls were popular events that drew hundreds of Nisei to YBA conferences. Contestant photographs and profiles were regularly featured in YBA newsletters and ethnic newspapers. "Miss Bussei" contests provided an opportunity for Nisei to

Figure 6.1. Eastern Young Buddhist League dance, Chicago, Illinois, circa 1950. Reproduced from Fred Yamaguchi Photograph Collection, Japanese American Services Committee, Chicago, IL.

celebrate a Nisei Buddhist version of an idealized femininity that announced their aspirations toward inclusion premised on Cold War heteronormativity and domestic gender norms.

Modeled after the Miss America pageant, the earliest Nisei beauty pageants were organized in the 1930s by ethnic entrepreneurs in Los Angeles' Little Tokyo district. As Lon Kurashige noted, beauty pageants were designed to attract Nisei investment and consumption in local ethnic businesses while also presenting a nonthreatening presentation of the community to the general population.[9] By the Cold War years, the racial liberal terms for assimilation—for Nisei Buddhists as for other racial minorities seeking entry into the middle class—was increasingly gauged by the performance of heteronormativity and the display of "proper" gender roles. As Rebecca Chiyoko King-O'Riain explained, Nisei and ethnic beauty contestant winners were expected to serve as exemplars of Nisei assimilation.[10]

As was true for other ethnic minority beauty queens, Miss Bussei winners were tasked with serving as cultural ambassadors on behalf of the BCA and its affiliated temples and churches. The first major Nisei Buddhist beauty contest was held in 1948 as part of the Golden Jubilee Festival. Marian Kono, a nineteen-year-old receptionist from Seattle, Washington, was honored as the festival queen in front of a crowd of seven hundred at the Fairmont Hotel in San Francisco.[11] Signaling an increasing acknowledgment of Nisei Buddhist potential for assimilation, a photo of Kono in a white evening gown attended to by members of her court appeared in the pages of *LIFE* magazine.[12]

By 1951, Kono continued to serve as a cultural ambassador, this time as part of an effort to improve public relations and develop transpacific trade networks between Seattle and Japan. In this regard, Kono and the other Nisei "hostesses" were described "wearing strictly modern off the shoulders evening gowns."[13] They joined three beauty queens from Japan for a Japanese trade fair produced for the general public at a cost of $500,000. The opening ceremony was attended by Shigemi Yokoo, Japan's minister of international trade; Seattle mayor William F. Devin; Washington governor Arthurs B. Lauglie; and Assistant Secretary of Commerce Thomas Davis. The trade fair itself contained "more than 6000 articles, ranging from industrial equipment to tiny handcraft objects, all from occupied Japan."[14]

Nisei publications regularly celebrated Miss Bussei queens and prominently displayed photos of smiling queens and contestants in formal gowns. Coverage obsessively described the appearance of contestants and noted their height, weight, and age, which ranged from late teens to early twenties.[15] Significantly, while posing for photographs and presenting their physical measurements, Miss Bussei contestants were also presented in ways that challenged the domestic ideal. Some coverage in Nisei Buddhist newsletters characterized contestants as intelligent, ambitious, career-oriented women who demonstrated leadership abilities and sought further education and employment. Sachi Kimura reported that the Visalia YBA was "proud to present Susie Yamashita as our first queen candidate for 'Miss CCYBA of 1955.'" She described Yamashita as "five feet 1 inch in height and a combination of brains, beauty, and talent." Kimura also noted that Yamashita was "an active member of the Visalia YBA" and had "proven her capabilities serving as vice-president and as co-editor of the carnival pamphlet."[16] Indeed, many of the candidates were all-around high achievers. Upon graduation from Clovis Union High School in 1952, Sue Kasamatsu, a Central California YBA Miss Bussei contestant that same year, was noted in the CCYBA *Bussei Review* for accolades including a life membership in the California Scholarship Federation, a Fresno State Scholarship, an American Legion Citizenship Award, and a National Forensics League Excellence Degree. Kasamatsu also served as editor of the school yearbook and as a speaker at high school commencement.[17] The four runner-up contestants in the 1953 Miss WYBL competition included a bookkeeper, a beautician, a student studying to become a medical secretary, and a student majoring in business administration. Masako Arita, the winner of the competition, was a student at Fresno State College with plans to become an elementary school teacher.[18]

It is striking that very few Miss Bussei contestants mentioned homemaking, even as a majority of Bussei women would marry and raise children as the era unfolded. When asked about current and future plans, an overwhelming majority of contestants from the late 1940s through the mid-1960s referenced continued education and careers in a range of occupations, from secretaries to office workers to teachers, nurses, social workers, physical therapists, cosmetologists, and dress makers. The emphasis on education and employment were driven by a combination of factors. As historian Valerie Matsumoto has demonstrated, employment opportunities for Nisei women, especially on the West Coast, gradually expanded in the decade after the end of World War II as a result of civil rights struggles and an American economy driven by Cold War defense spending. Limited to domestic and service work during the early resettlement period, Nisei women increasingly found work both within and beyond the ethnic community in a broad range of fields, from garment and clerical work to professions like teaching. Smaller numbers were able to enter the medical professions, academia, and the arts.[19]

Nisei Buddhist Family Formation and
Cold War Domesticity

At the 1951 WYBL conference held in Sacramento, California, discussion group topics including "Sunday School Program," "Teen-ager Group Problems," and a "Young Married Group" panel reflected new concerns among a growing number of Nisei who were married and raising children.[20] In developing programs attuned to emerging Nisei nuclear families, BCA's ministers and lay leadership, like much of the nation, were influenced by the emerging advice of social scientists, journalists, and popular writers who helped to usher in the emerging domestic revival of the postwar decades.[21]

Over the course of the 1950s and early 1960s, growing numbers of Nisei married and formed nuclear families, thus joining what Elaine Tyler May has described as a "familial consensus" around domestic revival resulting in "the most marrying generation on record."[22] While the Nisei search for security was driven by many of the same factors that led fellow Americans to embrace domesticity, Nisei shared with one another the distinct experience of forced incarceration and the WRA's assimilationist resettlement policies. These factors—together with persistent racial discrimination, including antimiscegenation laws, and pressure from Issei parents—shaped Nisei decisions to marry co-ethnics. According to Paul Spickard, despite higher rates of interracial marriage relative to the prewar years, when 2 to 3 percent of Nisei married non-Japanese, by the late-1950s only 10 percent of Nisei men and 17 percent of Nisei women married a spouse from a non-Japanese background.[23]

At the same time, the selection of marriage partners diverged from the Issei pattern of arranged marriage, resulting in greater independence for Nisei in their selection of partners. In contrast to Issei marriages in the prewar era, which were assisted or arranged by parents, many Nisei Buddhists in the postwar years chose marriage partners without first consulting their parents. In a 1964 survey of 1,100 Nikkei Shin Buddhist families living in rural, urban, and suburban neighborhoods in Southern California, Masami Nakagaki found that 47 percent of Nisei Buddhists chose their spouses without consulting their parents, while 53 percent consulted their parents.[24] Even Nisei relationships that followed Issei patterns were modified in ways that emphasized Nisei selection of a romantic partner. This modification was even true for some Nisei ministers. When Reverend LaVerne Sasaki's father, the Issei minister Sensho Sasaki, suggested that LaVerne Sasaki meet Helen Toshiko Yokoi, the young Nisei minister agreed and the couple were married soon after, in 1962. However, as Sasaki later recalled, despite their Issei parents' use of "go-betweens" in arranging their meeting, the choice to marry was the couple's. He recalled, "Either one of us could have called it off at any time, but we didn't. . . . Instead, impressed with her intelligence and poise on our sixth date, I proposed. And she said 'yes.'"[25] The emphasis on individual choice reflected shifting understandings of the meanings of these partnerships, and of weddings, from the Issei emphasis on the joining together of families to the Nisei emphasis on the joining together of two individuals.

Buddhist wedding ceremonies provided a key opportunity for Nisei couples to underscore their assimilation to white middle-class norms while also affirming their Buddhist faith. As Tetsuden Kashima has described, the ceremony was a blend of European American and Nikkei Buddhist tradition. Following European American traditions developed in the nineteenth century, the bride dressed in a white wedding gown and the groom dressed in a formal tuxedo. The couple entered the Buddhist temple accompanied by family and the music of Mendelssohn's "Wedding March" played on the temple organ. Couples offered incense before the altar, affirmed their faith in Amida Buddha and placed *ojuzu* (Buddhist prayer beads) over each other's hands. Kashima noted, "The *ojuzu* is given to both participants and with this *ojuzu,* both affirm their partnership to each other and to the Buddhist 'way of life.'"[26] After exchanging wedding vows and rings, the couple signed the marriage license in the presence of family and friends. Buddhist elements added to wedding ceremonies sought to instill a special bond between the couple and the sangha of family, friends, and fellow temple members grounded in shared Shin Buddhist teachings and ritual.[27]

The regular publication of announcements of engagements, weddings, and births in YBA publications, as well as in ethnic and local newspapers, underscore the pervasiveness of domestic revival among Nisei Buddhists. These announcements also had the effect of circulating and normalizing Nisei Buddhist family formation.[28] Wedding announcements were often accompanied with photographs of the bride or the couple. The 1953 edition of the *Bussei Review* released in conjunction with CCYBA's annual carnival featured photos and the announcement of the wedding of a number of couples, including Satoe Helen Kunishige and Seico Hanashiro. Kunishige and Hanashiro were wed at the Fresno Buddhist Church by Rinban J. Motoyoshi. The announcement included the names of the bride's parents and members of the wedding party, noting their attire and describing the arrangement of the bride's bouquet which "consisted of Lily of the Valley centered with a white orchid." The altar at the Fresno Buddhist Church was described as "beautifully decorated with potted palms banded with baskets of white stock." Following the ceremony, the eighty guests who attended the services were then greeted by the couple at a dinner reception at the Inn King Lum Restaurant in Fresno.[29]

Reflecting Cold War domestic ideology, many wedding announcements in Buddhist publications presumed or at least implied a single male breadwinner by noting the occupation of the groom while describing the bride solely in relation to her parents. Other announcements implied changes in occupation for the wife as a result of marriage. Alice Okano of Madera had been employed as a beautician until she married Yoshito Yamada and moved to his family farm in Kingsburg.[30] Helen Yokoi was a high school teacher in Sacramento; once she married Reverend LaVerne Sasaki in 1962, she became a homemaker and raised five children. Years later, she was again employed with the Workman's State Fund, Workman's Compensation Insurance.[31]

Despite domestic containment ideology's emphasis on distinct divisions between male breadwinners and female housewives, many Bussei families maintained two breadwinners. In his 1964 study of Nikkei Shin Buddhist families in Southern California, Masami Nakagaki found that 33 percent of Nisei and 53 percent of Kibei thought that women should be stay-at-home moms. However, another 40 percent of Nisei and 26 percent of Kibei thought that it was okay for women to work, while 26 percent of Nisei and 20 percent of Kibei thought that it was difficult to decide.[32] Despite these seemingly liberal views of working women among a portion of second-generation Bussei, the hold of domestic containment ideology remained strong. As Sylvia Yanagisako has shown in her study of Seattle Nikkei during the same period, while Nisei men defined their primary contribution to the family as breadwinners, women often emphasized the importance of being mothers. Meanwhile, working mothers, particularly those who worked while raising children, often felt compelled to qualify the reasons they continued to work, which they often attributed to economic necessity.[33]

Whether having one or two breadwinners, Bussei nuclear families grew from the late 1950s through the 1960s and appear to have been based on a deliberate decision to raise Sansei (third-generation) children, thus joining other American families in driving the postwar "baby boom." Nakagaki found that a majority of married Bussei couples in Southern California, both Nisei and Kibei, frequently discussed family planning. Neither Nisei nor Kibei disapproved of the use of birth control; 40 percent of Nisei and 30 percent of Kibei approved of the use of birth control, while 60 percent of both groups conditionally approved. When asked about the number of children that they wanted, 13 percent of Nisei and 7 percent of Kibei wanted five to ten children, while 40 percent of Nisei and 73 percent of Kibei wanted three to five children. Another 33 percent of Nisei and 13 percent of Kibei wanted between none and two children; 14 percent of Nisei and 7 percent of Kibei were uncertain about children.[34] In places like the Pacific Northwest, Nisei family fertility rates were closer to the national average.

In a study of Nisei families in the Seattle metropolitan region, Donna Leonetti found that most Nisei families had between two and three children, with older Nisei families having closer to two children and younger Nisei in the postwar years having closer to three children.[35]

Nisei Buddhist families also sought to fulfill the domestic revival ideal through gaining access to middle-class suburban neighborhoods. Given existing racial discrimination, spatial expansion into suburban neighborhoods did not occur seamlessly but evolved in relation to constant pushback from white residents, neighborhood associations, and realtors concerned with maintaining the racial homogeneity and corresponding property values accorded to white communities. Nevertheless, change unfolded gradually over time, in step with Cold War racial liberal discourse. As discussed earlier, early dispersion of the most "assimilated" Nisei to the Midwest and East Coast was encouraged and guided by the federal government working in concert with Christian and other benevolent organizations. Following WRA prescriptions, tens of thousands of Nisei, as well as smaller numbers of Issei, established themselves in new communities in the Midwest and eastern United States. While many returned to the West Coast, others stayed and contributed to growing postwar Buddhist churches and temples in cities like Chicago, Cleveland, Detroit, St. Paul, Minneapolis, New York, Seabrook (New Jersey), and Washington, DC.[36] In West Coast cities that had been central hubs of Issei communities, like Los Angeles and San Francisco, as well as in cities in which recent Nisei migration was predominant, such as Chicago and Detroit, limited housing opportunities led to early searches for housing beyond prewar ethnic centers.[37]

From the late 1940s through the 1950s, the continued spatial dispersion of BCA's Nisei population was driven by a number of additional factors. Access to new neighborhoods including previously all-white neighborhoods was created in some instances by white flight and in others by the gradual breakdown of racial barriers, particularly for Asian Americans, following the 1948 Supreme Court ruling in *Shelly vs. Kramer* that declared racially restricted housing covenants unconstitutional.[38] By the mid-to-late 1950s, Nisei, particularly those who were younger and more affluent, benefited from a series of high-profile racial liberal campaigns waged by early Asian American pioneers to suburban neighborhoods, together with sympathetic journalists and other political allies.[39] In Los Angeles County, for example, as Hillary Jenks has shown, Nisei gravitated toward suburban neighborhoods east, west and south of the center of the prewar Issei enclave of Little Tokyo, which was located in the heart of downtown Los Angeles.[40]

The movement of Nisei nuclear families to suburban neighborhoods led to the growth and expansion of BCA branch temples into independent temples in the San Francisco Bay Area and in Southern California. The growth of the West Los Angeles Buddhist Church in the Sawtelle District, from a small branch temple to a bustling independent affiliated temple, illustrated the broader trend. Established in 1926 as one of a number of small branch temples of the Los Angeles Hompa Hongwanji Buddhist Temple, by 1950 West LA Buddhist Church had established itself as an independent BCA-affiliated temple. With services filled to capacity, members raised $50,000 to construct a new larger building in 1955. By 1960, members had raised another $60,000 to add Sunday School classrooms and a meeting room, followed by another $140,000 to construct student dormitories, business offices, and a minister's residence, which was completed in 1966.[41]

Sunday School emerged as the centerpiece in efforts to promote family Buddhism. In addition to the recruitment of Nisei as Sunday School teachers for the Sansei, the program also drew lay leaders, ministers, and parents together to raise funds for classrooms and printed texts and to develop Buddhist curriculums. The push to expand and revise Sunday School programs began in the 1950s in response to the growing demographic of Sansei youth members. In one study of the Berkeley Buddhist Temple, the Reverend T. Suginari found that Sunday School attendance had grown by almost five times, from thirty-three children in the 1930s to 150 children in the 1950s. Similar growth occurred throughout BCA's branch churches and temples.[42]

Between the 1950s and mid-1960s, Sunday School classrooms were built or expanded in churches and temples in Parlier, Placer, Watsonville, San Jose, Oakland, Sacramento, San Francisco, Stockton, and West Los Angeles, California, as well as in Salt Lake City, Utah.[43] In 1958, parents in Parlier, California, began planning for a Sunday School annex that was to house more than 150 students. That same year in Watsonville, California, plans were made to develop a second annex "to alleviate the shortage of Sunday School classrooms." Church members volunteered their carpentry skills to reduce building costs, and four new classrooms were added in 1962. By 1973, the small temple had 150 students taught by twenty-one Sunday School teachers.[44] The Sacramento Buddhist Church responded to the doubling of attendance between 1961 and 1965, from 250 to 500 students, by constructing a fifteen-classroom building. The San Francisco Buddhist Church created a Classroom Building Committee in 1966, in order to address a shortage of Sunday School classrooms. The church raised funds leading to the development of a two-story 5,500-square-foot building with six classrooms.[45]

Growing demand for Sunday School programs also led to an expansion of efforts to recruit and train Sunday School teachers. Five hundred delegates attended the 1963 annual conference of the Federation of Western Buddhist Sunday School teachers, the largest such organization in BCA, encompassing

Buddhists delegates from California, the Pacific Northwest, and the Tri-State, Intermountain, and Eastern districts, along with Hawai'i and Canada. At the two-day conference, delegates learned about the reported results of a BCA membership survey report, attended a Buddhist "lesson presentation," participated in a "presentation of lessons," and reviewed Buddhist names and terms.[46] The highlight of the conference was an address by the religious education director, Reverend Takashi Tsuji. Tsuji noted the alignment of Buddhist education with the fundamental purpose of Buddhism. "The fundamental philosophy of Buddhist Education is synonymous with the supreme purpose of Buddhism which is to turn illusion into enlightenment." Tsuji advocated for the adoption of a Buddhist education program at every church, with the goal of inculcating Buddhist spirit in organizations, activities, and everyday life.[47]

"Going Our Aimless and Separate Ways": Perceptions of Decline in the YBA Movement

As Nisei gravitated toward insular nuclear families, youth-oriented Buddhist programs, especially the YBA organizations, once a stronghold of Buddhist activity, faced declining numbers and increasing criticism. YBA members, priests, and lay members repeatedly spoke of the need to instill proper Buddhist values and Buddhist spirit, particularly among youth, and sought to develop programs that would fulfill this. Yet, the struggle to recruit and retain youth also reflected a growing generational divide shaped by expanded social and civic opportunities beyond the ethnic enclave, as well as emerging fissures over Cold War containment culture.

As discussed earlier, estimated attendance to annual YBA conferences peaked in 1956, with numbers dropping off after that date. There are several long-term explanations for the decline in numbers. BCA continued to be dominated by Issei ministers with limited English-language ability, and youth had long complained about the language and cultural divide between themselves and ministers despite efforts by BCA to recruit and train English-speaking Nisei. Additionally, by the late 1950s, Bussei and Sansei Buddhists had many more social options than older Bussei had had in the early postwar years. Finally, former YBA members who were raising families and driving the growth of the Sunday School program were turning away from YBA participation. Even those older YBA members who remained active in Buddhist organizations increasingly joined the Young Adult Buddhist Associations or, for women, the Junior Fujinkai organizations.

In the face of declining numbers, Buddhist leaders including YBA members expressed concerns about declining Buddhist values and lack of "Buddhist spirit" among their younger members. In many respects, these criticisms echoed earlier concerns about an overemphasis on social activities at the expense of spiritual aspects at YBA conferences and gatherings. YBA members were also increasingly vocal about the need for promoting Buddhist spiritual values as a way to address the broader contours of American society amid escalating international Cold War tensions. In an editorial published in the 1951 *Berkeley Bussei,* Kimi Yonemura asserted,

> The youths of today are living in the oppressive shadow of extreme international tensions. Behind the apparent gaiety and carefree indifference lies a thwarted sense of insecurity—a feeling of foreboding uncertainty for a future that seems to promise nothing but war and destruction. Never before in our history has there been such widespread unrest and fear. . . . Living in this atmosphere of insecurity, our youths are either turning to a steadying faith in an existing religion to seek meaning in an otherwise meaningless existence, or throwing overboard all moral and spiritual values to seek gratification in a devil-may-care fashion.

Yonemura concluded, "In this state of complex social turmoil, it is the duty of each Bussei to re-evaluate the teachings of Buddha and come to realize the necessity for the preservation of ethical values to save the world from the shackles of misguided domination."[48]

Concerns about lack of Buddhist spirit persisted into the 1950s. In a 1952 WYBL conference panel titled "YBA Problems," some participants voiced concerns about a lack of "Buddhist spirit" in YBA activities despite a recognition of the important role that sports and other social activities had played in the postwar transition for Bussei. As a result, the panel's moderator, George Teraoka, proposed that all sports and social activities "commence with Gassho to remind contestants and all participants of the fundamental principle—Buddhism." WYBL leaders passed a resolution in support of Teraoka's proposal.[49] Two years later, in 1954, articles by members of the San Francisco YBA expressed concern about declining participation and engagement with the sangha of fellow YBA members. An editorial in the SFYBA's *Vista* noted, "We as members of the YBA have been going our aimless and separate ways for a long time. As a result, the feeling of Brotherhood which symbolizes Buddhism is slowly becoming but a myth."[50] Another piece, titled "Apathy," by an anonymous source, complained about the lack of participation in Buddhist religious services among YBA members. The author wrote, "Social affair? Great, let's go. Church? Oh, man, I'm too busy. Certainly, social affairs are fine things to have. That is not what is being criticized. It is your apathetic attitude towards attendance at, and moral support of, the Y.B.A. services."[51]

Miss Bussei contests were also criticized and modified as a result of their lack of spiritual focus. While asserting a Nisei Buddhist vision of gendered assimilation, concerns about the lack of Buddhist spirit in both Buddhist conferences and the selection of Miss Bussei led to reforms in the selection criteria of Miss Bussei candidates. Over the course of the 1950s, the selection process for local and regional Miss Bussei contestants and winners was modified to highlight Buddhist qualities in candidates, such as participation in Buddhist groups and knowledge of Buddhism. By the late 1950s, the rules and regulations of the national YBA added a requirement for a Buddhist minister to be included on the panel of judges; the national YBA also required that all Miss Bussei contestants be women at least seventeen years of age, who had been cardholding members for at least a year and were active members of their local YBA chapters. Contestants were to be judged in three categories: "character, personality and poise" constituted 35 percent of the assessment; "knowledge of Buddhism," based on questions from a Buddhist minister, constituted another 35 percent; the final 30 percent was based on "appearance."[52]

Despite limited measures by YBA to address complaints about lack of Buddhist spirit, criticism continued to grow and to include older Nisei who had formed separate Young Adult Buddhist Associations (YABAs). Many were former Nisei YBA leaders who had formed families. In 1959, Mary Maeno criticized the lack of discussion of religious topics at YABA conferences. Maeno proposed that YABA conferences could play an important role in the dissemination of Buddhist teachings, particularly with regard to the Buddhist family. She stated.

> The YABA conference can contribute to such problems as how we adult Buddhists can help to spread the religion or, even closer to home, how Buddhist parents can help their children to understand the meaning of Buddhism. . . . Many will say that this is the work of the Sunday School but the Sunday Schools are doing their best; the home must also do its share. After all Buddhism is not just a Sunday thing but an everyday thing. If we were to dig in and discuss problems like these, then those attending conferences would go home feeling that the intelligence and abilities of so-called Buddhist leaders were being put to good use.[53]

In an editorial note, *American Buddhist* editor Hiroshi Kashiwagi stated that Maeno's criticisms were equally applicable to YBA conferences, indicating "a real need for revamping and improving the conferences so that they will not be fly-by-night affairs. Some of the outmoded remnants of past conferences, such as picture-taking, and Miss Bussei contests, can surely be eliminated."[54]

Perhaps the culmination of criticism of lack of Buddhist values and spirit at YBA events came in April 1960, following reported "un-Buddhist like" behavior at the WYBL annual conference held at the Claremont Hotel in Berkeley. While the behavior was never discussed in great detail, it left a strong impression that was recalled in BCA's anniversary history book published fifteen years after the event. The behavior resulted in a BCA directive to all YBAs to send "adult chaperons to accompany the delegates to all future WYBL Conferences."[55]

When Allan Nagai reported on his experience at the 1961 WYBL conference held in Sacramento, attendance was already down by over 25 percent from the previous year's conference attendance. Arriving an hour late to the conference from San Francisco, Nagai found a number of delegates outside the Buddhist Church of Sacramento "strolling, standing and prating around" and assumed that the service was starting late. He was disappointed to learn that they were simply waiting for the religious service to end. Nagai recalled that "when they saw that the service was over, they happily went to their cars and drove off to the State Fair Grounds where the big events were going to take place."[56] Nagai described a symposium on "problems which young people are facing and had faced in the past," led by three veteran JACL members, as the "most stimulating event on that day."[57]

A year later, in 1962, Yoshio Shibata noted the further deterioration of YBAs in a report to the BCA on behalf of the Western Young Adult Buddhist League. Shibata characterized the YBA's recent decline as "alarming" and "a subject of much concern in our Buddhist movement." In contrast to the vibrant prewar movement, Shibata noted, "due to some unforeseen reasons it has suddenly taken a back seat during the last few years."[58] When the national YBA surveyed its membership in March 1962, it confirmed the concerns expressed in Buddhist publications, noting that "one thing stood out over others in that there was poor attendance at services, lack of interest, lack of leadership, etc."[59]

Connecting Buddhist Families to the Sangha: *Butsudan,* the Buddhist Life Program, and the Buddhist Sangha Award

At the 1960 WYBL conference that had stirred so much controversy about "un-Buddhist" behavior, the Reverend Taitetsu Unno gave a talk on the negative impact of wealth and consumerism on Buddhist spirit in families and communities. In "You Live in a Slum," Unno drew inspiration from a recent essay by Margaret Mead published in the *Los Angeles Times* on the negative effect that consumer culture was playing in shaping a spiritually impoverished family life. Unno noted,

> The father and the mother must shake off the lethargy of delegating the responsibility of parenthood to the expensive toy or the insurance fund and come to church to hear and awaken, to reflect and grow, so that, ultimately, [they] can provide for the children not a slum but a home. A spiritually enriching life, where there is real warmth, spontaneous joy and creative laughter, not a poverty stricken life, is the ideal home.[60]

Unno's address to YBA members about the importance of temple participation and spiritual engagement as an integral part of parenting acknowledged what many of those who attributed YBA decline to lack of Buddhist spirit missed, the fact that the configuration of the sangha was changing as former YBA members became parents. Thus, Unno's message to Nisei was that they had an obligation as parents to attend weekly services and engage with Buddhist teachings not only for their own sake but for that of their Sansei children.

The growing population of increasingly dispersed Nisei Buddhist families and its declining Young Buddhist Associations were thus, to a certain extent, interrelated phenomena. As cohorts of Nisei met partners, married, and started raising families, they often left the ranks of the YBAs. Some joined the Young Adult Buddhist Leagues or entered the ranks of BCA church or temple leadership. Others served as Sunday School instructors, sports coaches, or scout masters. Still others limited their participation in church activities to special occasions like weddings, funerals, and Buddhist holidays. Meanwhile, a cohort of Sansei (third-generation) Buddhists were emerging as BCA's newest demographic of young Buddhists.[61]

BCA engaged in efforts to ascertain the demographic composition of its membership in 1960 when it sent a membership survey to its affiliated temples and churches. Announced as a mechanism for determining the relative "fair share" that temples and churches needed to contribute in support of affiliated programs, the survey also aimed to produce a "standardization of the membership," which BCA could use to develop and support its current age cohorts. After fewer than half (twenty-six out of fifty-five) of the surveys from BCA's affiliated temples and churches had been returned, James Abe, director of the survey, expressed frustration with the lack of participation. Despite producing an incomplete picture of its total membership, the survey allowed BCA to gain valuable information about the changing composition of its membership in most of California, the state with the most members, as well as a few additional temples in Arizona, Oregon, and

Yakima, Washington. As a result, in addition to gaining a more accurate sense of the distribution of its age cohorts, BCA was also able to begin to chart some of the growing expansion of its Nisei families into suburban neighborhoods in Southern California and the San Francisco Bay Area.[62]

BCA's family Buddhism programs thus sought to respond to the changing composition of its membership, including its growing segment of Nisei families and Sansei youth. Perceptions of declining Buddhist spirit increased over the course of the 1950s and began to include characterizations of Nisei Buddhist families. In 1957, Nisei Eugene Sasai wrote about what he characterized as the declining Buddhist family home. Sasai complained about the abandonment of many of the "religious customs and practices of our Issei parents . . . in favor of something 'more modern.'" Sasai noted that "in many homes, the *Butsudan* (family shrine) has been shuttled off to some obscure corner to make room for television and high fidelity equipment. Gassho before and after meals is a thing of the past in many circles." He concluded, that "the average Nisei is a studying, working, and playing machine too busy to care too much about home and religion."[63]

Responding to growing concerns by Nisei like Sasai, BCA's Ministerial Research Committee initiated a series of annual themes that reflected an aspect of one of two broader themes, "Our Buddhist Family," and "The Buddhist Way of Life."[64] As Bishop Hanayama noted, while teachings related to these themes seemed "so obvious, . . . when it comes to actual daily practice, it is extremely difficult."[65]

The first annual theme, "Our Family Worships Daily before the Family Shrine," was introduced in 1963. Hanayama noted, "It is my fond hope that all members in the BCA will follow this theme and make worship a daily custom."[66] *Butsudan* shrine ritual traveled with Issei Shin Buddhists to America and involved lighting candles, chiming a bell, lighting incense, making small offerings, and reciting the *nembutsu*. While the design of the *butsudan* varied greatly, a typical *butsudan* was encased in a natural wood or black lacquer frame. The interior of the shrine included a *myōgō*, an image or statue of the Amida Buddha, or Japanese script for "Namu Amida Butsu" at its highest point of the altar. Although not strictly a part of Shin Buddhist doctrine, the *butsudan* also included space for ancestor veneration. The *butsudan* was where family kept *hōmyō* or posthumous Buddhist names of family members, as well as the family death register.[67]

As Jane Iwamura has explained, while the interior arrangement of the *butsudan* was more standardized, the placement of family photographs of deceased relatives and other objects with symbolic significance varied and was highly personal, reflecting individual and family choices. Significantly, Iwamura read the relation of the interior to exterior as opening up a dynamic and dialogic relation between individual and family practitioners and Buddhist teachings. Ima-mura concluded that the design of the *butsudan* "encourage[d] the devotee to make a series of associations (impermanence and Truth) and reciprocal exchanges (rice offering as both an expression of gratitude and in recognition of our own need for Amida's sustenance) that are meant to help her recognize the profound co-existence of the sacred and mundane."[68]

The annual theme was widely circulated as both a pamphlet and as an il-lustrated poster. The pamphlet, titled "The Family Shrine," likened the *butsudan* to a window, providing a "spiritual light of Amida Buddha" to the "hearts and minds" of Buddhist family members. The pamphlet reflected on the role that the *butsudan* played in the midst of difficult life challenges, noting, "When we are confronted with problems that cannot be solved we open the Butsudan panel and, in the midst of tears, we suddenly come face to face with the compassionate form of Amida Buddha. The form of Amida Buddha seems to speak, 'I see, I un-derstand, and I can quite see.'" As a result, "The troubling heart which is filled with suffering and sorrow seems to fill [with] comfort through the warm and understanding voiceless voice of the Buddha." The pamphlet concluded that the *butsudan* "gives strength to overcome all adversities and rise above the suffer-ing. The family Butsudan is a tower of strength."[69]

The pamphlet posited that a strong Buddhist family could, in addition to meeting life's unexpected challenges, overcome many of the "social problems" including "the rate of delinquency among our young people." The pamphlet stated, "It is certainly an exalting scene to see the entire family in gassho before the family shrine. Juvenile problems will never arise from such homes."[70] The program to revive family home rituals around the *butsudan* highlights similar actions taken by Chinese Americans during the same period. As Ellen Wu has shown, for Chinese Americans, a focus on juvenile delinquency offered a way "to stipulate their race and citizenship imperatives" by highlighting their shared con-cerns and needs around Chinese American juvenile delinquency while also high-lighting "exemplary" ethnic communities and households.[71]

In contrast to the text in the pamphlet, which was written in English and ac-companied by a photograph of a young Nisei nuclear family, with hands together before the *butsudan*, illustrated posters accompanying the campaign portrayed a Nisei-anchored family, with a husband, wife, son, daughter, and Issei grandpar-ents, with hands clasped and accompanied by the slogan "Our Family Worships Daily before the Family Shrine" printed in both English and Japanese.[72]

The annual theme focused on *butsudan* ritual sought to bring Nisei-anchored families, whether two or three generations, together in a daily prac-tice that was central to Shin Buddhism and that expressed and reinforced their

Figure 6.2. "The Family Shrine," pamphlet, 1963. Reprinted from Buddhist Churches of America, *1963 Annual Report*, January 1964, p. 17.

Figure 6.3. "Our Family Worships Daily Before the Family Shrine," 1963. Reprinted from Buddhist Churches of America, *1963 Annual Report*, January 1964, cover.

connection as a Buddhist family. The focus of the campaign on connecting extended families through Buddhist ritual was timely, responding to shifting perceptions of multigenerational cohabitation that were increasingly running up
against Cold War nuclear family norms. As Nakagaki found in his study of Southern California Nikkei Shin Buddhists, of Issei surveyed only 13 percent believed
that living separately was preferable to living with or in close proximity to their
married Nisei children. By contrast, 67 percent of Nisei stated a preference for
living separately from their Issei parents rather than living with or in close proximity to them.[73]

Moreover, the campaign provided encouragement for a practice that, like the
more public dimensions of participation in temple services and activities, was perceived as in decline. While Issei likely displayed a range of dedication and devo-
tion to the daily ritual, the *butsudan* remained a central focal point and symbol
of Shin Buddhism in the homes of BCA's Issei members. When queried about
whether they kept a *butsudan* in their home, 100 percent of Southern California
Issei and Kibei in Masami Nakagaki's 1964 study stated that they did. In contrast
87 percent of Nisei and only 33 percent of Sansei affirmed that they maintained a
butsudan in their home.[74]

Building on the 1963 focus on daily family home practice, the 1964 theme,
"Our Family Attends Church Regularly," sought to tie the Buddhist family to the
broader sangha of Buddhists. Accompanied by an image of a Nisei-anchored,
three-generation extended family, the slogan appeared in an *American Buddhist*
article titled "A Buddhist Affirms His Faith in the Buddha, Dharma and Sangha."
Significantly, the accompanying article focused not on Buddhist families but on
the individual Buddhists and their relations as part of the sangha. It stated, for
example, that "a Buddhist constantly hears the teaching of the Buddha by attending church regularly" and that "a Buddhist attends lectures and joins in discussion of the Teachings with other members of the church" noting that "from the
time of the first Sangha the disciples used the discourses of the Buddha and participated in active discussion."[75]

Even as BCA's ministers encouraged connections between daily family practice at home and greater participation of families at church, BCA's younger Nisei
leadership, working with Nisei minister Reverend Takashi Tsuji, director of
BCA's Buddhist Education Department, sought to create age standardizations
for Buddhist youth organizations and to develop mentoring programs for Nisei
and Sansei teenagers. In 1962, at the urging of members of the Young Adult
Buddhist Association, BCA sent approximately four thousand surveys to Nisei
and Sansei from its Pacific Coast and Western States districts. Polling a broad
age range of people, from teenagers to young adults, as to what they believed an

appropriate age affiliation for the Junior YBA, Senior YBA, and YABA organizations should be, BCA then adopted standard age ranges for its three organizations based on responses, with the Junior YBA including ages fourteen to eighteen; Senior YBA including eighteen to twenty-five; and YABA including twenty-five to forty.[76]

Based on responses to the youth surveys, Nisei ministers and younger Nisei leaders began to develop an umbrella program directed toward youth, from preteens to college students in their early twenties. In April 1962, national YBA leaders formed a research committee with Reverend Tsuji and BCA public relations chair William Nosaka to begin to develop a program to assess the situation. The committee concluded that leadership potential was underdeveloped and that YBA organizations lacked purpose, motivation, and long-term goals.[77] YBA leaders next began to introduce the problem to its membership. Repeating the findings of the research committee, Ted Abe, president of the San Francisco YBA, noted, "Presently, we as YBA members, seem to be floundering. We lack drive and initiative and we have no planned definite goals. In recent years much has been mentioned of such problems." Abe added, "In my opinion, these problems stack from a lack of organization and cooperation among members. The fault lies not in one particular person or group. We must all be responsible!"[78]

"We Are Not Interested in Making Bonsai Buddhists": The Buddhist Life Program

The result of these efforts was the development in 1963 of the Buddhist Life Program (BLP). A year earlier, BCA had approved a trial version of BLP at the Watsonville Buddhist Church. Fred Nitta described the trial program as an "adult counselor system." The Watsonville trial had run into some early challenges; Nitta stated that "the largest problem for this new program is lack of a systematized YBA curriculum to teach the Buddhist teachings to the members." Nitta also criticized the half-hearted effort of some of the older members who were skipping the general meetings held prior to the small group meetings.[79]

BLP aimed to "insure continuity of our Religious Education Program from early Sunday School age until mature adulthood, particularly through the high school and college range, where our present Religious Social Program is the weakest." National YBA president Yosh Isono explained in a report to the BCA that, while the voluntary program "cannot possibly solve all of our problems, the leaders of this project are optimistic that the Buddhist Life Program (BLP) can significantly improve the continuity of our present program."[80] The program sought to recruit and train volunteer adult counselors to join small groups of between eight to ten teenagers. Each group would have two or more counselors, "possibly a husband and wife team." The mentoring program was thus imagined as a way to create "mini-families" within a temple setting, further reinforcing connections between nuclear families and the sangha. To support the Buddhist Life Program, the National YBA council created and funded a new BCA youth director administrative position; Nisei Reverend Hogen Fujimoto was appointed to the position by Bishop Hanayama.[81]

In 1963, Fujimoto, working with Reverend Takashi Tsuji and YBA leaders, produced a twenty-one-page guidebook for BLP youth counselors. The introduction to the guidebook defined BLP as "designed to provide well-balanced wholesome youth activities for the development of spirit, mind and body." Focused on the "total person," BLP sought to "develop [a] true and devout Buddhist who understand[s] reality and is more comfortable in relation to it." The guidebook also noted, that the "opportunity this program brings for the adult leaders and youths to work together harmoniously in a variety of activities is also to be treasured."[82]

Essential for the success of BLP was the recruitment of Nisei mentors for teenagers transitioning from Sunday School, and from Junior YBAs to Senior YBA organizations. The BLP program sought to develop counselors as "spiritual advisers" who could be a "big brother" or "big sister" to youth. The training program noted that, "since both young girls and boys are involved in the group, a husband or wife team is most ideal to work as counselors." Nevertheless, the program guide stressed that the role was voluntary and noted that "anyone who is interested in the spiritual development of young people and is willing to grow with them in Amida's Wisdom and Compassion, is a worthy counselor."[83] As mentors and spiritual advisors working closely with youth, the counselor position was envisioned as an important link between BCA's ministers, participating parents, and children.[84]

Reverends Tsuji and Fujimoto and Nisei lay leaders who worked to formulate the Buddhist Life Program sought to develop a less hierarchical model of transmission than had been followed by ministers and lay teachers in the past. As Tsuji explained, curriculum for the Buddhist Life Program was to be tailored to meet the needs of a variety of young lay members, from children in Sunday School to college-age adults. A "notable feature" of the Sunday School curriculum, he explained, was "the consideration it gives to the psychological and social makeup of the children [which] tries to meet the spiritual needs at the level of their development and experience."[85] Moreover, Tsuji believed that education in both Sunday School and the Buddhist Life Program needed to follow a middle path between tradition and innovation, one that remained open and in dialogue with student participants. He explained, "We are not interested in making Bonsai Buddhists, whose growth is stunted, the branches trimmed, and the shape molded by adult standards." Refuting claims that he was abandoning previous traditions, Tsuji stated, "I am not suggesting that we must do away with tradition and adult supervision. Nor am I suggesting that children and youths should be completely free to express themselves."[86] Tsuji posited that, just as Shinran Shonin emerged after twenty years of study with a radically new view of monasticism, "in Buddhist Education children are taught to appreciate their rich heritage but at the same time guided to grow out of the past to discover fresh insights."[87]

Programs that sought to instill Buddhist values among Nisei families and to connect them to the broader sangha through church and temples activities met with mixed success. Ironically, but perhaps not surprisingly, long-standing social programs that had a built-in family component seemed to be most successful in fortifying this connection.

The evolution of the Buddhist Sangha Award for scouting provides an illustrative example. As Jane Iwamura noted, scouting represented one of a number of fronts in which BCA sought to instill home family *butsudan* practice.[88] Boy Scout troops affiliated with Buddhist temples and churches did exist prior to the war but did not garner significant attention from BCA until the postwar period. Efforts to establish a Boy Scout Sangha Award began in the 1950s. In 1954, the Boy Scouts of America recognized the Sangha Award as one among a number of religious awards for Protestants, Catholics, and Jews that could be earned by its scouts.[89] Because the award would apply to all Buddhists, the committee, originally initiated by a small group of BCA members led by Dr. Kikuo Taira, reached out to other Nikkei Buddhist sects in the continental United States and Hawai'i.[90] By 1957, requirements for the award were established. In 1971, attesting to the continued vibrancy of the program, requirements were streamlined and published in the *Young People's Introduction to Buddhism: A Sangha Award Study Book for Shin Buddhists,* a BCA guidebook published for the award by the Shin Buddhist convert minister Reverend Philipp Karl Eidman.

Requirements were organized around the three treasures of the Buddha, the Dharma and the Sangha, and divided into two "stages." In the first stage, scouts were to demonstrate a basic understanding of Buddhist concepts, teachings, ritual, and practice. In the second stage they were required to demonstrate a deeper understanding of each of these elements, culminating in a requirement of participation in a leadership role as a Sunday School teacher, youth leader, conference chair, or other leadership role recommended by ministers or counselors. By 1971, this culminating sangha project had been reduced to either a Buddhist minister or counselor-endorsed service project, or twenty-five hours of *dana* (volunteer charity work).[91]

The evolution of expectations for family and temple Buddhist services spoke to the impact of family Buddhist themes and campaigns in the early 1960s. Under the 1957 requirements, scouts were required to demonstrate a knowledge of family and temple shrines, including three months of daily care for the family shrine and leading at least seven family services at home. In addition to these requirements, scouts in the 1971 guidebook were also required to "show evidence of personal daily morning and evening meditation before the shrine."[92]

Both scouting and the Sangha Award proved relatively popular among young Nisei and Sansei from the late 1950s through the 1960s. By 1963, eighteen scouts had earned the award, and another thirteen had received first-stage cards.[93] Nine years later, in 1972, ninety-one additional scouts had earned the award. By 1975, nineteen of BCA's affiliated temples and churches sponsored a Boy Scout troop. A number of temples and churches also began to sponsor Camp Fire Girls, for which a Karuna (loving kindness) Award was established, following the model of the Sangha Award.[94]

In contrast to scouting, the Buddhist Life Program struggled to draw a critical mass of Nisei mentors and to maintain the interest of younger Nisei and Sansei. Following the successful yearlong trial run of the program in Watsonville, Reverend Fujimoto met with twenty-three groups of prospective counselors and youth participants in a series of rallies, discussions, and talks held in California and BCA's Tri-State and Northwest districts over the course of 1964. Despite his extensive efforts, Fujimoto reported on the challenges that he faced in the first year of the program's existence. He characterized the program as a "highly complicated one demanding dedicated adult leaders, enthusiastic youths, and [the] ardent support of parents." Fujimoto expressed frustration over the difficulties in recruiting mentors, noting that "to say that capable adult leaders are easy to find is an over-statement." He concluded that the program required "hard work, initiative and imagination of all concerned."[95]

In Fujimoto's view, some of the key challenges with recruitment and retention of mentors were driven by external factors in addition to those shaped by the demands of the program itself. He observed that many mentees eventually left the program to pursue college or as they joined youth associations with friends outside of church. Prospective counselors may have also been discouraged by unreasonably high qualification requirements and deficient educational support and training. They also faced heavy responsibilities that fell on the shoulders of a small number of volunteers, and lack of parental education. Fujimoto concluded that these factors were compounded by the particular challenges faced by present-day youth, compared with earlier generations.[96]

The following year, BCA attempted to jump-start the Buddhist Life Program by sponsoring National Buddhist Youth Week, which it held beginning March 14, 1965. BCA leadership announced that the goal of the week was "Firstly, to awaken youth consciousness among the church leaders and church members" and, secondly, "to arouse church consciousness among the youths themselves." Reported comments from both adults and youth were generally positive. Adults noted the attention brought to young people and youth issues. Adult commenters were impressed by the young people they encountered on panel discussions. One adult noted that participants appeared to be "more aware of the need of our spiritual education than we parents, . . . point[ing] out that although they could use some religion, the parents could stand to learn a little too." The youth noted that if "Church is good for us . . . why can't parents join us on Sundays?"[97]

By the end of 1965, the national Young Buddhist Association, whose leadership had worked with Fujimoto to support the BLP, also reported discouraging results regarding adult participation in youth programs. Reverend Hogen Fujimoto stated, "Our major problem, and this is particularly true with the Buddhist Life Program, deals with the lack of support by adults and counselors and advisors."[98] By the early 1970s, the program had been disbanded and was largely forgotten. Summarizing Fred Nitta's comments on the BLP in the *American Buddhist* in 1971, Paul Douglas Andrew explained that, in Nitta's view, despite the successful launch of the trial program at Watsonville, the BLP "was not so conscientiously carried out at other churches, and as a result Buddhist Life Program is not even a recognizable name to most present-day YBA members."[99]

The emphasis on "family Buddhism," by BCA priests and lay leaders was as much a recognition of the changing form and prospects of Nisei families as it was an effort to build new relations both among families, as well as between families and local temples and churches, through an emphasis on shared faith in Amida and moral living embodied through daily Buddhist practice. The efforts of BCA ministers and lay leaders to develop programs was most successful in growing its Sunday School program and traditional social programs like sports and scouting. While suffering from a lack of adult volunteers in an era when the YBAs were in decline, the focus of Buddhist leaders on issues of juvenile delinquency and lack of Buddhist spirit competed with national and world events that increasingly drew the attention of young Sansei Buddhists and convert Buddhists, including issues of civil rights, feminism, and the war in Vietnam. These issues and others would present new challenges to postwar BCA traditions and its established leadership.

CHAPTER 7

Dharma Bums, Social Activism, and Challenges to Nisei Buddhism

In 1968, Ryo Imamura, a Sansei medical student at the University of Hawaiʻi, led an antiwar march and demonstration at the Hompa Hongwanji Mission of Hawaiʻi on Memorial Day. Veterans of the 442nd, many of whom were Buddhists, had long used the temple's facilities as a clubhouse and had invited fellow veteran and US senator Daniel Inouye to speak as part of Memorial Day services. The student march was part of a larger series of student antiwar protests that erupted that spring in response to President Lyndon Johnson's activation of US Army and National Guard reserves, including members from Hawaiʻi, as part of the US escalation of the war in Vietnam.[1] Gathering at the University of Hawaiʻi campus, protesters marched through the city streets of Honolulu. As they emerged from a tunnel leading directly to the Hongwanji, some veterans urged calling the police. Others who identified Imamura at the head of the protesters urged restraint because he was the son of the Hongwanji's current Bishop, Kanmo Imamura. As he approached Senator Inouye, Imamura presented the group's petition and then offered to shake his hand, only to realize that Inouye, who had lost his right hand in combat during World War II, could not return the gesture. With closed hand, Imamura and Inouye improvised an alternative gesture. Following the presentation of the group's petition, the protesters disbanded from the temple.[2]

Ryo Imamura's antiwar activism and progressive views in defining and later ministering to a Buddhist sangha that challenged the presuppositions of Nisei Buddhism were inspired, on the one hand, by the social movements among young people in the 1960s but, on the other, were influenced by Imamura's exposure to the more open and progressive climate that first emerged in the 1950s in the BCA study group. As he later recalled, a "lot had to do with my upbringing—of the influence of my father and mother and all these people, like [those] who came to their study center in Berkeley. Always asking, questioning authority and wondering and wondering if there's more all the time."[3]

Born in the spring of 1944 at the Gila River WRA camp, Ryo Imamura was the son of Reverend Kanmo and Jane Imamura. His paternal grandfather was the Reverend Yemyo Imamura, first bishop of the Hompa Hongwanji Buddhist

Mission in Hawai'i, and his maternal parental in-laws were Reverend Issei Matsuura and Mrs. Shinobu Matsuura. Spending his formative years growing up in Berkeley where Kanmo had been the resident minister, Ryo, along with his three sisters Hiro, Rae and Mari, was raised in the hustle and bustle of the semipublic space of a minister's family, where the lines between family and sangha were blurred. They were surrounded by church members and YBA students, as well as the eclectic group of Buddhist study group participants that, over the course of the 1950s and early 1960s, would come to include future Nisei lay leaders and ministers, as well as Buddhist scholars and popularizers like Alan Watts, and Beat poets and writers including Gary Snyder, Jack Kerouac, Allen Ginsberg, and Philip Whalen.[4]

Even as BCA's institutions, programs, rituals, and social patterns associated with Nisei Buddhism were gradually elevated to the level of established orthodoxy over the course of the 1950s and 1960s, Nisei Buddhism, and in particular the Cold War racial liberal discourse in which ethnic Buddhism and family Buddhism had engaged in challenging racial and religious discrimination, met with its own detractors and critics. An emerging interest in Zen Buddhism and Beat Buddhist critiques of Cold War domestic containment ideology in the late 1950s initiated the pushback, particularly from a small but vocal group of white convert Buddhists together with a small group of enthusiastic Nisei. By the 1960s, a more significant challenge to Nisei Buddhism emerged from a younger generation of more progressive Nisei, Sansei, and white convert Buddhists from within BCA. While some criticized BCA's policies and institutional structures, others left BCA altogether to join more progressive political organizations and social movements.

The BCA Study Group and Beat Buddhism

Challenges to Nisei Buddhism's narrow sectarian traditions and practices, and to its gravitation toward an iteration of family Buddhism that resonated with US Cold War domestic ideology, first emerged from the margins of its membership in the 1950s, among a loosely affiliated group of Nisei and white convert Buddhists centered around the BCA Study Group in Berkeley, California. Those who participated tended to be more artistically inclined, politically progressive, and open to, or enthusiastic about, developing a Buddhist sangha that crossed lines of sect, ethnicity, and race.

The attraction of growing numbers of interested people from outside the Nikkei Shin Buddhist community was shaped by the open invitation to outsiders by BCA, particularly in Berkeley but also by broader historical developments. Scholars have addressed the growing interest in "things Japanese" in the postwar years as Japan was transformed into a Cold War ally and trading partner. Whether through business ventures or the influence of the occupation forces, this US presence produced new opportunities for those interested in learning about Japanese culture. As Meredith Oda has shown, this was particularly true for San Francisco and the surrounding Bay Area, as its civic and business leaders envisioned the city as a "gateway to the Pacific," centered on its relationship to the Pacific world and Japan in particular. New interest in Japan and Asian culture and people more broadly was reflected in the proliferation of popular films and novels and coverage in magazines, radio, and television. As Christina Klein has argued, emerging middlebrow Cold War Orientalist discourse reinforced the theme of connection between the United States and Asia. As Meghan Mettler has shown, this included an interest among the general public in Zen Buddhism.[5]

Under the guidance of Reverend Kanmo and Jane Imamura, the study group in Berkeley served as the central conduit between Nikkei and interested outsiders. As discussed previously, the study group had originally been established as part of efforts by BCA to recruit English-speaking ministers. While continuing to support that mission, under the guidance of the Imamuras, the study group drew scholars, students, artists, and the curious to share in discussion of the Buddhist teachings and concepts (Dharma) thus broadening the community of Buddhists (sangha). Early participants noted the diversity of backgrounds and perspectives of participants. Isao Fujimoto, a Nisei Berkeley undergrad from a Zen Buddhist family background, appreciated the "camaraderie" that grew among "all these people interested in Buddhism."[6] Vanita Meyer, a Berkeley graduate student, characterized the study group as a "happy conglomeration of people of different religions, races, ages and experiences." Meyer described a series of meetings during which the study group had gradually worked their way through a discussion of Junjiro Takakusu's *The Essentials of Buddhist Philosophy*. Meyer recalled Hitoshi Tsufura serving as moderator, trying to gently stir the group back from digressions. Meanwhile, "issues of importance" were addressed by Reverend Imamura together with Lama Tokwan Tada, a Japanese scholar of Tibetan Buddhism. Meyer concluded with a statement that celebrated the virtue of Dharma transmission through a gathering of the sangha, noting,

> The uniting of many minds on one problem results in a kind of learning very different from individual study, though that is necessary too. No matter how hard one works alone, his single light casts a shadow which leaves some things undiscovered. Working with others, those shadows can be dispersed, as the object of study is surrounded by the light of many minds.[7]

In the fall of 1955, Beat poets, writers, and artists including Allen Ginsberg, Philip Whalen, and Jack Kerouac began to participate in the group after Gary Snyder, who had joined months earlier, convinced them to attend meetings.[8] Among the small collection of poets and writers, Snyder was the key figure in introducing Buddhist thought to the group. Snyder and Whalen had first been introduced to Buddhist teachings as undergraduates at Reed College in the late 1940s. Snyder began reading the smattering of English-language translations of Buddhist sutras and secondary texts. In addition to H. C. Warren's *Anthology of Translations from the Buddhist Pali Cannon,* Snyder's interest in mountain climbing, which would later become mythologized in Kerouac's *Dharma Bums,* led him to read Marco Pallis' *Peaks and Lamas.* Originally published in 1939, *Peaks and Lamas* described Pallis' travels through Tibet and included discussions of the landscape, people, and culture. Through his reading of Pallis, Snyder first learned about Tibetan Buddhism; however, it was D. T. Suzuki's work that got Snyder interested in Zen. In 1951, he came across two volumes of edited works by Suzuki at the Metaphysical Bookstore in San Francisco, which motivated him to begin to prepare for Zen study in Japan. Snyder dropped out of a PhD program in linguistics at Indiana University and enrolled in the Oriental Languages Department at the University of California in preparation for travel to Japan to study Zen Buddhism.[9]

Snyder recalled years later, in a foreword to Jane Imamura's memoir *Kaikyo,* that as he entered the Berkeley Buddhist Church and joined the advanced study class, he "had not expected so familial and relaxed an atmosphere." His first experience attending study group was seeing "a mix of folks—students, children, and older people." Snyder was "given a gracious reception by a stylish Japanese-American lady who introduced me to the Reverend Imamura, and made me feel right at home. This was my first meeting with Jane and Kanmo (and Hiro, Rae, Mari and Ryo)."[10] For Snyder, the experience also challenged some of his preconceptions about Buddhist practice as well as what a "Buddhist" looked like. Snyder noted,

> It was just what I needed at that time to indeed break me out of my foolish attachments to the ideal of solitary accomplishment, and to see that the Dharma is practiced with other people; is actualized within a Sangha. Jane and Kanmo Imamura gave so many of us our first taste of Sangha. It was also paradoxically a great teaching for me, a bit of a rebel, to see the Imamura and other BCA families as—so American! So normal! A charming irony. "Normal" they may have been, but not cautious or conventional. The Reverend Imamura was quietly open to the experimental and creative spirit of the Bay Area fifties.[11]

Among the many public dimensions of her job as *bombori,* or wife of a Buddhist priest, Jane Imamura played a key role as cosponsor of the study group. In addition to contributing to the welcoming atmosphere, Jane was instrumental in maintaining connections with and among group members, many that lasted for decades. Along with her husband Kanmo, Jane also served as an important mentor to Nisei and served as an adviser for the *Berkeley Bussei,* a BCA-affiliated publication that would serve as the mouthpiece for expressing and articulating the scholarly and artistic voice that emerged from the Berkeley YBA and study group members during the 1950s.

Imamura's enthusiasm for the artistic bent of many of the study center newcomers came perhaps from her own prewar background as an aspiring artist. Prior to the onset of World War II, Jane had studied classical music under the direction of Swiss composer Rudolph Ganz at the Chicago Musical College. Her formal training was abruptly ended by her forced incarceration during the war.[12] Imamura fondly recalled the "core" of the study group regulars who spent time around the temple, as "scholars, poets, linguists, authors and artists and interested participants from all walks of life." Describing what many Issei and Nisei Buddhists would have likely dismissed as unconventional approaches to Buddhist teaching, Imamura recalled one study group session led by Snyder and Alex Wayman, a graduate student who would later become a pioneering scholar in Buddhist and Tibetan studies: "Once, Gary Snyder, even then the dedicated ecologist, arrived at a study class with a bag of all kinds of apples. Lining them up, he used them as subjects for a Dharma talk. Alex Wayman, another graduate student, followed this imaginative demonstration by composing a poem on all kinds of bread."[13] Imamura characterized regular study group participants as "erudite seekers often engaged in friendly bantering but mostly serious discussion," as "exceptional happenings with everyone in common search for the meaning of life."[14]

The ideas and approach of the study group germinated among its members and circulated through the *Berkeley Bussei,* joining a small but growing chorus of more progressive voices and publications within BCA, including the Issei Shin Buddhist reverend Itsuzo Kyogoku's *Tri-Ratna: Buddha, Buddhism, Buddhist,* which was published until his death, as well as the *American Buddhist,* which served as the official English-language publication of the BCA and ran from 1957 through the early 1970s. While not representing the dominant positions of BCA and its Nisei Buddhist lay leaders, these publications pushed the limits of discussion of Buddhism to include Shin Buddhist teachings, practice, and happenings, as well as trans-sectarian perspectives and contributions from a variety of participants, including BCA priests and laypersons, together with Asian, European, and European American scholars, students, and enthusiasts.[15]

Like the study group, these publications also diverged from typical BCA publications by demonstrating an openness and support of artistic and scholarly contributions. Gary Snyder published some of his earliest works in the *Berkeley Bussei,* beginning with the poem "Maitreya" in 1954.[16] Philip Whalen published "Unfinished, from 3: XII: 55" in the 1957 issue of *Berkeley Bussei.* In addition to publishing Kerouac's first poems, the 1960 issue published Kerouac's recollection of his encounter with D.T. Suzuki as well as an early version of Gary Snyder's "Marin-An."[17] Named after a meditation center that Snyder and friends had recently established in Mill Valley, "Marin-An" juxtaposed the quietude of the center with the morning commute across the Golden Gate Bridge into San Francisco.

Marin-An

The sun breaks over the Eucalyptus
Grove below the wet pasture,
The water's about hot enough
To wash dishes, I sit in
The open window and roll a smoke.
Distant dogs bark, a pair of
Cawing crows, the small voice
Of a pygmy nuthatch high in the pine.
From behind the cypress window
The mare moves up, grazing.
A soft continuous roar
Comes out of the far valley
Of the six-lane highway: thousands
And thousands of cars
Driving men to work.[18]

Some key Nisei members of the study group encouraged contributions of the Beat poets and shared their enthusiasm for the blending of Buddhist ideas and critiques of domestic containment culture. Hiroshi Kashiwagi, a contributor to the *Berkeley Bussei* and editor of the *American Buddhist* from 1957 to 1967, was among them. Like Jane Iwamura, Kashiwagi was also artistically inclined, with a longstanding interest in playwriting.

After Snyder left for Japan to study under a Zen roshi, study group members continued to update him on local happenings. Jane Imamura wrote to Snyder about Will Peterson, an artist loosely associated with the Beat scene and a study group participant, and about his plans to move to Japan shortly after he finished editing the 1957 *Berkeley Bussei*. She noted that while spring was usually "the time to be regenerated," Iwamura noted that there was "so much regeneration here all the time that I hardly feel it." Imamura also mentioned that Robert Jackson, a regular study group member, was lecturing on Buddhism at local universities and teaching BCA high school Sunday School courses, noting that "his energy shows no sign of exhausting which is a wonderful thing for us."[19] In another letter to Snyder, Kerouac reported on his participation in a study group meeting and the dinner that followed: "Last Sunday Claude [Dalenberg] spoke at the Buddhist meeting here and I met Mrs. Imamura again and that fine fellow [Hitoshi] Tsufura and they took us to dinner of eel at Fuji inn, which I guess Phil [Whalen] told you." Jane and Kanmo Imamura's interactions with convert participants such as Snyder would lead to friendships that spanned the next four decades.[20]

Ironically, the open spirit of the BCA study group and like-minded Nisei Buddhists resulted in new debates, criticisms, and countercharges in public discussions, in study group meetings, and in print. Some of these debates reflected earlier tensions within BCA between those emphasizing a narrower sectarian approach and those advocating for a broader vision of the sangha. Yet many of the criticisms from white convert Buddhists centered on the issue of the authenticity of various forms of Buddhist practice and teachings adopted by Nisei Shin Buddhists, including those adaptations that sought to meet postwar racial liberal proscriptions by presenting Buddhism as ethnic and in line with Cold War domestic containment ideology.

An additional source of debate was created by differences between Shin Buddhism and Buddhist schools including Zen. Criticism of programs associated with Nisei Buddhism emerged partly in response to the structure and form of Shin Buddhist practice and teaching, which some critics misread as too *similar* to Western religion. As discussed in the introduction, the Shin Buddhism adapted by Issei in the prewar years, and by Nisei during the period under study, retained what on the surface appeared to be doctrinal similarities to Christian Protestantism that many convert Buddhists found undesirable. One of the major differences between Shin Buddhist doctrine and that of other Buddhist schools such as Zen was the former's emphasis on *tariki* rather than *jiriki*. Shin Buddhism's founder Shinran emphasized *tariki,* or an acknowledgment of the "Other Power" of the Amida Buddha's compassion as the only necessary precondition to attaining enlightenment. This teaching stood in stark contrast to Zen Buddhism, which emphasized *jiriki,* or "Self-Power," which for the Sōtō school was generated through persistent and rigorous practice of zazen sitting meditation, something that many convert Buddhists found appealing. The emphasis on *tariki,* expressed through "faith" or gratitude to the Amida Buddha through the practice of devotional recitation, was often criticized for its perceived similarity to the Christian concepts of faith and redemption by the Christian God.[21]

The enthusiasm (and preference) for Zen Buddhism was facilitated by greater coordination among Japanese, European, and American scholars of Buddhism. Their collaborations were encouraged by successful independent businessmen, Japanese American communities, universities, and the US government. Universities, private institutions like the Ford and Rockefeller Foundations, and the federal government supported the development of Buddhist studies as an important subfield of Asian studies. While faculty and graduate students with interests in Buddhism existed at universities such as Berkeley, Stanford, Harvard, and Columbia, the first formal Buddhist studies program in the United States was established in 1962 at the University of Wisconsin by Richard Hughes Robinson, a participant in the BCA study group and contributor to BCA publications.[22]

The most prominent and influential figure in the popularization of Buddhism in the United States during the 1950s was Daisetz Teitaro Suzuki. In exploring why Suzuki and Zen captured the popular American imagination, Jane Iwamura noted that Suzuki's image was at least as critical as the way he presented Zen Buddhism. Iwamura concluded that "Suzuki is not viewed as simply a 'cultural ambassador' or 'translator' of the larger tradition but the embodiment of that tradition—the *icon* through which Zen Buddhism achieved meaning for those in the West."[23]

Returning to the United States after World War II, Suzuki was instrumental in the development of interest in and recognition of Zen. Suzuki first came to the attention of small groups of influential intellectuals, artists, and others interested in Asian religion and thought beginning in the early 1950s after he arrived in Hawai'i to attend the 1949 East-West Philosophers' Conference. He then moved to a visiting position at the Claremont Graduate School in Southern California, sponsored with funds raised by the Japanese American community.[24] After Claremont, Suzuki was invited by the Rockefeller Foundation to lecture at various American universities beginning in 1950; he held the position of visiting professor at Columbia University from 1952 to 1958.[25]

Over the course of the 1950s, Suzuki also attracted a growing readership who encountered him through his publications, which included the republished prewar work, *An Introduction to Zen Buddhism* (1949), *Mysticism: Christianity and Buddhism* (1957), *Zen and Japanese Culture* (1959), and the collaborative work, *Zen and Psychoanalysis,* written with psychologist Erich Fromm and Richard De Martino, a professor of religion at Temple University. However, it was in the late 1950s that coverage of Suzuki and Zen exploded into what *Time* magazine dubbed a Buddhist "boomlet." In 1957, discussion of Suzuki and Zen appeared in major national magazine publications including *Vogue, Time,* and the *New Yorker.* In April of that year, Suzuki appeared for an interview on the nationally televised NBC program *Wisdom.*[26]

In New York, Suzuki continued to maintain ties to the Shin Buddhist Japanese American community, giving talks and participating in cultural festivals such as the fiftieth-anniversary celebration of the establishment of the New York Buddhist Church (NYBC) in 1953 and the groundbreaking ceremony for the memorial to Shinran at NYBC in 1955.[27] Meanwhile, as Rick Fields has recounted, Suzuki's talks at Columbia University drew leading intellectuals and artists such as Erich Fromm, Karen Horney, John Cage, and lay practitioners (or future practitioners) such as Mary Farkas and Philip Kapleau.[28]

As they became increasingly familiar with BCA and Nisei Buddhist–led institutions and practices, some of the new recent-convert Buddhist arrivals raised criticisms of the modified practices. They believed that they were aiding these communities by steering them away from ostensibly misguided adaptations and back toward their own authentic origins. While acknowledging that racial and religious discrimination in the past might have led to use of the term "church," Calvin Steinmetz, a convert Buddhist who emerged in the 1950s and 1960s as a regular contributor to Buddhist publications, appealed to the BCA to change the term back to "temple," noting that he had learned from Buddhists in other countries—including (presumably) convert Buddhists in England—that they were "uniformly horrified at the idea of Buddhist 'churches.'" Steinmetz explained that "Buddhism is interesting to some of the best minds in the West because it is different enough from westernized religions that the contrast is striking." He concluded by advocating for the adoption of "Buddhist terms," by which he meant Japanese and Sanskrit terms.[29]

What many convert Buddhists found most unsettling were the same external modifications that shaped the presentation of American ethnic and family Buddhism. Convert Buddhists criticized what they described as the "Protestantized" modifications in Japanese American Shin Buddhist practices, such as Buddhist "temple worship." In a keynote address titled "Program for Buddhism in America" and presented to the Japanese American Western Young Buddhist League, Alan Watts, who would become a key popularizer of Zen Buddhism in the San Francisco Bay Area and then nationally over the course of the 1950s and 1960s, contrasted "American-Japanese" Buddhist group organizations in the United States with "purely American" groups, by which he meant convert Buddhist groups. "The former," he stated, "are organized as temples and churches, which pattern themselves more and more after the Protestant Christian Churches of the

West. The latter are organized as 'ashrams,' that is to say, as informal schools for the study and practice of Buddhist teachings." "Historically," Watts continued, "ashrams existed in Buddhism long before temples. Buddhism began as an ashram—a group of disciples studying under Gautama the Buddha. Temple life came later, as a way of paying respect or giving thanks to the Buddhas and Bodhisattvas for their compassion in pointing out the way of deliverance from illusion."[30]

If appeals to a historically based authenticity were not enough to persuade Japanese Americans to reconsider their forms of practice, Watts tapped into a source of anxiety for most Bussei by claiming that similarities in practice to Christianity threatened the future of Buddhism in the United States. Watts asserted,

> Temple-Buddhism is a very wonderful development—so long as it does not supplant or overshadow ashram-Buddhism. But this is just what is happening in Buddhism, particularly in the American groups of Japanese origin, and it is to be feared that if this course continues, these groups will die out, and fail to make their important contribution to Western life. . . . It is very understandable that Americans of Japanese origin want to adapt themselves to American life, and to fit in with the social patterns which they find in this country. But this copying of Christian church-organization is most unfortunate.[31]

Convert Buddhists also expressed displeasure with many of the external and organizational modifications that had produced the BCA's programs for ethnic national and family Buddhism: Buddhist priests who were addressed as reverends or ministers, Sunday School programs, Buddhist choirs, Young Buddhist Associations with basketball and baseball leagues that resembled YMCA and YWCA programs, and Buddhist Boy Scout troops and its Sangha Award. In a letter to the *American Buddhist,* the Reverend Jack Austin, editor of the *Western Buddhist,* stated that he "had no objection to any social activities and [was] in favor of Buddhist Youth organizations having all the sporting events possible, so long as this does not prevent the study of the Dharma, which is the main thing. But many of the [Japanese] American Buddhist magazines which reach us make one wonder if Buddhism is not the main thing but only an adjunct to baseball!"[32]

The publication of *On the Road,* in September 1957, made Jack Kerouac an instant national celebrity, with the novel receiving both strong praise and criticism. Kerouac followed *On the Road* a year later with the publication of *Dharma Bums,* a novel that shined a spotlight on the West Coast scene and introduced Beat Buddhism to the nation and world. The participation of Gary Snyder, Allen

Ginsberg, Phil Whalen, and Kerouac in BCA-affiliated circles that pre-dated the 1955 Gallery Six readings where Ginsberg and other Beat poets and writers gained notoriety also clearly excited and inspired a number of Nisei and convert Buddhists affiliated with the eclectic BCA Study Group.

As the Beat vision of Buddhism began to influence discussions among convert Buddhists, it was used as a point of contrast with those BCA members, particularly Nisei Buddhists, who were characterized as apathetic and conformist. Two months after the publication of *On the Road,* in November 1957, *American Buddhist* published an article by Robert Jackson, a Berkeley graduate in Asian studies, who became a high school teacher, active BCA member, and student of Buddhism living in the San Francisco Bay Area. Jackson's article, titled "Buddhism and the Beat Generation," celebrated the actions of a young postwar generation of Americans who could "hardly remember a thing before Hiroshima." Jackson described the Beat Generation as witness to "utopian dreams souring into a dismal swamp of jittering cities peppered by rains of Benzedrine and tranquilizers." He proposed that having rejected the "hollow life of production and consumption," the Beats had "come to the realization, however unspoken, of the first of the Buddha's four noble truths," that all life is suffering. They had "become 'beautified' as well for it [was] this experience, not a profession of mere belief, that [set] one upon the path of the bodhisattva." For Jackson, the Beat lifestyle and approach of white Buddhists embodied the true spirit of Buddhism even when compared to Japanese Americans who had been raised Buddhist. Jackson exclaimed that "in the brooding, nervous wandering across the continent and over oceans, these *hakujin* [white] Buddhists have built meditation into their lives" and that "while not all of these people care to be called Buddhist . . . they [knew] more about oneness, emptiness, wisdom and compassion than many whose Buddhism [was] a matter of no choice to them."[33]

A number of Nisei enthusiastically supported the contribution of Beat poets and writers and encouraged the growing interest in Beat Buddhism by those such as Jackson. One such Nisei was Hiroshi Kashiwagi, who served in BCA's office as executive secretary and as an editor of the *Berkeley Bussei* and editor of the BCA's English-language flagship publication, *American Buddhist.* Prior to his time with BCA, Kashiwagi had participated in a Nisei experimental writing group in Los Angeles with the future Beat poet Albert Saijo and his brother Gompers, among others, where he wrote *The Plums Can Wait* based on his family's experience in camp. To accompany Jackson's Beat Buddhism article Kashiwagi included reprints of poems that were first published in the *Berkeley Bussei* by Phil Whalen, Jack Kerouac, and Gary Snyder. In introducing the poems, Kashiwagi noted,

The expression of the "beat generation" is not *poesie,* but invection and a cry of awe out of the limitlessness of experience. It is often full of guts and spleen, caring little for literary purity, but rather for vision and liberation. At the Berkeley Buddhist Church, a group of writers now broadly being heard, once settled like cows on a fence, only long enough to make a group. One left for someplace, then all scattered. But their voices are still heard, not always sweet, but unmistakably true.[34]

Other Nisei shared Kashiwagi's enthusiasm. Roy Sato described Jackson's article on the beats as "stunning" and found the poems of Whalen, Kerouac, and Snyder reprinted from the *Berkeley Bussei* in the *American Buddhist* "even more stunning," noting that "they reveal a spirit of independence and adventure which might greatly serve the cause of Buddhism. I hope that the article and the poems shake awake these Nisei Buddhists who seem to be attempting to convey the idea that Gotama's religion is nothing more than sukiyaki dinners, parties, picnics, and bon-odoris."[35]

A year after the publication of "Buddhism and the Beat Generation," Jackson declared, "We are not looking for a popularized, watered-down version of Buddhism that will appeal to the lowest common denominator of the membership." Buddhist education needed to appeal to "individuals who will emerge from the apathetic run of people." Jackson concluded, "A Buddhist disciple is often unconventional, he does not ask for parables or stories to be minutely explained to him. He 'gets it,' 'digs' the teaching and often comes up with some startling ideas of his own."[36]

Criticisms that challenged the authenticity of Shin Buddhism and adapted Japanese American Buddhist practices were also met with criticism and counter challenges by those from the Japanese American Buddhist community. Japanese American Buddhists responded to challenges from convert Buddhists like Alan Watts and others in a number of ways. One was to point out the varying schools and traditions within Buddhism. David Iwamoto, a Nisei and former YBA member who had recently been ordained as a Shin Buddhist priest, addressed Watts' comments on Japanese American temple Buddhism with a pointed rebuttal. Iwamoto rejected Watts' characterization of Shin Buddhism as equivalent to or very similar to Christianity and also disagreed that Shin Buddhists needed to adjust their practice to an ashram format to remain significant. Invoking the long history and tradition of Shin Buddhism, Iwamoto called Watts' comments "a virtual insult not only to the Shin Sect order of America but to all who find the crystallization of Buddhism in Shinran Shonin's teaching." He added, "If [Watts] is the Buddhist scholar he claims to be, he must know that Shakyamuni Buddha made difficult truths intelligible to minds of various capacities and that this

Figure 7.1. American Buddhist staff, circa late 1950s. Left to right, editor Hiroshi Kashiwagi, Yukio Sugimoto, Robert Jackson, Elson Snow, and Taitetsu Unno. Reprinted from Jane Michiko Imamura, *Kaikyo*, 76.

diversity of provisions in Shakyamuni Buddha's teaching has been responsible for the establishment of various Buddhist sects." He concluded, "No one doubts today that the Shin Sect is an established Buddhist sect. People out of number have found joy in following the doctrine of the Shin Sect as the way to Enlightenment as propounded by Shakyamuni Buddha."[37]

Others affirmed the temple tradition, and in particular the important social and spiritual role that temples played, arguing that temples and churches had been important in sustaining an everyday sense of both collective and individual identity for Japanese Americans. Indeed, the Shin Buddhist tradition of gathering as a confraternity around the Buddhist temple could be traced at least back to the fifteenth century, when the Eighth Abbot Rennyo encouraged and systematized regular social-religious gatherings of Shin followers.[38] BCA study group member and future ministerial candidate John Doami reasoned that Buddhism was more "a way of life" than a "religion in the popular sense." In response to the question, "Is there really a need for temples and churches?" Doami stated, "I believe there is. To propagate a way of life that one believes in, the best way I know of is through word of mouth [in] a congregation." Doami then explained how the pursuit of individual understanding and community social interaction complemented each other. "Since Buddhism is an individual matter, a way of life seeking understanding of the self in order to achieve greater happiness in this world, intermingling would be an ideal, leading to a greater insight of one's thoughts and actions through observation of others [actions]."[39]

While sympathetic to the Beat vision portrayed in Jackson's article, Taitetsu Unno offered an alternative vision of Buddhism grounded in the teachings of the Buddha and the more ordinary workings of Buddhist lay communities. Unno argued that, while well intentioned, those celebrated by Jackson were misguided in their spiritual pursuits and often failed to engage Buddhist teachings on anything more than a superficial level. He wrote, "The earnest seek to go beyond this world of transiency and impermanence and realize their roots in a stable reality that is the ground of life. But so often they seek it in the wrong places." Quoting the Dhammapada, a text found within the Pali Canon, Unno observed that "men driven by fear go to many a refuge, to mountains and to forests, to sacred trees, and shrines," and added, "Today men go to resorts and psychiatrists, tranquillizers and drugs, effete philosophies and pseudo-religions. These are not solutions; the right path is clearly shown." Again quoting the Dhammapada, Unno proposed that, for a person who took "refuge in the Buddha, Dharma, and Sangha," and "who perceives in his clear wisdom the Four Noble Truths, . . . that verily is the safe refuge, that is the best refuge; after having gone to that refuge a man is delivered from all pain."[40]

Still others denounced *American Buddhist* articles that they viewed as heretically straying from traditional Shin Buddhist teachings. In one column, Jackson felt compelled to respond to sharply worded criticism from an unnamed but "respected source" on the recent "trend of American Buddhism." Jackson noted that the *American Buddhist* would continue to "remain open to the wider tradition of

Buddhism." Nevertheless, Jackson assured readers that "by no means is there a policy in the [BCA] or its publications of 'moving away from the Jodo-Shin-shu of their fathers in favor of a nebulous concoction composed of one part Zen, one part anti-Christianity (!) and one part metaphysical gymnastics' as the letter received put it. Nor is it true that faith in Amida would pass 'as soon as the last Issei is buried.'"[41]

Critiques of Nisei Shin Buddhist–adapted practices cut to the core of Nisei assumptions about their own religious practices, traditions, and identity. In responding to critics, Japanese American Buddhists invoked a particular vision of Buddhism that affirmed the acculturated practices and traditions developed in America over the previous sixty years. Whether supporting temple modifications, turning to their knowledge of Shin Buddhist teachings and general Buddhist sutras, or labeling articles heretical, Japanese American Buddhists clarified and thus crafted a renewed understanding of the content and form of Shin Buddhist practice. At the same time, by asserting their traditions and history, Japanese American Buddhists problematized Orientalist constructions of an idealized, ancient exotic form of Buddhism that reinforced its difference and distance from US national culture.

"I Think We Have to Democratize Our Buddhist Churches": Progressive Challenges to Nisei Buddhism in the 1960s and 1970s

In February 1967, the Western Adult Buddhist League (WABL) sponsored a "teen-age panel discussion" on the topic "The Buddhist Youth and His Perspective" as part of its annual conference held at the Fresno Buddhist Church. The panel was part of BCA's push to develop its Family Buddhism Program targeting youth, as was a talk that preceded it by the conference keynote speaker, Dr. Steven Abe, a staff psychologist with the California State Department of Juvenile Corrections. Moderated by Elaine Tashima, a student at the University of California–Davis, the panel was a roundtable discussion by four Sansei students from surrounding Fresno-area high schools.[42] Nisei WABL members, including many of the parents of the panelists, made up a majority of the audience. The moderator's opening statement tried to frame the conversation around the question of "preserving the Japanese heritage," including Buddhism, particularly in the aftermath of the construction of the stereotype of Japanese Americans as a "model minority."[43]

The panel revealed the nascent tension among a new generation of young Sansei Buddhists who felt increasingly alienated and disconnected from BCA's early

Cold War era programs. In some respects, the complaints raised at the panel around the issue of language and the transmission of Buddhist teachings echoed the complaints of Nisei raised decades earlier. One student stated, "Since most of our reverends come from Japan and speak Japanese there is a barrier between the Sansei and the reverends so the reverends can't convey their messages or what they want to teach about Buddhism."[44] Another student complained about what they perceived as a cultural gap between Sansei and Issei Buddhist priests: "I think when the ministers come from Japan they should have training in American society because I think they have unrealistic expectations of the country and people. The people outwardly treat the ministers respectfully but inside we don't think very much of them. What we need are ministers who can really convey their thoughts in their sermons."[45] The panel's moderator responded to complaints about gaps in language and culture by mentioning the BCA's new Buddhist Training Center and the fact that it would be directed toward the development of Buddhist priests from among the Sansei and Nisei.[46]

Yet, unlike their older Nisei (and Sansei) predecessors, these younger Sansei, along with a contingent of progressive Nisei, were also increasingly swept up in the social transformations that had unfolded over the course of the 1960s. The panelists raised criticisms that reflected growing frustration among younger Sansei and more progressive members about what they described as the undemocratic nature of both Buddhist families and temple relations among the sangha. One student complained about the lack of commitment of some Nisei audience members to an issue, which Sansei found relevant—the authoritarian style of parenting that had been passed down from the Issei. The Sansei panelist chastised Nisei in the audience for their complacency:

> I'd like to comment on Dr. Abe's talk. What he had to say was very relevant and it would have gone over much better had the majority of you people been awake. Unfortunately, I noticed that in every row there was at least one person asleep. If we are going to have this kind of complacent attitude then what he is saying can make no headway at all. He said the relationship between the Issei and Nisei was of an authoritarian, conditioned-response type. He said the relationship between Nisei and Sansei should be more democratic, explaining the "why's" and emphasizing the development of the individual. And yet you people just sit there and go to sleep.[47]

Other students directed their antiauthoritarian critique toward BCA and the Buddhist priests. One student called for Buddhist churches to be more "open."

The student described Buddhist priests as not having close personal relations with the sangha, explaining, "They are, in fact, a plateau above us." The student concluded, "I think this is authoritarian in nature and we have to democratize our Buddhist churches."[48]

Sansei frustrations expressed at the WABL panel confirmed Nisei lay leaders own concerns about generational division, which they attributed primarily to language barriers and to cultural divisions generally defined. As discussed earlier, BCA leaders viewed the development of English-speaking Nisei ministers as essential for resolving some of the tensions.

However, what emerged somewhat unexpectedly from the Sansei high school panelists, highlighted by the panelist who excoriated sleeping members in the audience, was a deeper frustration with what they defined as the antidemocratic "authoritarian" character of BCA and of Buddhist families. These and other criticisms by Sansei Buddhist youth were indicative of not only generational and general "cultural" divisions but also deeper ideological tensions that emerged between, on the one hand, an older generation of Nisei Buddhist cold warriors and, on the other, a younger generation of more progressive Nisei and Sansei who were increasingly critical of Cold War racial liberalism and containment ideology that had played a central role in defining BCA and its programs.

Scholars of Japanese Americans and Asian Americans during the 1960s have noted the emergence of an array of ideological political perspectives that emerged among these groups, which ranged from conservative to reform-oriented to radical.[49] Some of these perspectives challenged the model minority stereotype that attributed Japanese American "success," despite discrimination, to a Japanese cultural ethic that emphasized hard work, family unity, and respect for law and authority. In "Success Story, Japanese-American Style," penned for the *New York Times Magazine,* William Peterson attributed the transmission of Buddhism as a critical source of Japanese American morals and proposed that both Japanese American Buddhist and Christian churches were institutions that reinforced the value of authority among Japanese Americans. Published in January 1966, Peterson's article, which helped popularize the Asian American model minority stereotype, contrasted their successful navigation within the system with "problem" minorities engaged in civil rights protests and with students involved in the antiwar movement.[50]

In the case of Nikkei, the diversity of ideological perspectives partially reflected varying generational experiences and proclivities of older Nisei, younger Nisei, and Sansei. Sansei and younger Nisei have been portrayed as more likely to participate in radical, liberationist-oriented politics, in contrast to older Nisei who sought reform and assimilationist or integrationist policies.[51] Still, scholars have been careful to note that the divergence in political perspectives among Japanese Americans cannot be measured by generation alone. For example, as Daryl Maeda has shown, during the Third World Strike at San Francisco State College from November 1968 to March 1969, Asian American students, including a number of Sansei, were joined by a number of prominent Nisei progressives including Edison Uno, Raymond Okamura, Yori Wada, Lloyd Wake, and James Hirabayashi against the university president S. I. Hayakawa, a Canadian Nisei and Cold War racial liberal who sought to end the strike. Among the group, Wada was raised as a Shin Buddhist.[52] In his study of Los Angeles Nisei Week festivals, Lon Kurashige has demonstrated that, during the 1960s, the lines between Nisei and Sansei political ideologies could become blurred. A 1967 Japanese American Research Project survey found that a majority of Nisei and Sansei were in agreement in their *opposition* to social protest.[53] At the same time, Kurashige found that a small number of Nisei and Sansei liberals and radicals joined forces to challenge "group orthodoxy, leadership and relations to white America" espoused by an earlier generation of Nisei leaders with a new "radical cosmopolitanism."[54]

Domestic Containment and Cold War Civil Rights

The record of the BCA and its predominantly Nisei lay leadership and Issei priests from the resettlement era through the 1960s was consistent with Cold War domestic containment ideology and the racial liberal arguments that the organization and its Nisei leadership posited in arguing for full inclusion as American citizens. Ethnic Buddhist demonstrations of martial sacrifice, paired with family Buddhism programs that defined the sangha through heteronormative nuclear families with traditional gender roles, supported portrayals of Buddhist religion as contributing to the "success story" of Japanese Americans as a "model minority."

BCA's policies and statements on broader domestic and foreign policy issues such as civil rights and Cold War developments, particularly as they affected Buddhist nations or nations with significant numbers of Buddhists over the course of the 1950s and into the 1960s, reflected its transpacific connections to Buddhists in Japan and Asia as well as its adherence to Cold War racial liberalism. As discussed earlier, many Nisei Buddhists espoused a Cold War racial liberalism that, while committed to the general principle of racial equality, in practice prioritized issues affecting the Nikkei community. As was true in the broader general Nikkei community, BCA had been relatively silent on the issue of African American civil rights through the 1950s and early 1960s compared to other liberal religious groups. As Mark Brilliant has shown in the case of California, though civil rights activists from a diverse group of racial minorities occasionally crossed paths in the 1950s and 1960s, they did not converge into a broader long-term coalition.[55] As Greg Robinson noted, by the 1960s, among the handful of Nisei who had been active supporters of protests led by Reverend Dr. Martin Luther King and the Southern Christian Leadership Conference, "most Nisei expressed negative attitudes toward the black freedom movement which they considered at best as irrelevant to their interests and at worst as a threat to social stability. African Americans, conversely found little to share with their erstwhile allies."[56]

The actions of Black and white Protestant ministers and Jewish Rabbis who joined the Congress of Racial Equality and Student Nonviolent Coordinating Committee Interfaith Freedom Rides, in June 1961, were not mentioned in BCA publications. Not until August of 1963 did BCA's leadership take its first major public stand on the issue of civil rights. BCA's response came two months after President Kennedy had addressed the nation on the issue and as some 250,000 people took part in the March on Washington for Jobs and Freedom, on August 27, 1963. BCA ministers discussed civil rights during a three-day meeting that opened the same day as the march. In addressing "the race problem in the U.S.A.," BCA's ministers issued a public statement that unanimously supported the adoption of civil rights legislation by the federal government. The ministers noted their "stand on the basic principle of the Sangha—brotherhood of all men—in urging Congress to pass the Civil Rights legislation."[57] Meanwhile, BCA's 356-member board of directors passed a "strong civil rights resolution" to urge the passage of pending legislation. Like the BCA minister's resolution, the BCA board members' resolution also invoked the principle of the sangha as a brotherhood of all.[58]

BCA's ministers and lay leaders were more active in expressing opposition to local challenges to civil rights the following year, when they actively worked to oppose Proposition 14, a California voter initiative that would eliminate a California fair housing law established a year earlier. As Scott Kurashige has explained, Proposition 14 brought together every civil rights organization in the state of California. Japanese American organizations including the JACL, Buddhist and Christian churches, and others joined together with Mexican American and African American organizations and prominent leaders within the Democratic Party, including governor Edmund Brown.[59] BCA ministers' official endorsement of the "No on Proposition 14" position was published in the *American Buddhist* in October 1964.

> **Whereas** Buddhism is a religion which stands on the basic principle of Sangha—the dignity of the individual man and the brotherhood of all men; and **Whereas** we Buddhists who uphold this principle believe in basic human rights and equal justice for all peoples regardless of race,

creed and color; and **Whereas** we support the existing California Fair Housing Laws; and **Whereas** the proposed Constitutional Amendment will foster discrimination: Therefore be it **Resolved,** that we the Buddhist ministers of the Buddhist Churches of America, assembled at the annual Ministerial Conference in Gardena, California on August 25, 26, 27, 1964, do hereby unanimously express our opposition to the proposed California Constitutional Amendment on housing (Proposition 14); and be it: **Resolved** further, That copies of this resolution be distributed to all our churches urging our members to vote against Proposition 14.[60]

In a rare political editorial that took a strong position on civil rights, the *American Buddhist*'s editor, Hiroshi Kashiwagi, described Proposition 14 as legalizing discrimination in housing and as a threat to all minority groups including those of Japanese ancestry. He asked readers to consider, "Why is it that in San Francisco for example, the Japanese population is concentrated only in certain areas of the city? Why is it that there are so few if any Japanese in such districts as Lakeshore, Parkmerced, Pacific Heights, Sea Cliff, St. Francis Woods and Forest Hills?" Kashiwagi reasoned that "finance cannot be the reason, for there are many affluent Japanese who can easily afford to live in these districts."[61] He concluded that the passage of Proposition 14 could "easily undermine all the hard-won gains in human dignity and community acceptance of the Japanese people in California."[62] Striking a similar tone, Sandra Izumizaki refuted Proposition 14's claims of "reverse discrimination," noting that "the issue is whether privileged groups have the additional 'right' to discriminate by race, color or creed (this sounds almost unconstitutional) or whether the universal right of every man's human dignity will be recognized by the state."[63]

Outspoken public support for national civil rights legislation in 1963, and opposition to California Proposition 14 in 1964, challenge conventional representations of Japanese Americans and Buddhists as an apolitical model minority. Yet, they also represented Cold War liberal responses directed toward moderate reform through legislation. Over time, these limited responses to civil rights reform would be challenged by a younger generation of more progressive BCA members.

Containment Abroad

The hopeful sentiment shared by Nisei participants in the World Fellowship of Buddhists in elevating Buddhism as part of the process of decolonization in the 1950s was increasingly tempered by the late 1950s and into the 1960s. Following the 1963 coup in Burma (Myanmar) of U Nu's Socialist Buddhist government and the imprisonment of WFB's president at the time, the Burmese lay leader U Chan Htoon, WFB headquarters moved to Bangkok, Thailand, a key SEATO ally of the United States, and the Thai Princess Poon Diskul was elected president, a position that she would hold for the next twenty-two years. The inclusiveness of the organization—with representatives from nations throughout Asia, as well as the United States, Soviet Union, and an assortment of nations in Western Europe, in addition to the People's Republic of China and Taiwan (the Republic of China)—often meant that it was unable to find common ground on key issues.

BCA's Nisei Buddhist leaders did advocate for Buddhists in international affairs. This was relatively politically uncontroversial in anticommunist Cold War America, when they were advocating for Tibetan Buddhists after the People's Republic of China invaded Tibet in 1959. However, BCA was also willing to condemn the persecution of Buddhists by US ally Diem Ngo in South Vietnam that resulted in mass protests in 1963. In this respect, BCA's leaders were influenced by their connections to Buddhists throughout the world that, in the postwar period, had begun with their participation in the World Fellowship of Buddhists organization.

Despite their condemnation of Buddhist oppression, BCA's leaders also continued to support American Cold War foreign policy throughout the 1960s. Accepting the tenets of Cold War liberalism abroad as a corollary of racial liberalism at home, BCA's leaders presumed that an American presence and American leadership in Vietnam was necessary to address the persecution of Buddhists and other human rights abuses. In the aftermath of government suppression of Buddhists in May 1963, Buddhists in South Vietnam called on the government of Diem Ngo to support five demands. They asked that the government once again allow the Buddhist flag to fly; that Buddhists be treated as equals with Catholics; that arbitrary arrests of Buddhists in Hue and the victimization of Buddhists more generally be halted; that freedom of worship be extended to Buddhists; and that compensation be provided for those killed or injured in the violent suppressions. World Fellowship of Buddhist leaders and regional centers passed resolutions in support of the Buddhists.[64]

In the aftermath of the highly publicized self-immolation by the Buddhist monk Thich Quang Duc in June 1963 in protest of the Ngo government, BCA's Bishop Hanayama sent telegraph messages to President Kennedy, United Nations Secretary-General U Thant, Pope Paul VI, and President U Chan Htoon of the World Fellowship of Buddhists, pleading for "an early settlement to the problem."[65] As the crisis broadened and self-immolations continued, BCA's ministers established September 15 as South Vietnam Immolation Victims Memorial Service

Day, with all of BCA's churches conducting "a 24 hour vigil and a Memorial Service." Ministers wrote President Kennedy and Ambassador Henry Cabot Lodge "urging a speedy solution to the problem."[66]

BCA ministers also issued a statement in August 1963 that addressed the crisis, viewing it as "lamentable" and expressing hope that "peace and religious freedom will prevail in Vietnam." They urged their members to write their congressmen and senators in protest of "the use of American funds in supporting a government that uses violence against Buddhist monks and nuns and desecrates sacred places of worship."[67] Meanwhile, BCA's leadership received $1,375.25 from its member churches and temples after requesting that they take up a special collection during memorial services held on September 15, 1963, in support of Buddhist protestors in Vietnam. BCA then forwarded the money to the head monk in Saigon via the US embassy in South Vietnam.[68]

Despite these concerns, BCA leadership continued to express confidence in and support for American Cold War policy abroad. In the midst of President Lyndon Johnson's bid for reelection, two hundred delegates of the BCA general meeting passed a resolution in support of Johnson. An excerpt published in the February 1964 issue of *American Buddhist* read,

> Whereas the President's aim in these critical times is the ultimate attainment of peace for all mankind; and whereas this conforms to the accepted Buddhist principle of the oneness of all life; now therefore be it resolved that the Buddhists of America . . . go on record as highly commending the efforts of the President and pledge united support toward the realization of this objective.[69]

In his summary, "Notable Events of 1964," Bishop Shinsho Hanayama described the resolution as a "Pledge of Loyalty to President Johnson."[70]

By March 1965, President Johnson initiated a massive bombing campaign of North Vietnam and began to send American ground troops to Vietnam. As late as November 1965, BCA president Dr. Kikuo Taira delivered an address to the World Fellowship of Buddhists on behalf of Johnson, noting that the United States pledged to "work unstintingly for the attainment of peace, freedom, health and social opportunity for all."[71] While a departure from the apolitical representation of Japanese American Buddhists presented in the model minority stereotype, BCA's positions in support of US Cold War foreign policy, like its moderate positions on domestic civil rights, increasingly ran up against more radical critiques by younger Sansei and white members.

Challenges to the Cold War Racial Liberal Tenets
of Nisei Buddhism

By the 1960s, the Cold War domestic containment and racial liberalism endorsed by Nisei leaders would increasingly raise questions among a contingent of
younger, more liberal and progressive Nisei, Sansei, and white convert Buddhist members. These members were influenced by a decade of civil rights activism and burgeoning antiwar, second-wave feminist, and gay liberation social
and political movements that challenged the Cold War domestic ideology and
discourse around heteronormative nuclear families, gender roles, and normative
sexuality. As Robert Self has described it, the social movements initiated the
challenge to the "liberal version of the idealized nuclear family by demanding
rights not imagined by existing legal and political institutions."[72]

As discussed in chapter 6, Miss Bussei contests persisted, and complaints about
the contests grew over the course of the late 1950s and early 1960s. Added to complaints about lack of Buddhist spirit were criticisms of the focus on idealized
femininity and body image that foreshadowed protests of beauty pageants by second wave feminists in the late 1960s. Writing in 1964, Sansei Janice Nakao raised
a common long-standing criticism of YBA conferences when she pointed to an
overemphasis on social activities in contrast to religious ones. However, unlike
prior commentaries, Nakao's quickly turned to objections that she and others had
raised about both oratorical debates and Miss Bussei contests:

> The primary one is that they are *contests* and thus involve competition and
> conflict, while in Buddhism the emphasis has always been on cooperation
> and harmony. Therefore, it appears that the contests and the Teachings are
> in opposition to one another. To some also the Miss Bussei contests seem
> to have degenerated into a beauty contest with greatest criterion being per-
> sonality. In which case the contest does not seem necessary. The money
> and time could perhaps be used for other more meaningful purposes [em-
> phasis original].[73]

By 1969, in a move likely designed to counter charges of sexism in Buddhist
pageants, the Central California YBA allowed its young Buddhists to pick two
winners for its annual carnival celebration (and YBA conference) by combin-
ing the Miss Bussei contest with a Dream Man title.[74]

A rare subversion of Cold War heteronormativity and cis-gender norms established as part of Nisei family Buddhism also emerged in a YBA publication in
1962. In contrast to a vast array of photo collages over the course of the 1950s that

stressed heteronormative romantic socializing and distinct gender identities and roles, two portraits produced for the 1962 CCYBA publication used collage to present bodies and a variety of suggested social encounters and relations that seemed to playfully parody and destabilize the hegemony of heteronormative relations and cisgender identity. In one densely populated and fascinating collage titled "the search," an image of a young boy in the top-right corner of the collage was paired with cutout text, "... he knows ..." implying a very early internal and hidden acknowledgment about the subject(s) of the collage as a whole. Another image located at the bottom-left of the collage of a smiling young woman's head attached to a masculine torso posing in a t-shirt with a beer can in hand, was paired with photos of two men and the text "good looking," which seemed to be linked with an ambiguously placed cutout text of "man." A man at the center of the collage who appears to be the focal point of attention among an array of Nisei women and men is accompanied with the text, "**BEN-HUR ... loved Ben, hated Hur!" and the woman's photo paired with the text "sweetheart."[75]

A second collage, clearly produced by the same author(s) and titled, "Life in this here America/Scenes we'd like to See," included more Nisei Buddhists but branched out to include celebrities like Elizabeth Taylor, who was pictured with her hands on the shoulders of a young Nisei, who was accompanied by the word "Boredom." The collages also included commentary on the success-driven values of Nisei women, four of whom were teamed with an older white man and labeled as the investment management team, "Merrill, Lynch, Pierce, Fenner & Smith." A pair of male heads attached to female torsos in dresses were labeled, "almost human." Meanwhile a white couple is paired with "Why Worry?" and a number of Nisei women hold small heads or heads with torsos.[76] While breaking the gender binary in some ways, the collages still relied on male and female codes of the sex/gender system to do so. Still, the collages might have resonated with and affirmed fellow closeted gay, lesbian, and transgender Nisei Buddhists.

As the war in Vietnam escalated, it exposed growing ideological and age-cohort fissures that were emerging in BCA around the issue of Cold War liberalism at home and abroad. In contrast to BCA's official support for Cold War containment policy in Vietnam and elsewhere, beginning in 1965 and continuing through the early 1970s, BCA faced challenges from a small but vocal contingent of younger progressive Sansei, Nisei, and white convert Buddhists who expressed their opposition to the war and urged BCA to take a more critical position. BCA also faced the challenge of declining membership among its young adult members, with some joining more progressive social and political organ-

Figure 7.2. "The Search," CCYBA *Bussei Review,* 1962. Reprinted from CCYBA *Bussei Review,* 1962, p. 27, Buddhist Churches of America Archives, JANM.

izations. These mirrored larger developments among the American populace that emerged following the initiation in February 1965 of Operation Rolling Thunder, a massive aerial bombing campaign followed by President Johnson's extensive escalation of American ground troops in Vietnam beginning in March of 1965. The first of a wave of faculty- and student-led "teach-ins" was held on March 24, 1965, at the University of Michigan, spreading to other campuses nationwide including Berkeley. Meanwhile, the Students for a Democratic Society organized a demonstration against the war in Washington, DC, on April 17, 1965, in which twenty-five thousand participated.[77]

Growing concern about the war in Vietnam emerged regularly in oratorical speeches given by Sansei youth and then published in YBA newsletters and the *American Buddhist*. One Sansei, Joanne Uyeda, addressed the issue of the transformed approaches of Vietnamese Buddhists in an oratorical speech that took first place at a Northwest Buddhist League convention in 1965. Uyeda, a sixteen-year-old high school student, reflected on the transformation from nonviolent protests, including the highly publicized self-immolation by Buddhist priests, to more recent armed resistance, a transformation that she feared might lead to an increasingly negative perception of Buddhists, including those in the United States.[78] Uyeda thoughtfully noted the difficulty in interpreting these actions with only incomplete information. She asked, "Even though traditionally Buddhism has opposed violence, was it necessary for the South Vietnamese to turn to violence when other means of demonstration failed, or could what is happening in Vietnam be an example of the degradation of our Buddhist principles?"[79] Acknowledging the difficulty in answering this, she instead recounted a Buddhist doctrine that she had been taught:

> In this doctrine, the Buddha teaches us that no matter what the problem may be, we should not be swayed by the emotions of others and our own and we should accept nothing on hearsay, tradition, or dogma. He taught his disciples not even to accept his words without investigating all the principles of his teachings, and to try them out by every test or reason and by their application to everyday life.[80]

Returning to the question of Vietnam, Uyeda found herself "questioning their actions," because their intentions in resorting to violence and armed resistance were not clear.

A year later, Gary Yamamoto's speech, titled "Sangha in Action," which won both the CCYBA and WYBL's oratorical contest, addressed the suffering produced in race riots at home and the war abroad in Vietnam. Yamamoto noted,

Screaming with terror amidst the furious noises of war, a Vietnamese woman clutches her blood-drenched child; a Viet Cong prisoner's mouth and eyes are taped so as not to allow him to yell and spot friendly positions as he is taken back to a compound; a twenty-one year old American lies dead on a bed of spiked bamboo shoots. Malnutrition, fear, torture, sleeplessness, loneliness, filth, and death describe the Vietnamese way of life.[81]

"Why can't we do something before the tragedy occurs, why wait for the inevitable shock causing us to act?" Yamamoto asked. "Are these the fruits of Sangha: destruction, violence and misunderstanding?" In addressing how fellow Buddhists could respond to such a situation, Yamamoto noted the actions described in story he had read in the *Fresno Bee* about Mildred Lisette Norman, known as the "Peace Pilgrim," who by 1966 had walked 14,000 miles, across forty-eight US states, Canada, and Mexico. Yamamoto quoted Norman, who stated that she would continue, "until man learns the way of peace . . . and overcomes evil with good, falsehood with truth, hatred with love."[82] Yamamoto concluded by underscoring the notion of the sangha as "the idea of brotherhood of all human beings" noting that "we must be earnest, sincere and steadfast in our search for the realm of Sangha until we feel Amida's Compassion in our inner most hearts and truly experience the satisfaction offered by Sangha."[83]

Antiwar and prowar positions on Vietnam also emerged in *American Buddhist* from among the small but vocal group of white convert Buddhists. Calvin Steinmetz argued that Buddhists were not fighting a religious war, but rather fighting against Catholicism as a component of French colonialism. Given this, Steinmetz asked, "Should we therefore not listen more sympathetically to 'demonstrators' even in our own country and not be so quick to call them traitors and rioters? Do we really know for ourselves what the 'student movement' or the 'peace movement' or even facets of the 'communist' movement are all about?" Steinmetz concluded, with a plea, emphasized in boldface type, for a return to Buddhist temples and reflection on interdependence. "All ideas should flow through our Buddhist temples and study classes and no aspect of interdependence living should be avoided in our search for reality." [84]

Anticipating and seeking to placate controversy in his "Notes from the Staff," editor Hiroshi Kashiwagi stated, "We think you will form some definite opinions after reading the article by Calvin C. Steinmetz. Whether you agree with the writer or not, the problem he discusses is one that is with us and there is no getting around it."[85] Ideological divisions were not exclusive to ethnic Buddhists; Steinmetz received an angry letter a few months later from William J. Burtscher, another white

Buddhist who took a strong anticommunist position and chastised demonstrators both abroad and at home, concluding, "Demonstrations breed civil disorder and violence. This is not the way to correct inequities."[86]

Cyril Zimmerman complained in *American Buddhist*, "The field of civil rights, civil liberties, peace, the plight of farm labor, poverty, problems of educational reform all have escaped the attention of the Buddhist spokesmen." In contrast, Zimmerman noted that Japanese American Christians were more engaged in promoting social change. "They are to be found as participants in the labor and social movements and the peace movement. They apply their religious concepts to the problems of Japanese life." Zimmerman concluded that Buddhism had the potential to "revolutionize America and the world." For him, Buddhism was best suited "to seek and provide solutions for the individual and social suffering."[87]

Zimmerman's progressive agenda was refuted by Eugene Sasai, a Nisei who had long contributed to BCA publications and who defended Nisei Buddhism's racial liberal arguments as making a contribution to American society. Sasai stated,

> Why are American Buddhists so often maligned for not taking an active part in social problems, civil rights and liberties, or peace? In fact, where is the proof that this is true? I think we should point out to Mr. Zimmerman and others that every Buddhist "church" in America has been paid for partly with the blood and lives of American Buddhists. The countless numbers of Buddhist graves in our National cemeteries give cold and silent testimony.[88]

Sasai went on to endorse the model minority discourse of success that many Nisei in BCA had endorsed either in words or actions. He praised the work of Nisei Buddhists in the JACL and in the generation of teachers, doctors, and lawyers who had contributed to American society and who participated at the voting polls. Sasai asked, "Are they really less Buddhist because they don't burn draft cards?"[89]

The Cold War racial liberal politics of BCA's Nisei leaders like Sasai were increasingly viewed by younger and more progressive Buddhists as out of touch with rapidly changing events. By the late 1960s, some among BCA's Nisei leaders sought to steer BCA away from categorizing its younger members as juvenile delinquents or characterizing antiwar protest as a demonstration of lack of Buddhist spirit. In a 1968 article titled "Are We Blaming Student Attitudes for Our Own Shortcomings?" and published just months after the Tet Offensive and the assassinations of Reverend Dr. Martin Luther King Jr. in April and Democratic presidential nominee Robert Kennedy in June, Ricky Ito Taylor called for a reassessment of BCA's institutions and doctrine. Ito Taylor noted that "our young people don't dislike our Church system, they just ignore it," and continued, "Each year, the Church loses more bright young people for the wrong reasons. This is because they think the Church is dull, conformist, ethno-centered, only historical, doctrinaire, etc. and we haven't convinced them otherwise." In addressing the problem, Ito Taylor proposed that lay leaders begin "to recognize that today's youth is no longer interested in simply discussing the historical development of Buddhism, in the Japanese version of the Church and its functions." Instead, they "want the opportunity of practicing Buddhist philosophies and doctrines to help solve the great social issues of our time—ignorance, poverty, race relations and a dozen others."[90] Ito Taylor's article astutely pointed to the growing reality of the abandonment of BCA by its younger members as BCA's Cold War liberal positions on civil rights and Vietnam in 1963, which transitioned into more rigid and conservative reactionary politics in the mid-to-late 1960s, led many of its younger members to seek a home where they could reflect and act on the pressing concerns of the times.

Patty Hirota, whose father Tad had played a key role in guiding BCA through the tumultuous period of forced incarceration and resettlement was one such Sansei. Patty recalled her father's involvement as a leader in the Japanese American community as something that influenced her as well as her sister Sherry. Nevertheless, as a young person growing up in the 1960s, she was angered by what she viewed at the time as her father's "accommodationist" positions on adapting rather than resisting internment and joining the military.[91] As Hirota recalled, she "sort of rejected the Japanese American [Buddhist] church and all the traditional stuff." Instead, she got involved in progressive politics, working to repeal the McCarran Security Act and supporting Eugene McCarthy's 1968 campaign run before joining the Asian American Political Alliance and becoming active in the antiwar and Third World Liberation Front movements. Yet, rejecting the church never meant rejecting Buddhism. After moving to Illinois in 1971 with her first husband, professor Paul Wong, Patty enrolled in a course taught by Taitetsu Unno at the University of Illinois Urbana-Champaign. In 2011, Patty was ordained in the Sōtō Zen lineage of Shunryu Suzuki Roshi.[92]

Significantly, as she worked to create connections with the Japanese community of her youth, Hirota recalled that the most substantive factor fueling both her activism and search for community was anger generated by an awareness of Japanese American internment. After attending the University of California, she met up with like-minded Asian American students, noting, "There was a nisei student club and a Chinese American student club where Floyd Huen was president and I got really involved with that. The time was really ripe when AAPA, Asian

American Political Alliance was formed, and I felt like Ah! Those are my people."[93] As Daryl Maeda has explained, AAPA chapters were formed in Berkeley and San Francisco to draw individual Asian Americans together in coalition around New Left causes. They were active participants in the Third World Liberation Front strikes at San Francisco State University and the University of California, supported the Black Power movement and were against the war in Vietnam.[94]

In his youth, Ryo Imamura also recalled distancing himself from Buddhism. He noted, "When you're a preacher's kid, you get a negative view of the dynamics of the church, . . . and so I had no intention of becoming a minister myself." Instead, he studied mathematics at Berkeley and would later enter medical school at the University of Hawai'i. Imamura also became involved in antiwar and peace activism. Imamura's involvement also brought him back to Buddhism. After leading the protest discussed in the opening of this chapter, Imamura was confronted by the dean of the medical school, who described his participation in protests as "unbecoming of a doctor." Faced with an ultimatum, Imamura quit the medical school and decided to study for the priesthood. At the same time, Imamura's interest in Buddhism was driven by what he viewed as the shortcomings within activist circles. As he recalled,

> I was more and more troubled by the suffering in the world, focusing on Vietnam of course. I would go to all these peace rallies and marches and participate—and there seemed to be a lack of vision there. Even the peace groups would be competing and fighting against each other as to who would be in the front of the march, and criticizing each other. And somehow the Buddhist, it kept coming back to me. . . . I think I was snapped back into Buddhism after I got over being a preacher's kid, . . . began to see it in terms of my values, not only for myself, but in the context of the world and what was going on.[95]

Even as programs associated with Nisei Buddhism came to predominate the BCA, criticism of the Cold War racial liberalism that undergirded these programs was increasingly raised by a cohort of younger progressive Nisei, Sansei, and white convert Buddhists. Early challenges from convert Buddhists in the 1950s reflected a bias toward Zen Buddhism and a more exotic "Oriental" vision of what Buddhist practice and sangha looked like. Some convert Buddhists were unhappy with aspects of Shin Buddhist doctrine that stressed communal temple worship and the modified acculturated practices of Japanese Americans that resembled Protestantism. In contrast to the lively debates of the 1950s, by the 1960s, BCA's Cold War racial liberalism had gravitated from moderate toward a more conservative reactionary position, as it failed to adequately respond to rapidly changing political events and social transformations abroad, at home, and among its membership. While some of BCA's younger members sought to democratize the institution and push it toward a more progressive political agenda, others left BCA altogether, finding and working with like-minded political and social activists.

Conclusion

Nisei Buddhist leadership and Nisei Buddhism continued to dominate the Buddhist Churches of America until well into the 1990s. The Canadian-born Reverend Takashi Tsuji, the former head of the Buddhist Department of Education and a key Cold War liberal and proponent of family Buddhism, would become the first Nisei to be appointed bishop of the Buddhist Churches of America in 1968. He was succeeded by Reverend Haruo Yamaoka, BCA's first American Nisei to serve as bishop, from 1981 until 1996. Under Bishop Yamaoka's leadership, the Institute of Buddhist Studies was affiliated as a graduate school and seminary with the Graduate Theological Union in 1985.[1] In 2006, BCA completed construction of a new Jodo Shinshu Center in Berkeley at a cost of ten million dollars. Home to IBS, the JSC also included a Center for Buddhist Education for lay members and the general public, a Jodo Shinshu International Office for the global propagation of Shin Buddhism, and the Ryukoku University Berkeley Center to assist Ryukoku University students and faculty abroad, as well as conference facilities and lodging.[2]

Nisei also continued to maintain strong influence in BCA's national and local boards of directors for decades. Meanwhile, Nisei and Sansei ministers trained in Japan and at the Institute for Buddhist Studies joined new Issei ministers from Japan. In contrast to prewar Issei ministers, these ministers' importance in propagating Shin Buddhist teachings in communities did not translate into political power relative to BCA's lay leaders. Ministers circulated through BCA congregations, often with three-year terms, and the Minister's Association maintained a secondary political status. Meanwhile, the overall numbers of BCA's membership declined from a peak of an estimated 65,000 members in 1977 to 50,775 in 1995.[3] In 2021, BCA comprised sixty affiliated temples, with an estimated active membership of twelve thousand.[4]

These declining numbers stand in contrast to the vast growth in numbers of Asian Buddhist immigrants who arrived in the United States after the passage of the 1965 Immigration Act. The post-1965 wave of Asian Buddhist immigrants and refugees representing Theravada, Mahayana, and Tibetan Buddhist traditions arrived under a diverse set of circumstances, from war refugees in Southeast Asia to highly skilled professionals. While arriving in a different historical moment, these Buddhist immigrants also shared some of the challenges once faced by Shin Buddhists and other earlier Buddhist arrivals, to negotiate a place for themselves as racial and religious minorities in America. Even as the nation increasingly acknowledged its cultural and religious diversity, the mythology of an implicitly white Christian nation persisted.[5]

BCA's declining membership also stood in contrast to the rising popularity of Buddhism among non-Asian Americans. Growing numbers of Americans who had not been raised in a Buddhist tradition were increasingly drawn to Buddhism. The interest in Zen initiated by D. T. Suzuki and the Beats in the 1950s increased first within the American counterculture and then spread to the broader American society, where it spawned study centers and Buddhist publications such as *Tricycle: The Buddhist Review,* founded in 1990. Reflecting on the diversity of Buddhists in America, *Tricycle* editor Helen Tworkov stated, in 1992, that "the spokespeople for Buddhism in America have been, almost exclusively, educated members of the white middle class." In contrast, "even with varying statistics, Asian-American Buddhists number at least one million, but so far they have not figured prominently in the development of something called American Buddhism."[6]

In a letter to the editor, Ryo Imamura wrote that Tworkov's comments were "inaccurate and racist." Imamura noted the long history of Asian immigrants, including his grandparents and parents, who had transplanted Buddhism to America despite "white intolerance and bigotry," concluding that it was "Asian Buddhists who welcomed countless white Americans into our temples, introduced them to the Dharma, and often assisted them to initiate their own Sanghas when they felt uncomfortable practicing with us." Calling out Tworkov on her definition of "American Buddhism," Imamura stated, "It is apparent that Tworkov has restricted "American Buddhism" to mean "white American Buddhism," and that her statement is even more misleading than one claiming that Americans of color did not figure prominently in the development of American history."[7] Imamura's rebuttal sparked a debate among *Tricycle*'s board members and readership. Gary Snyder resigned from *Tricycle*'s board as a result of the controversy, and a special issue, "Dharma, Diversity and Race," was published in the fall of 1994.[8]

That the presence of Asian American Buddhists, including the Shin Buddhist members of the Buddhist Churches of America, could be so easily overlooked, even after almost one hundred years since its founding, attested to the racial discourse that had shaped and sought to preserve "Buddhism's" foreignness as well as direct its future development in a nation that, despite growing racial and religious diversity, continued to be imagined as a white Christian settler nation.

Yet, as this study has shown, together with American Orientalist discourse, during the transwar period, racial liberalism and the racial liberal strategies associated with Nisei Buddhism also played a role in sustaining this fictive imagining of American Buddhism.

Ironically, as this book has demonstrated, Nisei Buddhism's adaptations, which were developed in response to racial and religious discrimination and persecution, complemented efforts by convert Buddhists to maintain Buddhism as an idealized foreign religion. The ethnic and family Buddhist programs implemented in efforts to rebuild a prewar Nikkei sangha were celebrated not by white convert Buddhist practitioners and enthusiasts, but by conservatives interested in highlighting the contributions of Buddhism toward a neoliberal story of a Japanese American work ethic that purportedly enabled model minorities to assimilate, achieve economic and social mobility, and dissolve into the American mainstream.

Yet, even as Nisei Shin Buddhism appeared to have faded from the American national imaginary, new stories of regeneration emerged to meet the unfolding needs of an ever-changing sangha. Despite the maintenance of a relatively low national public profile beyond Shin Buddhist communities, Nikkei Buddhist communities would grow to include multiple generations of Sansei, Yonsei, Gosei, Hapa, new Issei, and an increasingly racially diverse group of non-ethnic Buddhists. Shin Buddhist institutions also reached out and engaged in greater intercultural and interreligious dialogue, and embraced greater diversity among its members in terms of class, race, gender, and sexuality.

Still others, who had been marginally involved in Shin Buddhist communities earlier in their lives, found themselves returning years later. The story of Keith Kojimoto, a Sansei from the San Francisco Bay Area, highlights the role that Shin Buddhist temples and their members continued to play in contemplating dying and death and in sustaining and regenerating the sangha. During most of his life, Kojimoto had little to no contact with Shin Buddhism or the Shin Buddhist community. In contrast, his father Mitsunobu, or "Mits," as he was known, had grown up as a Nisei around the Buddhist Church of San Francisco in the 1930s. An athletic youth, Mits played basketball and attended services. Mits married Sadame (née Hara) at BCSF in 1950. The couple had three children, including Keith, and two daughters Kathryn and Carrie, who were raised in an interreligious household. Mits served as a board member and in various other capacities at BCSF, while Sadame, a Christian, attended services at the nearby Japanese American Pine Methodist Church. As Mits recollected, "The kids are not a part of the church. Maybe it's our fault, but maybe those times, they always picture or remember the

Buddhist church in . . . Japanese. . . . You know, the sutras and all that stuff is kind of hard to . . . hear."[9]

Keith grew up a music fan, attending concerts and playing guitar. During high school, he joined antiwar marches and Black Panther Party rallies. He attended Berkeley in the 1960s and, like Patty Hirota, Keith found a like-minded community of social activists when he joined the Asian American Political Alliance. Keith joined the Third World Liberation Front strike at Berkeley in 1969. He was a community organizer for years before joining a large Japanese electronics corporation, and then a software corporation for three decades. Following his father's death in 2009, Keith found himself returning to the Buddhist church. As he recalled of his involvement, "When [my father] passed, they really gave me and our family so much support. Of course, I wanted to give back. . . . In the beginning, it was a little bit social." Over time, he and his wife, Priscilla, who was on a "spiritual journey" exploring Buddhism and Christianity, delved more deeply into Buddhist teachings. Keith noted that "since we're both atheists, it kind of struck me that what attracts us to Buddhism, besides the fact [that] I think the church is still important . . . in the Japanese community, is that maybe through all the political stuff, you lose a little bit of the focus that we're really just talking about people." Keith would go on to serve on the board of directors of the Buddhist Church of San Francisco.[10]

Keith Kojimoto's gravitation to the Buddhist church and Buddhist teachings highlights the recurring centrality of the sangha as a living force in the transmission of the dharma. It is a reminder that the historic struggles of BCA to maintain their temples and congregations, and a place in American national culture, was always interconnected with the ordinary, everyday struggles faced by sentient beings.

Notes

Introduction

1. Toshio Yoshida, Buddhist Golden Jubilee Committee, "Buddhist Golden Jubilee, Souvenir Program," August 21–29, 1948, San Francisco, California, p. 3, BCA Archives, Institute of Buddhist Studies, Berkeley, California.

2. "Buddhist Golden Jubilee, Souvenir Program"; Misao Nakamura, "Bussei Listen to Civic Leader," *Rafu Shimpo,* August 28, 1948, p. 1.

3. "Buddhist Jubilee: San Francisco Japanese Have 50th Anniversary," *LIFE,* September 20, 1948, p. 77.

4. For a discussion of *bukkyō tōzen* among the Issei, see Duncan Ryūken Williams and Tomoe Moriya, eds., *Issei Buddhism in the Americas* (Urbana: University of Illinois Press, 2010), ix–x; See, also, Duncan Ryūken Williams, *American Sutra: A Story of Faith and Freedom in the Second World War* (Cambridge, MA: Harvard University Press, 2019), 8–9.

5. For a discussion of Issei Shin Buddhism in America see, Tetsuden Kashima, *Buddhism in America: The Social Organization of an Ethnic Religious Institution* (Westport, CT: Greenwood Press, 1977); Michihiro Ama, *Immigrants to the Pure Land: The Modernization, Acculturation, and Globalization of Shin Buddhism, 1898–1941* (Honolulu: University of Hawai'i Press, 2011); Williams and Moriya, *Issei Buddhism in the Americas.*

6. For a discussion of American racial liberal ideology at home and abroad during the years between World War II and the Cold War, see Mae Ngai, *Impossible Subjects: Illegal Aliens and the Making of Modern America* (Princeton, NJ: Princeton University Press, 2004); Takashi Fujitani, *Race for Empire: Koreans and Japanese and Japanese as Americans During World War II* (Berkeley: University of California Press, 2011); Ellen D. Wu, *The Color of Success: Asian Americans and the Origins of the Model Minority* (Princeton, NJ: Princeton University Press, 2014).

7. Ellen Wu has coined the phrase "assimilating Others" to capture the impact of racial liberal discourse in reconstituting Asian Americans in relation to the American nation. See Wu, *Color of Success,* 4.

8. See Wu, *Color of Success;* Cindy I-Fen Cheng, *Citizens of Asian America: Democracy and Race during the Cold War* (New York: New York University Press, 2013); Jane H. Hong, *Opening the Gates to Asia: A Transpacific History of How America Repealed Asian Exclusion* (Chapel Hill: University of North Carolina Press, 2019).

9. Henry Yu, *Thinking Orientals: Migration, Contact and Exoticism in Modern America* (New York: Oxford University Press, 2001), 63–68.

10. Arissa H. Oh, *To Save the Children of Korea: The Cold War Origins of International Adoption* (Palo Alto, CA: Stanford University Press, 2015); David Hollinger, *Protestants Abroad:*

How Missionaries Tried to Change the World but Changed America (Princeton, NJ: Princeton University Press, 2017); Christina Klein, *Cold War Orientalism: Asia in the Middlebrow Imagination* (Berkeley: University of California Press, 2003).

11. Oh, *To Save the Children;* Ronit Stahl, *Enlisting Faith: How the Military Chaplaincy Shaped Religion and State in Modern America* (Cambridge, MA: Harvard University Press, 2017).

12. See Klein, *Cold War Orientalism,* 23.

13. James C. Dobbins, *Jōdo Shinshū: Shin Buddhism in Medieval Japan* (Honolulu: University of Hawai'i Press, 2002), 3, 24–27.

14. Nishi Honganji has often historically been romanized as "Nishi Hongwanji." I omit the "w" in this work, except where it appears in historical sources and citations. Kashima, *Buddhism in America,* 13–18; Ama, *Immigrants to the Pure Land,* 34–39.

15. Kashima, *Buddhism in America,* chapter 3; David Yoo, *Growing Up Nisei: Race, Generation, and Culture among Japanese Americans of California* (Urbana: University of Illinois Press, 2000), 44–45; BCA, *Buddhist Churches of America, Volume 1, 75 Year History, 1899–1974* (Chicago: Nobart, 1974).

16. For a discussion of Japanese American biculturalism in a secular context, see Lon Kurashige, *Japanese American Celebration and Conflict: A History of Ethnic Identity and Festival, 1934–1990* (Berkeley: University of California Press, 2002). For a discussion of the social and religious world of Nisei, see Yoo, *Growing Up Nisei,* especially chapter 2.

17. Ama, *Immigrants to the Pure Land,* 66–70.

18. In his classic history of Shin Buddhism in America, Tetsuden Kashima challenged earlier characterizations of Buddhist adaptations as representing the "Protestantized" assimilation of Buddhism to Christianity. While acknowledging external modifications to forms of practice, Kashima argued that Nikkei Buddhists continued to maintain core religious beliefs. See Kashima, *Buddhism in America.* Building on this distinction, Michihiro Ama characterized the acculturative process of Issei Shin Buddhism as a "blending process involving 'Japanization' and 'Americanization,'" with Shin Buddhist ministers responding to the introduction of Western religion and modernization in Meiji Japan, as well as to American nativism and traditions of religious pluralism and democracy in the United States. See Kashima, *Buddhism in America,* 15–16, 41–42; Ama, *Immigrants to the Pure Land,* 5–7.

19. Studies of racial minorities and Cold War cultural diplomacy include Mary L. Dudziak, *Cold War Civil Rights: Race and the Image of American Democracy* (Princeton, NJ: Princeton University Press, 2000); Penny Von Eschen, *Satchmo Blows Up the World: Jazz Ambassadors Play the Cold War* (Cambridge, MA: Harvard University Press, 2006); Cheng, *Citizens of Asian America;* Simeon Man, *Soldiering through Empire: Race and the Making of the Decolonizing Pacific* (Oakland: University of California Press, 2018); Hong, *Opening the Gates to Asia.*

20. In his study of the Los Angeles–based Nisei Week Festival, Lon Kurashige traced the emergence of a Nisei postwar strategy of "integration" that emphasized "inclusion" in mainstream social institutions, rather than an "immersion" into white America. Significantly, for Kurashige, integration did not necessitate an abandonment of ties with Japan. See Kurashige, *Japanese American Celebration and Conflict,* chapter 4, especially 120–121, 137–143. For a more recent study that situates Japanese Americans within transpacific networks of economic and cultural exchange, see Margaret Oda, *The Gateway to the Pacific: Japanese Americans and the Remaking of San Francisco* (Chicago: University of Chicago Press, 2019).

Chapter 1. Issei Buddhism to World War II

1. Shinobu Matsuura, *Higan: Compassionate Vow-Selected Writings of Shinobu Matsuura* (Berkeley: Matsuura Family, 1986), 67.

2. Jane Michiko Imamura, *Kaikyo, Opening the Dharma: Memoirs of a Buddhist Priest's Wife in America* (Berkeley, CA: Self-Published, 1998), 19.

3. Matsuura, *Higan,* 68.

4. For a discussion of immigrants and white settler-colonial discourse see, Alexander Saxton, *The Rise and Fall of the White Republic: Class Politics and Mass Culture in Nineteenth-Century America* (New York: Verso, 2003); Mae Ngai, *Impossible Subjects: Illegal Aliens and the Making of Modern America* (Princeton, NJ: Princeton University Press, 2004); Kornel Chang, *Pacific Connections: The Making of the U.S.-Canadian Borderlands* (Berkeley: University of California Press, 2012); Eiichiro Azuma, *In Search of Our Frontier: Japanese America and Settler Colonialism in the Construction of Japan's Borderless Empire* (Oakland: University of California Press, 2019). For a discussion of Buddhism in relation to American Orientalism, see Jane Iwamura, *Virtual Orientalism: Asian Religions and Popular Culture* (New York: Oxford University Press, 2011).

5. BCA, *Buddhist Churches of America, Volume 1, 75 Year History, 1899–1974* (Chicago: Nobart, 1974), 44–45; Historian Michihiro Ama situated the emergence of Issei Buddhism amid, on the one hand, Meiji-era modernization and imperial expansion and, on the other, US imperial expansion and processes of Anglo-Protestant exclusionism. See Michihiro Ama, *Immigrants to the Pure Land: The Modernization, Acculturation, and Globalization of Shin Buddhism* (Honolulu: University of Hawai'i Press, 2011), 5–6.

6. Roger Daniels, *Asian America: Chinese and Japanese in the United States since 1850* (Seattle: University of Washington Press, 1988), 100, 115.

7. Duncan Ryūken Williams, *American Sutra: A Story of Faith and Freedom in the Second World War* (Cambridge, MA: Harvard University Press, 2019), 276–277, ft. 39.

8. James C. Dobbins, *Jōdo Shinshū: Shin Buddhism in Medieval Japan* (Honolulu: University of Hawai'i Press, 2002), 3–7.

9. Yuji Ichioka, *The Issei: The World of the First Generation Japanese Immigrants, 1885–1924* (New York: The Free Press, 1988), 3–4, 102–110.

10. Tetsuden Kashima, *Buddhism in America: The Social Evolution of an Ethnic Religious Institution* (Westport, CT: Greenwood Press, 1977), 70.

11. Quoted in BCA, *Buddhist Churches of America, Volume 1,* 46.

12. Ichioka, *The Issei,* 17–22.

13. BCA, *Buddhist Churches of America, Volume 1,* 44–45. The origins of the formation of YMBAs in Japan is not completely clear. An American teaching at a university in Kyoto noted, in 1902, that Shin Buddhists priests and teachers in Tokyo had begun to consider the creation of Buddhist youth organizations along the lines of the Young Men's Christian Associations in the early 1880s. However, the first YMCAs appear to have been established in Japan in 1889. See Joseph A. Goodrich, "Young Men's Buddhist Association of Japan," *Public Opinion* 33, no. 14 (1902): 436. For a discussion of the establishment of Young Men's Christian Associations in Japan, see Jon Thares Davidann, *A World of Crisis and Progress: The American YMCA in Japan, 1890–1930* (Bethlehem, PA: Lehigh University Press, 1998), 40. Historian Stephen Prothero dates the formation of at least one YMBA in Japan to 1898, when Henry Steel Olcott, the American Buddhist sympathizer, visited the country. According to Prothero, Olcott, who played an

important role in the establishment of YMBAs in Sri Lanka in 1898, assisted in the establishment of a YMBA during his tour of Japan. See Stephen Prothero, *The White Buddhist: The Asian Odyssey of Henry Steel Olcott* (Bloomington: Indiana University Press, 1996), 6, 124–126.

14. James Ketelaar, *Of Heretics and Martyrs in Meiji Japan: Buddhism and Its Persecution* (Princeton, NJ: Princeton University Press, 1990); Judith Snodgrass, *Presenting Japanese Buddhism to the West: Orientalism, Occidentalism, and the Columbian Exposition* (Chapel Hill: University of North Carolina Press, 2003).

15. Snodgrass, *Presenting Japanese Buddhism,* 118–120.

16. Ama, *Immigrants to the Pure Land,* 24–27.

17. See Ketelaar, *Of Heretics and Martyrs,* chapter 4; Thomas A. Tweed, *The American Encounter with Buddhism, 1944–1912: Victorian Culture and the Limits of Dissent* (Chapel Hill: University of North Carolina Press, 2000), 31; Snodgrass, *Presenting Japanese Buddhism,* Introduction.

18. BCA, *Buddhist Churches of America, Volume 1,* 47; Ama, *Immigrants to the Pure Land,* 36.

19. Ama, *Immigrants to the Pure Land,* 39; Lori Pierce, "Buddhist Modernism in English-Language Buddhist Periodicals," in Duncan Ryūken Williams and Tomoe Moriya, eds., *Issei Buddhism in the Americas* (Urbana: University of Illinois Press, 2010), 87–88, 102.

20. Ama, *Immigrants to the Pure Land,* 40–41, 36. Nevertheless, as Eiichiro Azuma has argued, many of the developments in North America served as templates for future colonial endeavors in Asia. See Azuma, *In Search of Our Frontier: Japanese America and Settler Colonialism in the Construction of Japan's Borderless Empire* (Oakland: University of California Press, 2019).

21. See Ichioka, *The Issei,* especially chapter 5.

22. Ichioka, *The Issei,* 71–72.

23. Ama, *Immigrants to the Pure Land,* 88.

24. Ichioka, *The Issei,* 185–187.

25. Ichioka, *The Issei,* 185–187.

26. Ichioka, *The Issei,* 187–189; Brian Masaru Hayashi, *For the Sake of Our Japanese Brethren: Assimilation, Nationalism, and Protestantism among the Japanese of Los Angeles* (Palo Alto, CA: Stanford University Press, 1995), 29–30.

27. Ama, *Immigrants to the Pure Land,* 88.

28. Kashima, *Buddhism in America,* 17.

29. BCA, *Buddhist Churches of America, Volume 1,* 50.

30. Robert Spencer, "Japanese Buddhism in the United States, 1940–1946: A Study in Acculturation" (PhD diss., University of California Berkeley, 1946), 77.

31. Spencer, "Japanese Buddhism," 77.

32. David Yoo, "Enlightened Identities: Buddhism and the Japanese Americans of California, 1924–1941," *Western Historical Quarterly* 27, no. 3 (1994), 288.

33. Spencer, "Japanese Buddhism," 77.

34. Ichioka, *The Issei,* 226, 252–254.

35. Ichioka, *The Issei,* 200–202.

36. Ama, *Immigrants to the Pure Land,* 65–68.

37. BCA, *Buddhist Churches of America, Volume 1,* 53.

38. David Yoo, *Growing Up Nisei: Race, Generation, and Culture among Japanese Americans of California, 1924–49* (Urbana: University of Illinois Press, 2000), 38, 46.

39. Hiroshi Kashiwagi, *Starting from Loomis and Other Stories* (Boulder: University of Colorado Press, 2013), 32.

40. BCA, *Buddhist Churches of America, Volume 1,* 11, 53.

41. Yoo, *Growing Up Nisei,* 46.

42. Yoo, *Growing Up Nisei,* 46–51.

43. As part of the Geneva Peace Accord Agreements, some limited indirect communication via the government of Spain existed, but for the most part, Japanese Buddhist institutions were isolated.

44. Tetsuden Kashima, *Judgment without Trial: Japanese American Imprisonment during World War II* (Seattle: University of Washington Press, 2003), 49; Duncan Ryūken Williams, *American Sutra,* 67.

45. Greg Robinson, *By Order of the President: FDR and the Internment of Japanese Americans* (Cambridge, MA: Harvard University Press, 2001), 62; Kashima, *Judgment without Trial,* 228; Williams, *American Sutra,* 31.

46. As Stephen S. Fugita and Marilyn Fernandez have noted, in contrast to the targeting of Buddhist priests, Christian ministers of Japanese ancestry were not singled out by the government but were forcibly relocated with their parishioners months later. See Stephen Fugita and Marilyn Fernandez, *Altered Lives, Enduring Community: Japanese Americans Remember Their World War II Incarceration* (Seattle: University of Washington Press, 2004), 175–180.

47. Kashima, *Judgment without Trial,* ix; Williams, *American Sutra,* 19.

48. Bill Hosokawa, *Nisei: The Quiet Americans* (Boulder: University of Colorado Press, 2002), 256.

49. Lawrence E. Davies, "20 Aliens on Coast Seized with Arms," *New York Times,* February 11, 1942, p. 12.

50. Davies, "20 Aliens on Coast Seized with Arms," *New York Times,* 12.

51. Lawrence E. Davies, "6 Japanese Spies Seized on Coast," *New York Times,* March 22, 1942, p. 20.

52. Kashima, *Judgment without Trial,* 31.

53. Reverend Kenryo Kumata, Notes of Conference with Attorney Kido, San Francisco, CA, January 6, 1942, 1–3, BCA Collection, Japanese American National Museum (hereafter JANM); National Young Buddhist Association. National Young Buddhist Association, Minutes of the Emergency Meeting of the Buddhist Churches of America, December 19, 1941, BCA Collection, JANM. For a discussion of JACL's rising influence during this period, see Brian Masaru Hayashi, *Democratizing the Enemy: The Japanese American Internment* (Princeton, NJ: Princeton University Press, 2004), 73–75.

54. Reverend Kenryo Masara Kumata, Notes of telephone conversations with United States Naval Intelligence, December 26, 1941, to March 10, 1942, BCA Collection, JANM.

55. Williams, *American Sutra,* 60–61.

56. Buddhist Churches of America, "Minutes of the Emergency Meeting," San Francisco, California, February 15, 1942, 1–2, BCA Collection, JANM.

57. California Young Buddhist League Leaders, "Minutes of the Emergency Meeting," San Francisco, California, January 4, 1942, BCA Collection, JANM.

58. Reverend Kenryo M. Kumata to the Young Buddhist Associations in the United States, January 13, 1942, BCA Collection, JANM.

59. Williams, *American Sutra,* 58–60.

60. Kashima, *Buddhism in America,* 48.

61. Lon Kurashige, *Japanese American Celebration and Conflict: A History of Ethnic Identity and Festival, 1934–1990* (Berkeley: University of California Press, 2004), 79.

62. See Kashima, *Buddhism in America,* chapter 4.

Chapter 2. Forced Incarceration, Resettlement, and the Rise of Nisei Buddhism

1. Duncan Ryūken Williams, *American Sutra: A Story of Faith and Freedom in the Second World War* (Cambridge, MA: Harvard University Press, 2019), 102–103; Greg Robinson, *Tragedy of Democracy: Japanese American Confinement in North America* (New York: Columbia University Press, 2009), 131.

2. Williams, *American Sutra,* 114, 130–132.

3. Takashi Fujitani, *Race for Empire: Koreans as Japanese and Japanese as Americans* (Berkeley: University of California Press, 2011), 108–117.

4. Mae Ngai, *Impossible Subjects: Illegal Aliens and the Making of Modern America* (Princeton, NJ: Princeton University Press, 2004), 177. See also Brian Masaru Hayashi, *Democratizing the Enemy: The Japanese American Internment* (Princeton, NJ: Princeton University Press, 2004); John Howard, *Concentration Camps on the Homefront: Japanese Americans in the House of Jim Crow* (Chicago: University of Chicago Press, 2008); Ayanna Yonemura, *Race, Nation, War: Japanese American Forced Removal, Public Policy and National Security* (New York: Routledge, 2019).

5. Fujitani, *Race for Empire,* 108–109.

6. Yonemura, *Race, Nation, War,* 17–19.

7. Robinson, *Tragedy of Democracy,* 185–186.

8. Williams, *American Sutra,* 184–185. Eric L. Muller, *American Inquisition: The Hunt for Japanese American Disloyalty during World War II* (Chapel Hill: University of North Carolina Press, 2007), 47.

9. *A Challenge to Democracy,* War Relocation Authority with the Office of War Information and the Office of Strategic Services, nd. Record Group 210: Records of the War Relocation Authority, National Archives at College Park, http://www.archive.org/details/Challeng1944.

10. Art Takemoto, interview by James Gatewood, May 19, 1998, *REgenerations: Oral History Project, Rebuilding Japanese American Families, Communities and Civil Rights in the Resettlement Era,* vol. 2 (Los Angeles, 2000), 397, JANM.

11. Patty Hirota, Biography of Tad Hirota (unpublished), chapter 2, p. 1, chapter 4, p. 5; *Bussei Life,* May 15, 1943, p. 1–2, Topaz, Utah, JERS Collection, The Bancroft Library, University of California, Berkeley (hereafter JERS Collection).

12. *Bussei Life,* May 15, 1943, p. 1, Topaz, Utah, JERS Collection.

13. *Bussei Life,* August 29, 1943, cover and p. 1, Topaz, Utah, JERS Collection.

14. BCA, *Buddhist Churches of America, Volume 1,* 64–65.

15. *Bussei Life,* May 15, 1943, p. 5, Topaz, Utah, JERS Collection.

16. "National Confab Revitalization Planned," *Bussei Life,* June 6, 1943, p. 1, Topaz, Utah, JERS Collection.

17. Patty Hirota, Biography of Tad Hirota (unpublished), chapter 4, p. 5; "YBA Meet Reports," *Bussei Life,* June 6, 1943, p. 1, Topaz, Utah, JERS Collection.

18. For a brief discussion of the impact of trans-sectarian services and Sunday Schools on jōdo Shinshū Buddhists congregants, see, BCA, *Buddhist Churches of America, Volume 1,* 64.

19. "YBA Meet Reports," *Bussei Life,* June 6, 1943, p. 1, Topaz, Utah, JERS Collection.

20. "Myer Pleased with YBA Plans," *Bussei Life*, June 20, 1943, p. 1, Topaz, Utah, JERS Collection.

21. Charles F. Ernst, "Voice from Administration," *Bussei Life*, May 15, 1943, p. 1,Topaz, Utah, JERS Collection.

22. "Editorial Reprint: Totalitarian Beliefs," *Bussei Life*, August 29, 1943, p. 3, Topaz, Utah, JERS Collection.

23. Quoted in "Relocated Buddhists," *Newsweek*, January 3, 1944, p. 60.

24. "Former Engineering Student Sent to National Office," *Ogden Standard-Examiner*, August 24, 1945, p. 11.

25. "National Confab Revitalization Planned," *Bussei Life*, June 6, 1943, p. 4, Topaz Utah, JERS Collection.

26. Reverend Newton Ishiura, "Thoughts from National Meet: Time for Busseis to 'Carry On' Work," *Bussei Life*, June 20, 1943, p. 3, Topaz Utah, JERS Collection.

27. Barry Saiki, "Bussei Speak," *Bussei Life,* June 6, 1943, p. 5, JERS Collection.

28. "Bottrell Speaker Y.P. Service," *Buddhist Digest* 1, p. 1, Heart Mountain, WY, June 12, 1943, JERS Collection.

29. "Director Voices Views on Future," *Bussei Life,* June 20, 1943, Topaz, Utah, JERS Collection.

30. "Fund Drive Started: YBA to Raise 300 Dollars for Headquarters Fund," *Bussei Life,* June 20, 1943, p.1, Topaz Utah, JERS Collection.

31. Donald R. Tuck, *Buddhist Churches of America Jodo Shinshu* (Lewiston, NY: Edwin Mellon, 1987), 284.

32. Robert F. Spencer, "Japanese Buddhism in the United States, 1940–1946: A Study in Acculturation" (PhD diss., University of California, Berkeley, 1946), 186–187.

33. Tuck, *Buddhist Churches of America*, 1.

34. State of California, Office of the Secretary of State, Articles of Incorporation of the Buddhist Churches of America, May 2, 1944, Corporation Number 194746.

35. See Charlotte Brooks, "In the Twilight Zone between Black and White: Japanese American Resettlement and Community in Chicago, 1942–1945, *Journal of American History* 86, no. 4 (2000): 1661; Allan W. Austin, "Eastward Pioneers: Japanese American Resettlement during World War II and the Contested Meaning of Exile and Incarceration," *Journal of American Ethnic History* 26, no. 2 (2007): 62–63.

36. Brooks, "In the Twilight Zone," 1678–1679.

37. Tamotsu Shibutani, "The Initial Phases of the Buddhist Youth Movement in Chicago," October 1944, unpublished paper, Japanese Evacuation and Resettlement Study, JERS Collection, 23; "Dr. I. Tashiro, Aided U.S.-Japan Ties," *Chicago Tribune*, December 21, 1983, section 2, p. 11. For a discussion of JERS workers and their participation in WRA resettlement, see Matthew Briones, *Jim and Jap Crow: A Cultural History of 1940s Interracial America* (Princeton, NJ: Princeton University Press, 2012), especially chapters 4 and 5.

38. Much of the discussion in this section relies on a study produced by Tamotsu Shibutani while he served as a JERS researcher and was subsequently enrolled as a graduate student at the University of Chicago. Shibutani went on to earn a PhD in sociology from the University of Chicago and taught at the University of California, Santa Barbara. For a study of Shibutani's relation to the JERS study and its impact on his own interpretive methodology, see Karen M.

Inouye, *The Long Afterlife of Nikkei Wartime Incarceration* (Palo Alto: Stanford University Press, 2016), chapter 1. Shibutani, "Initial Phases," p. 23, JERS Collection.

39. Shibutani, "Initial Phases," JERS Collection, 24.
40. Arthur Takemoto interview, *REgenerations*, 392–394.
41. Shibutani, "Initial Phases," JERS Collection, 26, see fn. 6.
42. Shibutani, "Initial Phases," JERS Collection, 37–38.
43. Quoted in Shibutani, "Initial Phases," JERS Collection, 36.
44. Quoted in Shibutani, "Initial Phases," JERS Collection, 42.
45. Shibutani, "Initial Phases," JERS Collection, 42–45.
46. Quoted in Shibutani, "Initial Phases," JERS Collection, 60.
47. Shibutani, "Initial Phases," JERS Collection, 42; Claimed by Shinran, founder of Jōdo Shinshū, as the first of seven patriarchs of Pure Land Buddhism, Junirai was regularly chanted at prewar Japanese American services.
48. Shibutani, "Initial Phases," JERS Collection, 46–47.
49. Shibutani, "Initial Phases," JERS Collection, 47.
50. Shibutani, "Initial Phases," JERS Collection, 126, fn 24.
51. Shibutani, "Initial Phases," JERS Collection, 123.
52. Shibutani, "Initial Phases," JERS Collection, 125.
53. Shibutani, "Initial Phases," JERS Collection, 126.
54. Scott Kurashige, *Shifting Grounds of Race: Blacks and Japanese Americans in the Making of Multiethnic Los Angeles* (Princeton, NJ: Princeton University Press, 2008), 166–167; Charlotte Brooks, *Alien Neighbors, Foreign Friends: Asian Americans, Housing, and the Transformation of Urban California* (Chicago: University of Chicago Press, 2009), 163–168.
55. BCA, *Buddhist Churches of America, Volume 1*, 160.
56. BCA, *Buddhist Churches of America, Volume 1*, 160; Williams, *American Sutra*, 237.
57. BCA, *Buddhist Churches of America, Volume 1*, 160.
58. Takeo Yamamoto interview by Jeffrey Gifford and Sylvia Lieu, Buddhist Church of San Francisco Oral History Project, November 20, 1996, p. 13.
59. "Buddhist Hostel Opened in LA," *Topaz Times*, 1, JERS Collection.
60. "Buddhist Hostel, 1336 W. 35th Place, Los Angeles, near the University of Southern California," WRA photographs of Japanese-American Evacuation and Resettlement, Series 12, V46, Section E, WRA no. H-782, with photograph by Charles E. Mace, June 25, 1945, JERS Collection.
61. Takemoto interview, *REgenerations*, 405.
62. Takemoto interview, *REgenerations*, 401.
63. "Attempt to Burn Jap Hotel Made in Watsonville," *Santa Cruz Sentinel*, Santa Cruz, CA, September 25, 1945; Williams, *American Sutra*, 237–239.
64. Shinobu Matsuura, *Higan: Compassionate Vow-Selected Writings of Shinobu Matsuura* (Berkeley, CA: Matsuura Family, 1986), 69.
65. Section 4 of the 1924 Immigration Act included, in the "Non-Quota Immigrant" category, any immigrant or spouse and/or children of an immigrant who sought to enter the United States for the sole purpose of ministering to a religious denomination.
66. War Relocation Authority, *People in Motion: The Postwar Adjustment of the Evacuated Japanese Americans* (Washington, DC: GPO, 1947), JERS Collection, 11–12; Roger Daniels, *Asian America: Chinese and Japanese in the United States Since 1850* (Seattle: University of Washington Press, 1988), 288–289.
67. BCA, *Buddhist Churches of America, Volume 1*, 141.

Chapter 3. Memorialization and Ethnic American Buddhism

1. "Tribute Paid to Nisei at Hero's Last Rites," *Los Angeles Times,* May 2, 1948, p. 3; Williams, *American* Sutra, 164; James C. McNaughton, *Nisei Linguists: Japanese Americans in Military Intelligence Service during World War II* (Washington, DC: Department of the Army, 2006), 115, fn 76.

2. "Tribute Paid to Nisei," 3; *Nisei Vue,* Summer 1948, BCA Collection, Japanese American National Museum (hereafter JANM), 31.

3. "Tribute Paid to Nisei," 3.

4. "Tribute Paid to Nisei," 3.

5. For a discussion of the impact of the Cold War in shaping US government policies of racial liberalism, particularly in relation to Japan and Asia more broadly, see Lon Kurashige, *Japanese American Celebration and Conflict: A History of Ethnic Identity and Festival, 1934–1990* (Berkeley: University of California Press, 2002), 124–125; Takashi Fujitani, *Race for Empire: Koreans as Japanese and Japanese as Americans* (Berkeley: University of California Press, 2011), especially chapter 5; Jane Hong, *Opening the Gates to Asia: A Transpacific History of How America Repealed Asian Exclusion* (Chapel Hill: University of North Carolina Press, 2019), 116–127. See also Naoko Shibusawa, *America's Geisha Ally: Reimagining the Japanese Enemy* (Cambridge, MA: Harvard University Press, 2006), Introduction.

6. For a discussion of Cold War racial liberalism that utilizes a multiracial lens, see Mark Brilliant, *The Color of America Has Changed: How Racial Diversity Shaped Civil Rights Reform in California, 1941–1978* (New York: Oxford University Press, 2010); Scott Kurashige, *Shifting Grounds of Race: Blacks and Japanese Americans in the Making of Multiethnic Los Angeles* (Princeton, NJ: Princeton University Press, 2008). For a discussion of Nisei soldiers in occupied Japan, see Simeon Man, *Soldiering through Empire: Race and the Making of the Decolonizing Pacific* (Oakland: University of California Press, 2018); Fujitani, *Race for Empire.*

7. Greg Robinson, *By Order of the President: FDR and the Internment of Japanese Americans* (Cambridge, MA: Harvard University Press, 2001), 163–169; Fujitani, *Race for Empire,* 81–82.

8. Kelli Y. Nakamura, "'They Are Our Human Secret Weapons': The Military Intelligence Service and the Role of Japanese-Americans in the Pacific War and in the Occupation of Japan." *The Historian* 70, no. 1 (Spring 2008): 58.

9. Franklin Odo, *No Sword to Bury: Japanese Americans in Hawai'i during World War II* (Philadelphia: Temple University Press, 2004), 182–183, 219.

10. Odo, *No Sword to Bury,* 9.

11. Hosokawa, *Nisei: The Quiet Americans* (Boulder: University of Colorado Press, 2002), 271.

12. Robinson, *By Order of the President,* 165–169.

13. Greg Robinson and Takashi Fujitani have made this argument most strongly. Each noted the contrast between public and private discussions of key leaders in making the decision. See Robinson, *By Order of the President,* 167–169; Fujitani, "The Reischauer Memo: Mr. Moto, Hirohito and Japanese Soldiers," *Critical Asian Studies* 33, no. 3 (2001): 396.

14. Quoted in Masayo Duus, *Unlikely Liberators: The Men of the 100th and 442nd* (Honolulu: University of Hawai'i Press, 1987), 57.

15. Robinson, *By Order of the President,* 162–163.

16. Quoted in Duus, *Unlikely Liberators,* 57.

17. Robinson, *By Order of the President,* 170; According to Mike Masaoka, Dillon Myer wrote the speech and mentioned that the OWI's Elmer Davis had penned the last sentence. See Mike Masaoka and Bill Hosakawa, *They Call Me Moses Masaoka: An American Saga* (New York: William Morrow, 1987), 127.

18. Hosokawa, *Nisei,* 402–409.

19. Duus, *Unlikely Liberators,* 214.

20. Shibutani, "The Reischauer Memo," 391.

21. Memo of Record Telephone Conversation between Colonel Davison and Colonel Scobey, May 3, 1943, RG 107, Box 48, Folder 8, National Archives and Records Administration, College Park, MD (hereafter NARA).

22. "Robert T. Mizukami, Obituary," *Seattle Times,* May 16, 2010.

23. Mike Masaoka and Bill Hosakawa, *They Call Me Moses Masaoka: An American Saga* (New York: William Morrow, 1987), 25–30.

24. Masaoka and Hosakawa, *They Call Me Moses Masaoka,* 115, 140, 144.

25. Masaoka and Hosakawa, *They Call Me Moses Masaoka,* 144.

26. Masaoka and Hosakawa, *They Call Me Moses Masaoka,* 145.

27. Duus, *Unlikely Liberators,* 90–91.

28. Duus, *Unlikely Liberators,* 112.

29. Duus, *Unlikely Liberators,* 128.

30. Milton Bracker, "Nisei Troops Take Mountain in Italy: Japanese-American Infantry Returns from France—Foe Stiffens in East," *New York Times,* April 9, 1945, p. 8.

31. Lt. Hall to Colonel Scobey, February 9, 1943, p. 1, RG 107, box 47, folder 4, NARA.

32. Lt. Scobey to Col. Pence, April 24, 1943, RG 107, box 47, folder 10, NARA.

33. Lt. Scobey to Col. Pence, April 24, 1943, RG 107, box 47, folder 10, NARA.

34. Mike Masaoka, *They Call Me Moses Masaoka,* 135.

35. Ronit Stahl, *Enlisting Faith: How the Military Chaplaincy Shaped Religion and State in America* (Cambridge, MA: Harvard University Press, 2017), 96–99.

36. Stahl, *Enlisting Faith,* 99.

37. *Nisei Vue: The Japanese American Magazine,* January 1949, p. 8, Yokomizu Family Papers, BCA Collection, Institute for Buddhist Studies Archives (hereafter IBS Archives).

38. "War Department Asked to Recognize Buddhism as One of Religions," *Pacific Citizen,* September 18, 1948, p. 1.

39. "Buddhist Continue Drive for Army Recognition," *Pacific Citizen,* November 13, 1948, p. 3.

40. *Nisei Vue,* January 1949, p. 6, Yokimizu Family Papers, BCA Collection, IBS Archives.

41. *YBA Times,* January 1949, p. 1, BCA Collection, JANM; NYBCC, "NYBCC Progress Report," 1948, p. 3, box BCA Admin 46–52, folder 25B Correspondence 47–50, BCA Collection, JANM.

42. John Chiaverina, "Meditating Soldiers, a Giant Crossword Puzzle, and Yoga Mat Toilet Paper: Maryam Jafri on Her Exhibition, 'War and Wellness,'" *Art News,* January 19, 2018, https://www.artnews.com/art-news/artists/meditating-soldiers-giant-crossword-puzzle-yoga -mat-toilet-paper-maryam-jafri-exhibition-war-wellness-9664/.

43. "Campaign by Results in Proposal for Change in Army Designation of Faiths," *Pacific Citizen,* January 15, 1949, p. 1.

44. "Army Proposal on New Religious Designation Satisfies Buddhists," *Pacific Citizen,* January 22, 1949, p. 1.

45. Matthew Frye Jacobson, *Whiteness of a Different Color: European Immigrants and the Alchemy of Race* (Cambridge, MA: Harvard University Press, 1999), 102–103.

46. "I Am a Buddhist," *YBA Times,* February 1949, BCA Collection, JANM.

47. "GI Burial Set," *Rafu Shimpo,* May 3, 1948, p. 1.

48. "Military Rites Set for Nisei," *Salt Lake Tribune,* May 3, 1948, p. 14; "GI Burial Set," p. 1.

49. The Shin Buddhist tradition is distinct in presenting Buddhist names to the living. See Jeff Wilson, "The Great Matter of Life and Death: Death and Dying Practices in American Buddhism," in Lucy Bregman, ed., *Religion, Death and Dying,* vol. 3 (Santa Barbara, CA: Praeger, 2010), 162.

50. BCA, Commission on Research and Publication, *Buddhism and Jodo Shinshu* (San Francisco, 1955), 287–289. See also Tetsuden Kashima, *Buddhism in America: The Social Evolution of an Ethnic Religious Institution* (Westport, CT: Greenwood Press, 1977), 127–128.

51. BCA, Commission on Research and Publication, *Buddhism and Jodo Shinshu,* 287.

52. Hong, *Opening the Gates to Asia,* 116–123.

53. Masaoka and Hosakawa, *They Call Me Moses Masaoka,* 187; Kurashige, *Shifting Grounds of Race,* 191; Hong, *Opening the Gates to Asia,* 116–123.

54. Masaoka and Hosakawa, *They Call Me Moses Masaoka,* 135.

55. NYBCC, "NYBCC Progress Report," 1948, 3, box BCA Admin 46–52, folder 25B Correspondence 47–50, BCA Collection, JANM.

56. "New L.A. Chapter Elects First President," *Pacific Citizen,* June 19, 1948, p. 2.

57. Harold Y. Shimizu, "Guild of Being Different" Advertisement, *Pacific Citizen,* October 18, 1947, p. 8.

58. Claude N. Settles, *American Legion Magazine,* October 1943, pp. 21, 51, American Legion Digital Archive.

59. Alexander Gardiner, *American Legion Magazine,* October 1943, p. 21, American Legion Digital Archive.

60. According to Mike Masaoka, the idea of a review was initiated after he contacted John McCloy at the Pentagon. See Masaoka and Hosakawa, *They Call Me Moses Masaoka,* 190–191. "Truman Stands in Rain to Cite Nisei GI Outfit," *Washington Post,* July 16, 1946, p. 1.

61. Elizabeth Spalding argues that Truman's pragmatic and ecumenical view of religion, including the importance of bringing world religions into coalition, played an important yet understudied role in shaping his Cold War politics and policies. See Elizabeth Spalding, *The First Cold Warrior: Harry Truman, Containment and the Remaking of Liberal Internationalism,* (Lexington: University of Kentucky Press, 2006), 205–211.

62. Kurashige, *Shifting Grounds of Race,* 200–201.

63. Kurashige, *Japanese American Celebration and Conflict,* 123.

64. "From the Mayor's Office," *Sangha,* Los Angeles Young Buddhist League, October 11, 1946, quoted in William Charles Rust, "The Shin Sect of Buddhism in America: Its Antecedents, Beliefs and Present Condition" (PhD diss., University of Southern California, 1951), 231. Bowron raised similar sentiments a month later as the guest of honor at a highly publicized JACL banquet. See, Kurashige, *Shifting Grounds of Race,* 191.

65. See Mary L. Dudziak, *Cold War Civil Rights: Race and the Image of American Democracy* (Princeton, NJ: Princeton University Press, 2000).

66. "Nisei Will Form Honor Guard at GI Funeral," *Los Angeles Times,* May 1, 1948, p. 5.

67. BCA, Commission on Research and Publication, *Buddhism and Jodo Shinshu* (San Francisco: Buddhist Churches of America, 1955), 288.

68. *Rafu Shimpo,* May 3, 1948, p. 4.

69. "Tribute Paid to Nisei," p. 3; A *Rafu Shimpo* photograph confirms that Bowron addressed a crowd at the funeral ceremony. See *Rafu Shimpo,* May 3, 1948, p. 4.

70. "Nisei Will Form Honor Guard," p. 5; *Rafu Shimpo,* May 3, 1948, p. 4.

71. *Greenfield Daily Reporter,* Greenfield, IN, May 4, 1948, p. 2; *News-Herald,* Franklin, PA, May 4, 1948, p. 2; *Logansport Pharos-Tribune,* Logansport, IN, May 5, 1948, p. 16; *Daily Republican,* Monongahela, PA, May 7, 1948, p. 1; *Mount Pleasant News,* Mount Pleasant Iowa, May 8, 1948; Delphos *Daily Herald,* Delphos, OH, May 10, 1948, p. 3; *Kane Republican,* Kane, PA, May 10, 1948, p. 6; *Albuquerque Journal,* May 13, 1948.

72. "Buddhists Pay Tribute to Nisei War Dead," *Pacific Citizen,* September 4, 1948, p. 6.

73. "Buddhists Pay Tribute," p. 6.

74. "Cpl. Kokubu Former Portlander Killed," *Minidoka Irrigator,* Hunt, ID, November 11, 1944, p. 1; "Remains of Corporal Kokubu Join Graves of Two Other Nisei Dead at Arlington Cemetery," *Northeast Times,* Seattle, WA, September 25, 1948, Densho Digital Collection.

75. "People in the News: Nisei War Heroes to Be Buried Friday in Arlington; First Time in History," *Washington Post,* May 30, 1948, M2.

76. Tosuke Yamasaki, "Two Nisei Soldiers Will Be Buried at Arlington Cemetery," *Pacific Citizen,* May 29, 1948, pp. 1–2.

77. Yamasaki, "Two Nisei Soldiers," p. 2.

78. Micki McElya, *The Politics of Mourning: Death and Honor in Arlington National Cemetery* (Cambridge, MA: Harvard University Press, 2016), 182–190.

79. Marc C. Mollan, "Honoring Our War Dead," *Prologue: The Journal of the National Archives* 35, no. 1 (2003): 64.

80. McElya, *Politics of Mourning,* 218.

81. Sam Zagoria, "Truman Leads in Honoring 2 Wars' Dead," *Washington Post,* November 12, 1947, B2.

82. "Washington Honors War Dead Today," *Washington Post,* November 11, 1947, p. 3.

83. "Remains of Corporal Kokubu," September 25, 1948, Densho Digital Collection.

84. "Mike Masaoka Writes," NYBCC Progress Report, 1948, p. 3, JANM, BCA Collection, box Admin 46–52, file F25B.

85. "Mike Masaoka Writes," NYBCC Progress Report, 1948, p. 3, JANM, BCA Collection, box Admin 46–52, file F25B.

86. "Mike Masaoka Writes," NYBCC Progress Report, 1948, p. 3, JANM, BCA Collection, box Admin 46–52, file F25B.

87. "National Young Buddhist Groups Seeks Recognition by Army of Religious Cemetery Markers." *Pacific Citizen,* February 25, 1949, p. 2; *YBA Times,* January 1949, p. 1, BCA Collection, JANM.

88. "Bodhi Tree to Embrace National Cemetery," *YBA Times,* February 1949, BCA Collection, JANM; "Memorial Honors Buddhist War Dead," *Pacific Citizen,* August 27, 1949, p. 2.

89. "Army Grants Recognition to Buddhist Mark," *Pacific Citizen,* September 3, 1949, p. 1.

90. Marc C. Mollan, "Honoring Our War Dead," 64.

91. "The Buddhist Gravemarker," 24th Territorial YBA Convention, August 8–11, 1957, 39, BCA Collection.

Chapter 4. Institutional Politics, Ministerial Training, and the Ascendance of Nisei Buddhism

1. "U.S. Bishop Head Dies in Los Angeles," *Pacific Citizen,* June 26, 1948, p. 1; BCA *Buddhist Churches of America, Volume 1, 75 Year History, 1899–1974* (Chicago: Nobart, 1974), 66.

2. "Funeral Rites Held for Top U.S. Buddhist: 43 Priests Take Part in Final Rites for Bishop Matsukage," *Pacific Citizen,* July 3, 1948, p. 2.

3. "Funeral Rites Held," 2.

4. Arthur Takemoto, "A Jubilee Dedication," Golden Jubilee Souvenir Program, San Francisco, CA, August 21–29, 1948, p. 5, BCA Collection, Japanese American National Museum (hereafter JANM).

5. BCA, *Buddhist Churches of America, Volume 1,* 67–68.

6. BCA, *Buddhist Churches of America, Volume 1,* 67–68.

7. "Facts on the NYBCC," *Berkeley Bussei,* 1950, p. 12, BCA Collection, JANM.

8. New York Young Buddhist Association, *Bliss of Nirvana* 2, no. 2 (1946): 14–19, 22, 27–29, BCA Collection, JANM. As Duncan Williams and Tomoe Moriya have explained, *bukkyō tōzen* was reimagined and invoked in the late nineteenth and early twentieth centuries by Issei overseas Buddhist missionaries in arguing for Buddhism's important role in bringing Japanese culture and values to the West. See Duncan Ryūken Williams and Tomoe Moriya, eds., *Issei Buddhism in the Americas* (Urbana: University of Illinois Press, 2010), Introduction.

9. BCA, *Buddhist Churches of America: A Legacy of the First 100 Years* (San Francisco: BCA, 1998), 18; Tetsuden Kashima, *Buddhism in America: The Social Evolution of an Ethnic Religious Institution* (Westport, CT: Greenwood Press, 1977), 169–170, 146.

10. William P. Woodard, *The Allied Occupation of Japan and Japanese Religion* (Leiden: Brill, 1972), 203–205; Kashima, *Buddhism in America,* 171. For SCAP's impact on traditional branches of Buddhism including Shin Buddhism, see Woodard, *Allied Occupation,* chapter 21.

11. National Young Buddhist Coordinating Council Minutes, February 25, 1952, 1, BCA Collection, JANM.

12. BCA, *Buddhist Churches of America, Volume 1,* 105–106.

13. "Organizers to Hold Confab," *Rohwer Outpost,* February 3, 1943, p. 4; "Co-op Notes," *Rohwer Outpost,* Rohwer WRA Center, Rohwer, AR, April 3, 1943, p. 2.

14. NARA Internment file; BCA, *Buddhist Churches of America, Volume 1,* 41; interview with Hiroshi Kashiwagi, by the author, San Francisco, California, October 17, 2002.

15. BCA, *Buddhist Churches of America, Volume 1,* pp. 41, 66; BCA, *Buddhist Churches of America: A Legacy,* 2–3.

16. "Buddhist Jubilee," *Nisei Vue,* Winter, 1948, p. 31.

17. "Buddhist Jubilee," 31.

18. "Topaz YBA to Hold First Confab Mar. 20–21," *Topaz Times,* Topaz WRA Center, Topaz, UT, March 13, 1943, p. 6.

19. Toshio Yoshida, Golden Jubilee Souvenir Program, August 21–29, 1948, p. 2, BCA Collection, JANM; "Articles of Incorporation of Buddhist Churches of America," Office of the Secretary of State, California, Corporation Number 194746, filed May 2, 1944, p. 2.

20. Yoshida, "Golden Jubilee Souvenir Program," 2, BCA Collection, JANM.

21. "National YBA Will Be Reactivated," *Pacific Citizen,* June 26, 1948, p. 2; "YBA Delegates to Jubilee Listed," *Rafu Shimpo,* August 21, 1948, p. 1.

22. The number is based on delegate participation in a Thursday evening banquet. See, Masao Nakamura, "Bussei Listen to Civic Leader," *Rafu Shimpo*, August 28, 1948, p. 1.

23. "U.S. Buddhist Head Dies," p. 1; " New U.S. Head," *Pacific Citizen*, July 10, 1948, p. 1. See also BCA, *Buddhist Churches of America, Volume 1*, 67–68.

24. Golden Jubilee Souvenir Booklet, August 21–29, 1948, p. 7, BCA Collection, JANM.

25. See for example, the *Pacific Citizen, Rafu Shimpo,* and *Nisei Vue.*

26. Golden Jubilee Souvenir Booklet, August 21–29, 1948, p. 7, BCA Collection, JANM.

27. Golden Jubilee Souvenir Booklet, August 21–29, 1948, p. 10; BCA Collection, JANM; Misao Nakamura, "Bussei Listen to Civic Leader," 1.

28. Misao Nakamura, "Bussei Listen to Civic Leader," 1.

29. Golden Jubilee Souvenir Booklet, August 21–29, 1948, p. 11, BCA Collection, JANM.

30. NYBCC, "Progress Report on NYBCC Office, Report #1, 1948, 1, box BCA Admin 46–42, folder 25B, BCA Collection, JANM; BCA, *Buddhist Churches of America, Volume 1,* 107.

31. Misao Nakamura, "Buddhist Jubilee Closes amidst Gaiety," *Rafu Shimpo*, August 30, 1948, p. 1; BCA, *Buddhist Churches of America, Volume 1,* 107.

32. Matthew Frye Jacobson, *Whiteness of a Different Color: European Immigrants and the Alchemy of Race* (Cambridge, MA: Harvard University Press, 1999); Judith Snodgrass, *Presenting Japanese Buddhism to the West: Orientalism, Occidentalism and the Columbian Exposition* (Chapel Hill: University of North Carolina Press, 2003), 21–25.

33. Eiichiro Azuma, *Between Two Empires: Race, History and Transnationalism in Japanese America* (New York: Oxford University Press, 2005), 91–93; Williams and Moriya, *Issei Buddhism in the Americas.*

34. Interview with Arthur Takemoto, *REgenerations,* 392, JANM.

35. Arthur Takemoto, "A Jubilee Dedication," Golden Jubilee Souvenir Program, San Francisco, CA, August 21–29, 1948, p. 5, BCA Collection, JANM.

36. Ruth Kodama, "The Golden Jubilee 1898–1948," Golden Jubilee Souvenir Program, San Francisco, CA, August 21–29, 1948, p. 6, BCA Collection, JANM.

37. Kodama, "Golden Jubilee 1898–1948," 6, BCA Collection, JANM.

38. NYBCC, "Progress Report on NYBCC Office, Report #1, 1948, 1, box BCA Admin 46–42, folder 25B, BCA Collection, JANM.

39. NYBCC, "Progress Report on NYBCC Office, Report #1, BCA Collection, JANM.

40. NYBCC, "Progress Report on NYBCC Office, Report #1, BCA Collection, JANM.

41. NYBCC, "Progress Report on NYBCC Office, Report #1; "News Release," Eastern Buddhist League, October 1949, p. 1, box BCA Admin 46–42, folder 25B, BCA Collection, JANM.

42. "News Release," Eastern Buddhist League, BCA Collection, JANM.

43. Minutes of the NYBCC Board Meeting, San Francisco, CA, February 25, 1952, pp. 2–4, BCA Collection, JANM.

44. BCA, *Buddhist Churches of America, Volume 1,* 68.

45. John W. Dower, *Embracing Defeat: Japan in the Wake of World War II* (New York: W. W. Norton, 1999), 267–273.

46. For a discussion of Nikkei civilian relief aid and the Chicago Committee for the Relief of Displaced People in Japan, see Masako Iino, "Licensed Agencies for Relief in Asia: Relief Materials and Nikkei Populations in the United States and Canada," in Lane Ryo Hirabayashi, Akemi Kikumura-Yano, and James A. Hirabayashi eds., *New Worlds, New Lives: Globalization and People of Japanese Descent in the Americas and from Latin America in Japan* (Palo Alto, CA: Stanford University Press, 2002), 69; Keyes Beech, "Nisei Spokesman Arrives in Tokyo to

'Preach the Blessings of Democracy,'" *Corpus Christi Caller-Times,* November 26, 1947, p. 14; "Mikado Grateful for U.S. Relief," *Oakland Tribune,* January 9, 1948, p. 14.

47. Bishop Enryo Shigefuji to Teruo Mukoyama, May 13, 1949, box Adm 1946–1952, folder 25 B, document 75, BCA Collection, JANM.

48. BCA, *Buddhist Churches of America: A Legacy,* 24.

49. See Naoko Shibusawa, *America's Geisha Ally: Reimagining the Japanese Enemy* (Cambridge, MA: Harvard University Press, 2010); John W. Dower, *War without Mercy: Race and Power in the Pacific War* (New York: Pantheon Books, 1986).

50. BCA Press Release to the city editor, *Sacramento Bee,* January 22, 1952, pp. 1–2, box "Visitors, Lord Ohtani's Visit 1952," folder 5, BCA Collection, JANM.

51. Jack Morrison, "Buddhist Head Here: Leader of Shinshu Sect Predicts Prosperous Democratic Japan," *San Francisco Chronicle,* February 4, 1942, p. 5, box "Visitors, Lord Ohtani's Visit 1952," folder 5, BCA Collection, JANM.

52. "Buddhists Pay Tribute to Japan Leader," *Fresno Bee,* December 7, 1951, p. 27.

53. Morrison, "Buddhist Head Here," 5, box "Visitors, Lord Ohtani's Visit 1952," folder 5, BCA Collection, JANM.

54. *Los Altos News,* Los Altos, California, February 22, 1952, p. 1, box BCA Admin 46–52, folder 4, BCA Collection, JANM.

55. "Top Buddhist of Japan Visits in Utah," *Salt Lake City Tribune,* January 8, 1952, p. 34.

56. "Buddhists Visit City," *Tacoma News Tribune,* January 23, 1952, box BCA Admin 46–52, folder 4, BCA Collection, JANM.

57. BCA, *Buddhist Church of San Francisco, 1898–1978* (San Francisco, BCSF, 1978), 41, 88; "Buddhist Abbot Guest Here," *New York Times,* January 3, 1952, p. 46.

58. BCA, *Buddhist Churches of America, Volume 1,* 68–69, box "Visitors, Lord Ohtani's Visit 1952," folder 5, BCA Collection, JANM.

59. Reverend Sensho Sasaki, Buddhist Church of Sacramento, "Conformation Ceremony (Kikyoshiki)," box "Visitors, Lord Ohtani's Visit 1952," folder 5, BCA Collection, JANM.

60. "Buddhist Leader Will Visit Salinas Church," *Salinas Californian,* February 9, 1952, p. 5, box BCA Admin 46–52, folder 4, BCA Collection, JANM.

61. "Application for 'Kikyoshiki,'" Salinas, California, 1–5, box "Visitors, Lord Ohtani's Visit 1952," folder 5, BCA Collection, JANM.

62. "Gold Razor Hails 200 to Buddhism," *Ogden Standard-Examiner,* January 11, 1952, p. 17.

63. BCA, *Buddhist Churches of America, Volume 1,* 68–69, box "Visitors, Lord Ohtani's Visit 1952," folder 5, BCA Collection, JANM; "Japan's Chief Abbot Studies Policies Here," *Fresno Bee,* December 8, 1951, p. 1.

64. Western Young Buddhist League, "Minutes of the Official Delegates' Meeting," San Jose, CA, February 23, 1952, p. 2, BCA Collection, JANM.

65. Minutes of the NYBCC Board Meeting, San Francisco, CA, February 25, 1952, p. 2, BCA Collection, JANM.

66. Minutes of the NYBCC Board Meeting, San Francisco, CA, February 25, 1952, p. 3, BCA Collection, JANM.

67. Jane Michiko Imamura, *Kaikyo, Opening the Dharma: Memoirs of a Buddhist Priest's Wife in America* (Berkeley, CA: Self-Published, 1998), 32; Shinobu Matsuura, *Higan: Compassionate Vow-Selected Writings of Shinobu Matsuura* (Berkeley, CA: Matsuura Family, 1986), 103.

68. For a discussion of Bishop Yemyo Imamura, see Tomoe Moriya, *Yemyo Imamura: Pioneer American Buddhist* (Honolulu: Buddhist Study Center Press, 2000).

69. Reverend Kanmo Imamura, "Panorama," *Berkeley Bussei*, 1953, p. 1.

70. In later accounts the study group in Berkeley has been referred to as both the "Berkeley Buddhist Study Group" and the "BCA Study Group."

71. "A Time for Action," *Berkeley Bussei*, 1952, p. 22. The proportion of students had increased significantly since 1941, when thirty-one out of seventy of the members were students.

72. M. Paulina Hartono, "The Founding of the Institute of East Asian Studies at UC Berkeley," website of the UC Berkeley Institute of East Asian Studies, published, August 2012, https://ieas.berkeley.edu/ieas-home/about-ieas/history-ieas.

73. Imamura, *Kaikyo*, 30–31.

74. Imamura, *Kaikyo*, 32–33.

75. Kimi Yonemura (Hisatsune), Minutes, Buddhist Study Group, 1949, copy in author's possession; "Buddhist Study Group," *Berkeley Bussei*, 1950, p. 7, BCA Collection, JANM.

76. Kimi Yonemura (Hisatsune), Minutes, Buddhist Study Group, 1949, copy in author's possession.

77. "Buddhist Study Group," *Berkeley Bussei*, 1950, p. 7, BCA Collection, JANM.

78. See for example, "Buddhist Study Group," *Berkeley Bussei*, 1950, p. 7, BCA Collection, JANM; Taitetsu Unno, interview by author, November 18, 2002.

79. Isao Fujimoto, interview by author, October 16, 2002, Davis, California.

80. Jeff Schroeder, "The Insect in the Lion's Body: Kaneko Daiei and the Question of Authority in Modern Buddhism," in Hayashi Makoto, Otani Eiichi, and Paul Swanson, eds., *Modern Buddhism in Japan* (Nagoya: Nanzan Institute for Religion and Culture, 2014).

81. "Religious Section, Introduction," *Berkeley Bussei*, 5, BCA Collection, JANM.

82. Notes on the back of photograph, "1952 BCA Summer Seminar, August 9–11, 1952," Admin 46–52, folder 4 AB Info 1950s, BCA Collection, JANM.

83. Hitoshi Tsufura, "Buddhist Seminar," *Berkeley Bussei*, 1953, pp. 28, 36, BCA Collection, JANM; Jane Imamura, *Kaikyo*, 33–34, 48–49.

84. A.B., "Notes on the Buddhist Seminar: New Experience," *Tri-Ratna*, September-October, 1952, p. 16.

85. A.B., "Notes on the Buddhist Seminar," 16.

86. Tsufura, "Buddhist Seminar," 28.

87. Tsufura, "Buddhist Seminar," 28.

88. A.B., "Notes on the Buddhist Seminar," 15–16.

89. BCA, *Buddhist Churches of America, Volume 1*, 240.

90. Imamura, *Kaikyo*, 48.

91. Taitetsu Unno, interview by the author, November 18, 2002, Anaheim, California; see, *Berkeley Bussei*, 1950, BCA Collection, JANM.

92. Taitetsu Unno, interview by the author, November 18, 2002, Orange County Buddhist Church, Anaheim, California.

93. Unno, interview by the author, November 18, 2002.

94. Taitetsu Unno, "Faced with a Dilemma," *Berkeley Bussei*, 1951, p. 16, BCA Collection, JANM.

95. Unno, interview by the author, November 18, 2002.

96. Unno, interview by the author, November 18, 2002.

97. LaVerne Senyo Sasaki, interview by the author, April 22, 1996, San Francisco, California, 6–7.

98. LaVerne Senyo Sasaki, *Out of the Mud Grows the Wisteria: Life Journey and Essays of a Japanese American Jodo Shinshu Minister* (San Francisco, Self-Published, 2017), 41–42.

99. Sasaki, interview by the author, April 22, 1996, pp. 6–7.

100. Sasaki, *Out of the Mud,* 44–45.

101. Sasaki, *Out of the Mud,* 42.

102. Sasaki, *Out of the Mud,* 50.

103. Sasaki, *Out of the Mud,* 41–42.

104. "Buddhist Plan 4-PT. National Project," *Pacific Citizen*, October 30, 1953, p. 4.

105. "Buddhist Executive Secretary Appointed," *Pacific Citizen*, August 21, 1953, p. 7.

106. Buddhist Churches of America Headquarters, "List of Board of Directors, 1955–1958," box Adm 1946–1952, folder 18, BCA Collection, JANM; "BCA Organizational Chart," *BCA Annual Report*, 1960, n.p. For a list of ministers and their university affiliations, see BCA, *Buddhist Churches of America: A Legacy,* 53–179.

107. BCA, *Buddhist Churches of America, Volume 1,* 70; BCA Special Projects Fund, "An Urgent Appeal to You," Pamphlet, 1957, box Admin 46–52, folder F18, BCA Collection, JANM.

108. BCA, *Buddhist Churches of America, Volume 1,* 70; BCA Special Projects Fund, "An Urgent Appeal to You."

109. Manimai Ratanamani "History of Shin Buddhism in the United States" (MA thesis, University of the Pacific, 1960), 86; BCA, *Buddhist Churches of America, Volume 1,* 70.

110. Reverend Kanmo Imamura, "A House for Our Hopes," *Berkeley Bussei*, 1952, p. 2, BCA Collection, JANM; BCA, *Buddhist Churches of America, Volume 1,* 240.

111. BCA, *Buddhist Churches of America, Volume 1,* pp. 69, 85; Imamura, *Kaikyo,* 58–59.

112. "BCA Scholarships Now Available to Ministers and Students of Buddhism," *American Buddhist*, September 1, 1957, p. 3. The author expresses gratitude to the late Hiroshi Kashiwagi for allowing him access to his personal collection of *American Buddhist.*

113. Imamura, *Kaikyo,* 66.

114. "Special Projects Fund Announces Program," *American Buddhist*, April 1, 1957, p. 4.

115. "BCA Ministerial Training Center in Full Swing," *American Buddhist*, August 1, 1957, p. 3.

116. "Full Curriculum for Ministerial Students Established," *American Buddhist*, August 1, 1957, p. 3.

117. "BCA Ministerial Training Center in Second Year," *American Buddhist*, May 15, 1958, p. 3.

118. "Special Projects Fund Announces Program," p. 4; "Buddhist Groups Pushing $50,000 Seminary Drive," *Pacific Citizen*, June 7, 1957, p. 1; "Full Curriculum for Ministerial Students Established," p. 3.

119. "BCA Award Scholarships to Ministers and Students," *American Buddhist*, February 15, 1958, p. 3.

120. Rev. Gyoyu Hirabayashi, "The Ministerial Training Center—Regarding Its Future," July 16, 1958, trans. Kikuo Taira, 2, box BCA Admin 46–52, folder 18, BCA Collection, JANM.

121. Hirabayashi, "The Ministerial Training Center," 1–2, box BCA Admin 46–52, folder 18, BCA Collection, JANM.

122. BCA, "Press Release," August 31, 1958, box BCA Admin 46–52, folder 18, BCA Collection, JANM.

123. Bishop Haruo Yamaoka, interview by the author, May 31, 2016, Jodo Shinshu Center, Berkeley, California.

124. Reverend John and Mrs. Koko Doami, interview by the author, October 9, 2015, Cerritos Library, Cerritos, California.

125. Reverend John and Mrs. Koko Doami, interview by the author, October 9, 2015, Cerritos Library, Cerritos, California.

126. BCA, *Buddhist Churches of America: A Legacy,* 143.

127. Yamaoka, interview by the author, May 31, 2016.

128. Yamaoka, interview by the author, May 31, 2016.

129. Yamaoka, interview by the author, May 31, 2016.

130. Yamaoka, interview by the author, May 31, 2016.

131. Yamaoka, interview by the author, May 31, 2016.

132. Yamaoka, interview by the author, May 31, 2016.

133. Yamaoka, interview by the author, May 31, 2016.

134. James Dobbins has described the *Kyōgyōshinshō* as "a difficult work, but . . . the most extensive exposition of Shinran's religious thought." See Dobbins, *Jōdo Shinshū: Shin Buddhism in Medieval Japan* (Honolulu: University of Hawai'i Press, 2002), 31.

135. Bjarje Frellsevig, *A History of the Japanese Language* (Cambridge, UK: Cambridge University Press, 2010), 258.

136. Bishop Seigan (Haruo) Yamaoka, interview by the author, May 31, 2016, Jodo Shinshu Center, Berkeley, California.

137. Bishop Seigan (Haruo) Yamaoka, interview by the author, May 31, 2016.

138. Bishop Seigan (Haruo) Yamaoka, interview by the author, May 31, 2016.

139. Bishop Seigan (Haruo) Yamaoka, interview by the author, May 31, 2016.

140. A handful would also serve in Canada. See BCA, *Buddhist Churches of America: A Legacy.*

141. Ben Sato, "Chairman's Report, Special Projects Fund," BCA Annual Report, 1962, p. 14.

142. Ratanamani "History of Shin Buddhism," 83.

143. "Guest Minister Tours East," *American Buddhist*, August 1960, p. 4; Ryosetsu Fujiwara, "Professor Fujiwara Bids Farewell," *America Buddhist*, February 1963, p. 4.

144. "BSC Activity Report," BCA Annual Report 1960, p. 28; "President's Report," BCA Annual Report 1961, pp. 18–19.

145. Bishop Shinsho Hanayama, "Report—Office of the Bishop," Pt. I, BCA 1962 Annual Report, February 1963, p. 3; "Ministerial Research Committee," BCA 1962 Annual Report, Pt. II, February 1963, p. 43.

146. Bishop Junsho Ota, "Message," BCA 1962 Annual Report, Pt. I, p. 3.

147. "Ministerial Research Committee," BCA 1962 Annual Report, Pt. II, February 1963, p. 43.

148. BCA, 1964 Annual Report, January 1965, p. 4; BCA 1965 Annual Report, January 1966, p. 27; Bishop Shinsho Hanayama, "Institute for Buddhist Studies for Ministerial Training," *American Buddhist*, February 1967, p. 1.

149. Shinso Hanayama, "Report—Office of the Bishop," BCA Annual Report 1964, p. 20.

150. Hanayama, "Report," 20.

151. Hanayama, "Report," 21.

152. Kikuo Taira, "Taisaku Iinkai Report (Ministerial Recruitment and Development Committee)," BCA 1965 Annual Report, January 1966, p. 141.

153. Bishop Taijun Toyohara, "Message," BCA 1965 Annual Report, Pt. I, February 1966, p. 1.

Chapter 5. Nisei in the Buddhist World

1. For a discussion of the role of religion in shaping postcolonial nationalism, see Partha Chatterjee, *The Nation and Its Fragments* (Princeton, NJ: Princeton University Press, 1993), especially chapter 5; for a discussion of the third world nonalignment movement see "Bandung," in Vijay Prashad, *The Darker Nations: A People's History of the Third World* (New York: The Free Press, 2007).

2. George D. Bond, *The Buddhist Revival in Sri Lanka: Religious Tradition, Reinterpretation and Response* (Columbia: University of South Carolina Press, 1988), 76; Yoneo Ishii, *Sangha and State: Thai Buddhism in History* (Honolulu: University of Hawai'i Press, 1986), 122; Juliane Schober, *Modern Buddhist Conjunctures in Myanmar: Cultural Narratives, Colonial Legacies, and Civil Society* (Honolulu: University of Hawai'i Press, 2011), 79.

3. World Fellowship of Buddhists, *Report of the Inaugural Conference* (Ceylon: WFB, 1950), 1–2.

4. World Fellowship of Buddhists, *Report of the Inaugural Conference* (Ceylon: WFB, 1950), 22–28.

5. For a discussion of long-standing transregional Theravada connections, see Sujit Sivasundaram, "Ethnicity, Indigeneity, and Migration in the Advent of British Rule in Sri Lanka," *American Historical Review* 115, no. 2 (2010): 434.

6. World Fellowship of Buddhists, *Report of the Inaugural Conference* (Ceylon: WFB, 1950), 33.

7. World Fellowship of Buddhists, *Report of the Inaugural Conference* (Ceylon: WFB, 1950), 34, 32.

8. World Fellowship of Buddhists, *The Constitution of the World Fellowship of Buddhists* (Rangoon: The Fellowship Burma Centre, nd), 1.

9. Sunao Miyabara, *A History of The World Fellowship of Buddhists* (Bangkok: WFB Headquarters, 2000), 14.

10. World Fellowship of Buddhists, *Constitution of the World Fellowship*, 2.

11. World Fellowship of Buddhists, *Constitution of the World Fellowship*, 9–10.

12. World Fellowship of Buddhists, *Constitution of the World Fellowship*, 9–10.

13. For a discussion of the distinct formation of Japanese settler-colonial discourse, see Eiichiro Azuma, *In Search of Our Frontier* (Oakland: University of California Press, 2019).

14. Alan Sponberg, "A Report of Buddhism in the People's Republic of China," *Journal of the International Association of Buddhist Studies* 5, no. 1 (1982): 109–110, 113.

15. World Fellowship of Buddhists, *Constitution of the World Fellowship*, 15; World Fellowship of Buddhists, *Report of the Inaugural Conference*, 83. On Miyabara's proposal, see Miyabara, *History of the World Fellowship*, 4.

16. Miyabara, *History of the World Fellowship*, 5, 9.

17. Miyabara, *History of the World Fellowship*, 7. For a discussion of early efforts by organizations such as the Maha Bodhi Society to restore sacred sites such as Bodh Gaya, see Stephen Prothero, *The White Buddhist: The Asian Odyssey of Henry Steel Olcott* (Bloomington: Indiana University Press, 1996), 158–162.

18. G. P. Malalasekera, *The Buddhist Flag of South Asia* (Colombo, Sri Lanka: Buddhist Publishers, 1951), 1.

19. See the "Publishers Note," in Malalasekera, *Buddhist Flag of South Asia*.

20. Malalasekera, *Buddhist Flag of South Asia*, 29.

21. Malalasekera, *Buddhist Flag of South Asia*, 6, 16, 38.

22. World Fellowship of Buddhists, *Report of the Inaugural Conference*, 28–32.

23. World Fellowship of Buddhists, *Report of the Inaugural Conference*, 30–31.

24. World Fellowship of Buddhists, *Report of the Inaugural Conference*, 29.

25. Miyabara, *History of The World Fellowship*, 5.

26. World Fellowship of Buddhists, *Report of the Inaugural Conference*, 86.

27. World Fellowship of Buddhists, *Report of the Third Conference* (Burma: WFB, 1954), 2.

28. World Fellowship of Buddhists, *Report of the Third Conference* (Burma: WFB, 1954), 37.

29. Bond, *Buddhist Revival in Sri Lanka*, 75.

30. World Fellowship of Buddhists, *Report of the Inaugural Conference*, 1.

31. The Chaṭṭha Sangayana is recognized as the 6th Buddhist Council in the Burmese tradition. Other Buddhists recognize different numbers of councils. For example, Thailand recognized nine councils prior to 1789. See Ishii, *Sangha and State*, 12.

32. Bond, *Buddhist Revival in Sri Lanka*, 76; Schober, *Modern Buddhist Conjunctures*, 60.

33. Miyabara, *History of the World Fellowship*, 3–4.

34. *Minutes of the Official Delegates' Meeting*, Western Young Buddhist League Convention, San Jose, California, February 23, 1952, p. 3, box 12, BCA Collection, JANM; "Delegates," *Young East* (Tokyo, December, 1952), 27, (Honolulu: Buddhist Study Center Library) (hereafter BSC Library).

35. Tamotsu Muryama," "Tokyo Newsletter," *Pacific Citizen*, January 29, 1953, p. 2.

36. G. P. Malalasekera, "Transcript of Memorial Service Sermon," *Tri Ratna* 7, no. 3 (May/June 1953): 1 (Fresno, California).

37. Malalasekera, "Transcript of Memorial Service Sermon," 3.

38. Malalasekera, "Transcript of Memorial Service Sermon," 2–3.

39. Malalasekera, "Transcript of Memorial Service Sermon," 5.

40. Manabu Fukuda, "The Coming Religion," *Berkeley Bussei*, 1953, p. 13, BCA Collection, JANM.

41. Dr. Kikuo Taira, "2nd World Buddhist Conference," *Berkeley Bussei*, 1953, pp. 25–26, BCA Collection, JANM.

42. Taira, "2nd World Buddhist Conference," 26.

43. See, for example, "Will Show Pictures," *Fresno Bee*, December 14, 1952, p. 18; "Lions Club Hears Japanese Doctor Buddhist Delegate," *Fowler Ensign* (Fowler, CA), January 13, 1954, p. 1.

44. Dr. Kikuo H. Taira, "Thoughts on Buddha's Birthday." Reprinting of radio address (date of broadcast unknown), in *The Call to Adventure: Twentieth Anniversary*, Central California Buddhist Radio Broadcast, Fresno, 1970, pp. 29–31, BSC Library.

45. *Report of the Third Conference of the World Fellowship of Buddhists* (Burma: WFB, 1954), 24.

46. LaVerne Senyo Sasaki, "A Recommended One-Year Buddhist Curriculum for High School Seniors in the Buddhist Churches of America" (MA thesis, University of the Pacific, 1965), v.

47. LaVerne Sasaki, "In Reminiscing Our Travel to India, Nepal and Ceylon (pt. 3)," *Young East* (Summer 1956): 29 (Tokyo), BSC Library.

48. Sasaki, "In Reminiscing Our Travel to India, Nepal and Ceylon (pt. 2)," *Young East* (Spring 1956): 28, 30–31 (Tokyo), BSC Library.

49. Sasaki, "In Reminiscing Our Travel (pt. 3)," 30–32.

50. Sasaki, "In Reminiscing Our Travel (pt. 2)," 30.

51. Sasaki, "In Reminiscing Our Travel (pt. 3)," 30.

52. Sasaki, "In Reminiscing Our Travel (pt. 3)," 30.

53. Sasaki, "In Reminiscing Our Travel (pt. 3)," 33.

54. Sasaki, "A Recommended One-Year Buddhist Curriculum for High School Seniors," 2.

55. James C. Dobbins, *Jōdo Shinshū: Shin Buddhism in Medieval Japan* (Honolulu: University of Hawai'i Press, 2002), 79, 150.

56. Michihiro Ama, *Immigrants to the Pure Land: The Modernization, Acculturation and Globalization of Shin Buddhism, 1898–1941* (Honolulu: University of Hawai'i Press, 2011), 26.

57. Imre Galambos, "An English Participant in the Japanese Exploration of Central Asia: The Role of A.O. Hobbs in the Third Ohtani Expedition," in Irina Popova ed., *Russian Expeditions to Central Asia at the Turn of the 20th Century* (St. Petersburg: Slavia, 2008), 197.

58. Charles Elliot, *Japanese Buddhism* (London: Curzon, 1994), 389; republication of 1935 monograph.

59. Minoru Kiyota, "Buddhism in Postwar Japan: A Critical Survey," *Monumenta Japanica* 24, nos. 1/2 (1969): 121.

60. Galen Amstutz, *Interpreting Amida: History and Orientalism in the Study of Pure Land Buddhism* (New York: SUNY Press, 1997), 37. There is some disagreement among scholars as to how much this affected Jōdo Shinshū as compared to the other major established branches of Japanese Buddhism.

61. Amstutz, *Interpreting Amida,* 38; Hiroko Kawanami, "Japanese Nationalism and the Universal Dharma," in Ian Harris, ed., *Buddhism and Politics in Twentieth Century Asia* (New York: Continuum, 1999), 117.

62. Eiichiro Azuma, *Between Two Empires: Race, History and Transnationalism in Japanese America* (New York: Oxford University Press, 2005), 105–107.

63. Ama, *Immigrants to the Pure Land,* 36.

64. Nihon Kirsutokyo Kyogikai; Nihon Kirisutokyo Remmei; Fellowship of Christian Missionaries in Japan, *Japan-Christian Yearbook,* vol., 48, 1959 (Tokyo: Christian Literature Society), 27.

65. "Southern California YABA Discussion with Lord Abbot," *American Buddhist* 3, no. 3 (1959): 6.

66. Reverend Takashi Tsuji, "Ignorance Is Not Bliss," *American Buddhist,* October 1959, p. 5.

67. "A Message from the Lord Abbot Kosho Ohtani," *American Buddhist* 5, no. 1 (1961): 1.

68. BCA Documents 1961, p. 3, box BCA Administrative, 1959–1963, BCA Collection, JANM.

69. "Minutes of BCA General Meeting," San Francisco, February 28, 1959, p. 3, box Adm Board Minutes, 1948–67, BCA Collection, JANM.

70. Interview with Hiroshi Kashiwagi, by the author San Francisco, CA, October 17, 2002; "Japanese Hostesses Feted Here," *The Times* (San Mateo, CA), April 1, 1963, p. 8.

71. BCA Annual Report, 1960, p. 2, box General Meeting Annual Reports 1960–1965, BCA Collection, JANM.

72. Bishop Shinsho Hanayama, "Office of the Bishop," BCA 1961 Annual Report, February 1962, p. 1.

73. Buddhist Churches of America, "Tour No. 1: 10—Day Tour Visiting Tokyo, Kyoto, Nara, Atami, Hakone, Kamakura and Nikko," box "Administrative, Board Minutes, 1948–1967," folder 24, BCA Collection, JANM.

74. Buddhist Churches of America, "Tour No. 1: 10—Day Tour," BCA Collection, JANM.

75. "Attendance at 700th Shinran Service Planned," *American Buddhist,* October 1959, p. 6; "A Tour of Buddhist Sites," *American Buddhist,* October 1960, p. 4.

76. "A Tour of Buddhist Sites," *American Buddhist,* 4; "1,000 Members to Attend Memorial Service," *American Buddhist,* January 1961, p. 4.

77. BCA Annual Report, 1960, p. 59, box General Meeting Annual Reports 1960–1965, BCA Collection, JANM.

78. Haruo Yamaoka, "Recitation of Nembutsu Is Most Impressive," *American Buddhist* 5, no. 4 (April 1961): 2.

79. Yamaoka, "Recitation of Nembutsu," 2.

80. Hanayama, "Office of the Bishop," BCA 1961 Annual Report, February 1962, p. 5.

81. The Junirai or "twelve adorations of Amida Buddha" was penned by Nagarajuna (150–250 CE) venerated by Shinran as the first of the seven patriarchs of Pure Land Buddhism. Yamaoka, "Recitation of Nembutsu," 2.

82. "Honbu Report No. 219," BCA Headquarters, November 7, 1960, Administrative Board Minutes, 1948–1967, folder 24, BCA Collection, JANM.

83. Haruo Yamaoka, "Lord Abbot Stresses the Need for True Faith," *American Buddhist,* April 1961, 4.

84. Haruo Yamaoka, "Special Article—Young Buddhist Conference at Kyoto," *BCA Documents 1961 Bound,* np, box BCA Admin 1959–63, BCA Collection, JANM.

85. Yamaoka, "Special Article—Young Buddhist Conference," np.

86. "American Buddhist Academy," BCA 1961 Annual Report, February, 1962, p. 28.

87. "Buddhist Statue Here: Gift from Hiroshima Unveiled as a Symbol of Peace," *New York Times,* September 12, 1955, p. 18.

88. "Buddhist Statue Here," *New York Times,* 18.

89. "American Buddhist Academy," BCA 1961 Annual Report, p. 28.

90. Ohtani quoted by Hanayama, "Office of the Bishop," BCA 1961 Annual Report, February 1962, p. 1.

91. Hanayama, "Office of the Bishop," 1.

92. Hanayama, "Office of the Bishop," 1.

93. "1959 Report of the Buddhist Churches of America Headquarters," *American Buddhist,* April 1960, pp. 3, 6; BCA, *Buddhist Churches of America, Volume 1* (Chicago: Nobart, 1974), 69.

94. BCA Minutes of the Board of Directors Meeting, December 6, 1959, p. 2, box Administrative Board Minutes, 1948–1967, folder 24, BCA Collection, JANM.

95. "Bishop Hanayama—Official Duties and Trip: Shinran Shonin 700th Anniversary, Solicitation of Donations," Bishop's Report, BCA 1960 Annual Report, 1961.

96. BCA, "Report of Shinran Shonin 700th Memorial Offering," BCA 1960 Annual Report, February 15, 1961, p. 62.

97. Shinsho Hanayama, "Office of the Bishop," BCA 1961 Annual Report," 1962, 2.

98. BCA, "Report of Shinran Shonin," pp. 62–64.

99. Yamaoka, "Recitation of Nembutsu," 2.

100. Interview with Bishop Haruo Yamaoka by the author May 30, 2016, Jodo Shinshu Center, Berkeley, California.

101. "BCA Dana Choir on Goodwill Tour of Japan," *American Buddhist,* June 1961, 3.

102. May Nimura, "A Trip to Japan—Dana Choir Group," *American Buddhist,* October 1961, 3.

103. May Nimura, "A Trip to Japan—Dana Choir Group, Part II," *American Buddhist,* November 1961, 3.

104. Nimura, "A Trip to Japan—Dana Choir Group," 3.

105. Nimura, "A Trip to Japan—Dana Choir Group," 3.

106. BCA Press Release, July 21, 1961, *Documents 1961,* BCA Collection Administrative 1959–1963, BCA Collection, JANM.

107. Nimura, "A Trip to Japan—Dana Choir Group," 3–4.

108. Hiroshi Kashiwagi, "The History of Buddhist Music in America," *American Buddhist,* June 1961, p. 1.

109. Kashiwagi, "History of Buddhist Music," 1.

110. Kashiwagi, "History of Buddhist Music," 1.

111. Kashiwagi, "History of Buddhist Music," 1.

112. Kashiwagi, "History of Buddhist Music," 1–2.

113. Kashiwagi, "History of Buddhist Music," 2.

114. Azuma, *In Search of Our Frontier.*

115. Kashiwagi, "History of Buddhist Music," 2.

116. Nimura, "A Trip to Japan—Dana Choir Group," 3.

117. Nimura, "A Trip to Japan—Dana Choir Group, Part II," 3.

118. Nimura, "A Trip to Japan—Dana Choir Group, Part III," *American Buddhist,* December 1961, p. 4.

119. Nimura, "A Trip to Japan—Dana Choir Group, Part IV," *American Buddhist,* February 1962, 3.

120. Tomiye Sumner (May Nimura), interview by the author, May 30, 2016, Berkeley Buddhist Temple, Berkeley, California.

121. Tomiye Sumner (May Nimura), interview by the author, May 30, 2016.

122. Tomiye Sumner (May Nimura), interview by the author, May 30, 2016.

Chapter 6. Domestic Revival and Family Buddhism

1. "The Buddhist Family," *American Buddhist,* January 1964, 1.

2. "The Buddhist Family," 1.

3. For a discussion of domestic revival during the Cold War, see Elaine Tyler May, *Homeward Bound: American Families During the Cold War Era* (New York: Basic Books, 2017); Cindy I-Fen Cheng, *Citizens of Asian America: Democracy and Race during the Cold War* (New York: New York University Press, 2013), 58–67.

4. Tetsuden Kashima, *Buddhism in America: The Social Evolution of an Ethnic Religious Institution* (Westport, CT: Greenwood Press, 1977), 132; Sylvia Junko Yanagisako, *Transforming the Past: Tradition and Kinship among Japanese Americans* (Palo Alto: Stanford University Press, 1985), 74.

5. "Minutes of the Cabinet and Board of Directors' Meeting," WYBL, Oakland, CA, August 8, 1953, p. 1, BCA Collection, Japanese American National Museum (hereafter JANM); "Young Buddhists Meet," *Los Angeles Times,* March 26, 1955, p. 8; BCA, *Buddhist Churches of America, Volume 1, 75 Year History, 1899–1974* (Chicago: Nobart, 1974), 107; *Los Angeles Times,* March 14, 1956, p. 32; Reverend LaVerne Sasaki, interview by author, 1997, pp. 1–2; "19th Annual Young Buddhist Conference," *American Buddhist,* April 1961, p. 4; "President Harvey Takikawa Installed Other Events at the 20th Annual WYBL Conference," *American Buddhist,* April 1962, p. 4.

6. "Buddhist League 25th Anniversary," *Greely Tribune*, Greely, CO, December 19, 1958, p. 13.

7. Reverend LaVerne Sasaki, interview by the author, San Francisco, CA, 1997, pp. 1–2.

8. Reverend LaVerne Sasaki, interview by the author, 1997, 1–2.

9. Lon Kurashige, *Japanese American Celebration and Conflict: A History of Ethnic Identity and Festival, 1934–1990* (Berkeley: University of California Press, 2002), 43–44.

10. Rebecca Chiyoko King-O'Riain, *Pure Beauty: Judging Race in Japanese American Beauty Pageants* (Minneapolis: University of Minnesota Press, 2006), 63–64.

11. "Buddhist Jubilee Closes amidst Gaiety," *Rafu Shimpo*, Los Angeles, CA, August 20, 1948, p. 1.

12. "Buddhist Jubilee: San Francisco Japanese Have 50th Anniversary," *LIFE*, September 20, 1948, p. 78.

13. "Seattle Trade Fair Shows Japan Goods," *Bakersfield Californian*, Bakersfield, CA, June 19, 1951, p. 6.

14. "Seattle Trade Fair," *Bakersfield Californian*, 6.

15. See, for example, CCYBA, *Bussei Review*, 1952, p. 11, BCA Collection, JANM; "Buddhist League 25th Anniversary," *Greeley Tribune*, 19.

16. Sachi Kimura, "Visalia Reflects," CCYBA, *Bussei Review*, 1955, p. 23, BCA Collection, JANM.

17. CCYBA, *Bussei Review*, 1953, pp. 16, 18, BCA Collection, JANM.

18. WYBL Conference Program, 1953, p. 13, BCA Collection, JANM.

19. Valerie J. Matsumoto, *City Girls: The Nisei Social World in Los Angeles, 1920–1950* (New York: Oxford University Press, 2014), 190–203.

20. *San Francisco YBA Bulletin*, April 19, 1951, box 12, BCA Collection, JANM.

21. May, *Homeward Bound*. See also Joanne Meyerowitz, ed., *Not June Cleaver: Women and Gender in Postwar America, 1945–1960* (Philadelphia: Temple University Press, 1994).

22. May, *Homeward Bound*, 20–23.

23. Paul Spickard, *Mixed Blood: Intermarriage & Ethnic Identity in Twentieth Century America* (Madison: University of Wisconsin Press, 1991), 58.

24. Masami Nakagaki, "A Study of Marriage and Family Relationships among Three Generations of Japanese American-Family Groups" (MA thesis, University of Southern California, 1964), 71–81.

25. LaVerne Senyo Sasaki, *Out of the Mud Grows the Wisteria: Life Journey and Essays of a Japanese American Jodo Shinshu Buddhist Minister* (San Francisco: Self-Published, 2017), 77.

26. Kashima, *Buddhism in America*, 130.

27. Kashima, *Buddhism in America*, 130.

28. See, for example, San Diego YBA, "Post-Scripts," *Bussei Scripts*, January 27, 1953, p. 3, BCA Collection, JANM.

29. "Helen Kunishige Becomes Bride of Seico Hanashiro," CCYBA, *Bussei Review*, 1953, p. n.p, BCA Collection, JANM.

30. "Alice Okano and Yoshito Yamada Are Wed," CCYBA, *Bussei Review*, 1953, n.p, BCA Collection, JANM.

31. LaVerne Senyo Sasaki, interview by the author, April 22, 1996, San Francisco, California, p. 5.

32. Nakagaki, "Study of Marriage and Family Relationships," 114.

33. Yanagisako, *Transforming the Past*, 111–115.

34. Nakagaki, "Study of Marriage and Family Relationships," 100–103.

35. Donna Lockwood Leonett, "Fertility in Transition: An Analysis of the Reproductive Experience of an Urban Japanese-American Population" (PhD diss., University of Washington, 1976), 106, 119.

36. BCA, *Buddhist Churches of America, Volume 1.*

37. Meredith Oda, *The Gateway to the Pacific: Japanese Americans and the Remaking of San Francisco* (Chicago: University of Chicago Press, 2019), 38; Scott Kurashige, *Shifting Grounds of Race: Blacks and Japanese Americans in the Making of Multiethnic Los Angeles* (Princeton, NJ: Princeton University Press, 2008), 68. For a discussion of housing prospects for resettling Nisei in Chicago and Detroit, respectively, see Charlotte Brooks, "In the Twilight between Black and White: Japanese American Resettlement and Community in Chicago, 1942–1945," *Journal of American History* 86, no. 4 (2000): 1673–1678; Greg Robinson, *After Camp: Portraits of Midcentury Japanese American Life and Politics* (Berkeley: University of California Press, 2012), 51.

38. Cheng, *Citizens of Asian America,* 47–55.

39. Charlotte Brooks, *Alien Neighbors, Foreign Friends: Asian Americans, Housing, and the Transformation of Urban California* (Chicago: University of Chicago Press, 2009), 216–221.

40. Hillary Jenks, "Seasoned Long Enough in Concentration: Suburbanization and Transnational Citizenship in Southern California's South Bay," *Journal of Urban History* 40, no. 1 (2014): 9–10.

41. BCA, *Buddhist Churches of America, Volume 1,* 410–11.

42. Jane Michiko Imamura, *Kaikyo, Opening the Dharma: Memoirs of a Buddhist Priest's Wife in America* (Berkeley, CA: Self-Published, 1998), 57.

43. BCA, *Buddhist Churches of America, Volume 1,* 162, 169, 176, 191, 195, 205, 216, 244.

44. "Parlier Buddhists to Build New SS Annex," *American Buddhist,* December 1958, p. 3; "Watsonville Church to Build SS Annex," *American Buddhist,* December 1958, p. 4; BCA, *Buddhist Churches of America, Volume 1,* 224–225.

45. BCA, *Buddhist Churches of America, Volume 1,* 153, 147.

46. "BCA Sunday School Lessons Orientation at Conference," *American Buddhist,* February 1963, p. 4; Takashi Tsuji, "New Horizons in Buddhist Education," *American Buddhist,* May 1963, p. 1.

47. Tsuji, "New Horizons in Buddhist Education," 1.

48. Kimi Yonemura, "Editorial," *Berkeley Bussei,* 1951, p. 4, BCA Collection, JANM.

49. WYBL, "Minutes of the Official Delegates' Meeting," WYBL Convention, San Jose Civic Auditorium, February 23, 1952, p. 5, BCA Collection, JANM.

50. "General Meeting," *Vista* 1, no. 1 (1954): 1, BCA Collection, JANM.

51. "Apathy," *Vista* 1, no. 1 (1954): 2.

52. NYBA, "Rules and Regulations of Miss Bussei Contest," Western Young Buddhist League Handbook Committee, April 1958, BCA Collection, JANM.

53. Mary K. Maeno, "What Is the Purpose of YBA and YABA Conferences?" *American Buddhist,* January 1959, pp. 2, 5.

54. Maeno, "What Is the Purpose?" 2.

55. BCA, *Buddhist Churches of America, Volume 1,* 107.

56. Allan Nagai, "Eccentric Glimpse of WYBL Convention," SF YBA, *Vista,* April 1961, p. 3, BCA Collection, JANM.

57. Nagai, "Eccentric Glimpse," 5.

58. Yoshio Shibata, "BCA Age Standardization for Affiliated Organizations," BCA 1962 Annual Report, pp. 54–55.

59. Yoshio Isono, National Young Buddhist Association, "Buddhist Life Program," BCA 1962 Annual Report 1962, pp. 66–67.

60. Taitetsu Unno, "You Live in a Slum," SF YBA, *Vista*, May 1960, p. 3, BCA Collection, JANM.

61. The issue of Nisei ascendance to positions of leadership within BCA was addressed extensively in an editorial and articles about contributions of the Young Adult Buddhist League members in the August 1962 edition of *American Buddhist*, 1–4.

62. Albert Kosakura, "President's Report," BCA 1960 Annual Report; James Abe, "BCA Membership Survey," BCA 1961 Annual Report, 54–55.

63. Eugene Sasai, "Religion at Home," *American Buddhist*, April 1, 1957, p. 8.

64. Bishop Shinsho Hanayama, "Report, Office of the Bishop," BCA 1962 Annual Report (January 1963), 16–17.

65. Hanayama, "Report, Office of the Bishop," BCA 1962 Annual Report, 17.

66. Hanayama, "Report, Office of the Bishop," BCA 1962 Annual Report, 17.

67. Jane Iwamura, "Altered States: Exploring the Legacy of Japanese American Butsudan Practice," *Pacific World: The Journal of the Institute of Buddhist Studies* 3, no. 5 (2003): 276.

68. Iwamura, "Altered States," 277–278.

69. Reverend Bunyu Fujimura, "The Family Shrine," included in BCA 1963 Annual Report (January 1964), 1–2.

70. Fujimura, "The Family Shrine."

71. Ellen D. Wu, *The Color of Success: Asian Americans and the Origins of the Model Minority* (Princeton, NJ: Princeton University Press, 2013).

72. Hanayama, "Report, Office of the Bishop," BCA 1963 Annual Report, 17.

73. Nakagaki, "Study of Marriage and Family Relationships," 88.

74. Nakagaki, "Study of Marriage and Family Relationships," 142.

75. "A Buddhist Affirms His Faith in the Buddha, Dharma and Sangha," *American Buddhist*, February 1964, p. 1.

76. Yoshio Shibata, "BCA Age Standardizations for Affiliated Organizations," BCA 1962 Annual Report, 54–55.

77. Yoshio Isono, National Young Buddhist Association Report, BCA 1962 Annual Report, 66–67.

78. Ted Abe, "The President's Message," SF YBA *Vista*, 1962, p. 34, BCA Collection, JANM.

79. Fred Nitta, "How YBA Buddhist Life Program Works," *American Buddhist*, February 1963, pp. 2, 4.

80. Isono, National Young Buddhist Association Report, 51–52.

81. Isono, National Young Buddhist Association Report, 51–52.

82. Reverend Hogen Fujimoto, *Buddhist Life Program Guide*, 1963, BCA Youth Department, Bureau of Buddhist Education, 1, BCA Collection, JANM.

83. Fujimoto, *Buddhist Life Program Guide*, 3.

84. Fujimoto, *Buddhist Life Program Guide*, 3.

85. Takashi Tsuji, "New Horizons in Buddhist Education," *American Buddhist*, May 1963, p. 3.

86. Tsuji, "New Horizons in Buddhist Education," 3.

87. Tsuji, "New Horizons in Buddhist Education," 3.

88. Jane Iwamura, "Altered States," 16.

89. Tamotsu Murayama, "Sangha Award Adopted by Boy Scouts of America to Deserving Bussei," *Pacific Citizen,* August 20, 1954, p. 1.

90. BCA, *Buddhist Churches of America, Volume 1,* 100.

91. "Boy Scout Buddhist 'Sangha' Award Requirements" (Sangha Award Committee, USA), *Young East,* Spring 1957, 30–31 (Honolulu: Buddhist Study Center Library)

92. "Boy Scout Buddhist "Sangha" Award Requirements," 30–31; Reverend Phillip Karl Eidman, *Young People's Introduction to Buddhism: A Sangha Award Study Book for Shin Buddhists* (San Francisco: BCA, 1971), 134–135, BCA Collection, JANM.

93. Dr. Kikuo Taira, Committee on Scouting, BCA 1963 Annual Report, 58.

94. BCA, *Buddhist Churches of America, Volume 1,* 100–101.

95. Fujimoto, "BCA Youth Department Report," 43.

96. Fujimoto, "BCA Youth Department Report," 43.

97. Fujimoto, "BCA Youth Department Report," 55.

98. Mas Hashimoto, "National Young Buddhist Association Report," BCA 1965 Annual Report, San Francisco, CA, February, 1966, p. 70.

99. Paul Douglas Andrew, "A Brief Look at Young Buddhist Association History in California," *American Buddhist,* March 1971, 4.

Chapter 7. Dharma Bums, Social Activism, and Challenges to Nisei Buddhism

1. Ryo Imamura interview by Stephen Fugita (primary) and Erin Kimura (secondary), segment 17, August 3, 1999, Olympia, WA, Densho Visual History Collection, Densho Digital Archive. Simeon Man addresses the broader climate of antiwar activism in the spring of 1968 in Hawai'i as a result of mobilization; see Man, *Soldiering through Empire: Race and the Making of the Decolonizing Pacific* (Oakland: University of California Press, 2018), 93–98.

2. Ryo Imamura interview by Stephen Fugita (primary) and Erin Kimura (secondary), segment 17, August 3, 1999.

3. Ryo Imamura interview by Stephen Fugita (primary) and Erin Kimura (secondary), segment 16, August 3, 1999.

4. Ryo Imamura interview by Stephen Fugita (primary) and Erin Kimura (secondary), segments 1, 15, August 3, 1999.

5. See John W. Dower, *Embracing Defeat: Japan in the Wake of World War II* (New York: W.W. Norton, 1999), 206–207; Naoko Shibusawa, *America's Geisha Ally: Reimagining the Japanese Enemy* (Cambridge, MA: Harvard University Press, 2006); Meredith Oda, *The Gateway to the Pacific: Japanese Americans and the Remaking of San Francisco* (Chicago: University of Chicago Press, 2019), 3; for a discussion of middlebrow cultural production about Asia, see Christina Klein, *Cold War Orientalism: Asia in the Middlebrow Imagination, 1945–1961* (Berkeley: University of California Press, 2003). For a discussion of Zen Buddhism, see Megan Mettler, *How to Reach Japan by Subway: America's Fascination with Japanese Culture, 1945–1965* (Lincoln: University of Nebraska Press, 2018).

6. Vanita Meyer, "Advanced Study Group," *Berkeley Bussei,* 1953, p. 29, BCA Collection, Japanese American National Archives (hereafter JANM); Isao Fujimoto, interview by the author, October 16, 2002, Davis, CA, in author's possession.

7. Meyer, "Advanced Study Group," 29.

8. "Buddhist Study Group," *Berkeley Bussei,* 1950, p. 7, BCA Collection, JANM; Hitoshi Tsufura, "Buddhist Seminar," *Berkeley Bussei,* 1953, p. 28, BCA Collection, JANM; Gary

Snyder, "Introduction," in Jane Michiko Imamura, *Kaikyo, Opening the Dharma: Memoirs of a Buddhist Priest's Wife in America* (Berkeley, CA: Self-Published, 1998), iii; Gary Snyder interview by the author, February 7, 2002, Nevada City, CA; Alfred Bloom, "The Unfolding of the Lotus: A Survey of Recent Developments in Shin Buddhism in the West," *Buddhist-Christian Studies* 10 (1990): 158.

9. Gary Snyder interview by the author, February 7, 2002.

10. Gary Snyder, "Foreword," in Imamura, *Kaikyo,* iv.

11. Snyder, "Foreword," in Imamura, *Kaikyo,* iv.

12. Imamura, *Kaikyo,* 9.

13. Imamura, *Kaikyo,* 38–39.

14. Vanita Meyer, "New Experience: Notes on the Buddhist Seminar," *Tri-Ratna: Buddha, Buddhism, Buddhist,* September/October 1953, p. 15 (Honolulu: Buddhist Study Center Library) (hereafter BSC Library); Isao Fujimoto, interview by the author, October 16, 2002. Snyder, "Introduction" in Imamura, *Kaikyo,* iii; Imamura, *Kaikyo,* 39.

15. For example, the 1955 *Berkeley Bussei* was primarily produced by and included contributions from BCA Study Group members, including Lily Fujioka, Kimi Hisatsune, Jane Imamura, Reverend Kanmo Imamura, Robert Jackson, Hiroshi Kashiwagi, Vanita Meyer, Gary Snyder, Tokwan Tada, Hitoshi Tsufura, Taitetsu Unno, Alan Watts, and Alex Wayman. Kashiwagi reflected back on the goals of the *American Buddhist* in 1964, after serving as editor for the previous seven years. See Kashiwagi, "Progress Report," *American Buddhist* 8, no. 1 (1964): 2.

16. Gary Snyder, "Maitreya," *Berkeley Bussei,* 1954, p. 14, BCA Archives, JANM; Gary Snyder, "Epistemological Fancies," *Berkeley Bussei,* 1955, p. 15, BCA Archives, JANM.

17. See for example 1953, 1957, and 1958 editions of the *Berkeley Bussei.* The 1960 edition of the *Berkeley Bussei* includes a reprint of Jack Kerouac's recounting of his meeting with D. T. Suzuki; Hiroshi Kashiwagi, "1957 *Berkeley Bussei* Exceeds Previous Editions," *American Buddhist* 1, no. 5 (1957): 4.

18. Gary Snyder, "Marin-An," *Berkeley Bussei,* 1960, BCA Archives, JANM.

19. Jane Imamura to Gary Snyder, February 20, 1957, folder 46, box 85, series II, Gary Snyder Papers, D-050, Special Collections, UC Davis Library, University of California, Davis (hearafter Gary Snyder Papers).

20. Jack Kerouac to Gary Snyder, May 24, 1957, folder 38, box 94, series II, Gary Snyder Papers; see introductions by Jane Imamura and Gary Snyder in Imamura, *Kaikyo.*

21. Galen Amstutz, *Interpreting Amida: History and Orientalism in the Study of Pure Land Buddhism* (New York: SUNY Press, 1997), 8–10. See for example, Robert Jackson, "Zen and Shin," *American Buddhist,* June 15, 1958, p. 5. Despite his continued preference for Zen and Beat-styled Buddhism, Jackson began to develop a more comprehensive understanding of faith as expressed in Shin Buddhism versus Christianity. See Robert P. Jackson, "Buddhism and Christianity," *American Buddhist* 5, no. 5 (1961): 2.

22. For a discussion of the development of Asian studies as a component of area studies during the Cold War years, see Bruce Cummings, "Boundary Displacement: Area Studies and International Studies during and after the Cold War," in Christopher Simpson, ed., *Universities and Empire: Money and Politics in the Social Sciences during the Cold War* (New York: New Press, 1998); Vicente L. Rafael, "The Cultures of Area Studies in the United States," *Social Text* 41 (Winter 1994): 91–111; "Buddhist Studies at the University of Wisconsin," *American Buddhist* 5, no. 1 (1961): 3; see also Douglas Dunsmore Daye, "Memorial Tribute to Richard Hugh Robinson, 1926–1970," *Philosophy East and West* 22 (1972): 291.

23. Jane Iwamura, *Virtual Orientalism: Asian Religions and American Popular Culture* (New York: Oxford University Press, 2011), 25.

24. Rick Fields, *How the Swans Came to the Lake: A Narrative of Buddhism in America* (Boston: Shambhala, 1992), 195–196.

25. Joseph M. Kitagawa, "Daisetz Teitaro Suzuki, 1870–1966," *History of Religions* 6 (1967): 265–269.

26. "Zen," *Time,* February 4, 1957, pp. 67–68; Winthrop Sergeant, "Great Simplicity," *New Yorker,* August 31, 1957, pp. 34–35.

27. "Buddhism's 'Heavenly Children' Parade," *New York Times,* March 23, 1953, p. 26.

28. Fields, *How the Swans Came,* 196.

29. Calvin C. Steinmetz, "What's In a Name: The Question of Temple or Church," *American Buddhist* 6, no. 6 (1962): 2, 4.

30. Alan Watts, "A Program for Buddhism in America," *Berkeley Bussei,* 1952, p. 21, BCA.

31. Watts, "Program for Buddhism," 21.

32. Rev. Jack Austin, "Letters from Readers," *American Buddhist* 1, no. 7 (1957): 4.

33. Robert P. Jackson, "Buddhism and the Beat Generation," *American Buddhist* 1, no. 8 (1957): 1. The author expresses gratitude to the late Hiroshi Kashiwagi for allowing him access to his personal collection of *American Buddhist.*

34. "GUTS AND SPLEEN: Some Poems from the Berkeley Bussei," *American Buddhist,* November 1957, p. 5.

35. "Letters from Readers," *American Buddhist,* January 15, 1958, p. 2.

36. Robert P. Jackson, "On Buddhist Education," *American Buddhist* 2, no. 7 (1958): 1.

37. David Iwamoto, "The Shin Sect Doctrine in America," *Tri-Ratna,* 1953, 7–8, Buddhist Study Center Library.

38. Michihiro Ama, *Immigrants to the Pure Land: The Modernization, Acculturation and Globalization of Shin Buddhism, 1898–1941* (Honolulu: University of Hawai'i Press, 2011), 43.

39. John Doami, "The Social Utility of the Church," *American Buddhist* 2, no. 10 (1958): 6.

40. Taitetsu Unno, "Some Insights into Life from the Dhammapada: A Collection of the Sayings of Buddha," *American Buddhist* 2, no. 8 (1958): 1, 6.

41. Robert P. Jackson, "The Relationship of Shin Shu and General Buddhism," *American Buddhist* 1, no. 6 (1957): 1, 5.

42. "Buddhists Plan Fresno Gathering," *Fresno Bee,* February 11, 1967.

43. "Notes on Panel Discussion," WABL Conference, March 1967, Fresno, California, 1, BCA Collection, JANM.

44. "Notes on Panel Discussion," WABL Conference, March 1967, p. 2.

45. "Notes on Panel Discussion," WABL Conference, March 1967, p. 2.

46. "Notes on Panel Discussion," WABL Conference, March 1967, p. 2.

47. "Notes on Panel Discussion," WABL Conference, March 1967, p. 1.

48. "Notes on Panel Discussion," WABL Conference, March 1967, p. 3.

49. See, for example, Jere Takahashi, *Nisei/Sansei: Shifting Japanese American Identities* (Philadelphia: Temple University Press, 1997); Daryl Maeda, *Chains of Babylon: The Rise of Asian America* (Minneapolis: University of Minnesota Press, 2009); Diane C. Fujino, *Heartbeat of Struggle: The Revolutionary Life of Yuri Kochiyama,* (Minneapolis: University of Minnesota Press, 2009).

50. William Peterson, "Success Story, Japanese-American Style," *New York Magazine,* January 8, 1966.

51. Takahashi, *Nisei/Sansei*, 154–156.

52. Maeda, *Chains of Babylon*, 62; Yori Wada, "Working for Youth and Social Justice: The YMCA, the University of California, and the Stulsaft Foundation," 1990, Bancroft Library, https://calisphere.org/item/61febe6e9d604f1fbdcd711791c26c51/.

53. Lon Kurashige, *Japanese American Celebration and Conflict: A History of Ethnic Identity and Festival, 1934–1990* (Berkeley: University of California Press, 2002), 155.

54. Kurashige, *Japanese American Celebration and Conflict*, 153.

55. Mark Brilliant, *The Color of America Has Changed: How Racial Diversity Shaped Civil Rights Reform in California, 1941–1978* (New York: Oxford University Press, 2010): 125–127.

56. Greg Robinson, *After Camp: Portraits in Midcentury Japanese American Life and Politics* (Berkeley: University of California Press, 2012), 217.

57. "Ministers Discuss Vietnam Crisis, Civil Rights, and Other Issues at Annual Conference," *American Buddhist*, September 1963, p. 4.

58. "Aid for Vietnam Buddhist Reported at Board Meeting," *American Buddhist*, September 1963, p. 4.

59. Scott Kurashige, *Shifting Grounds of Race: Blacks and Japanese Americans in the Making of Multiethnic Los Angeles* (Princeton, NJ: Princeton University Press, 2008), 259–264.

60. "BCA Ministers Oppose Proposition 14," *American Buddhist*, October 1964, p. 1.

61. Hiroshi Kashiwagi, "Proposition 14 Would Legalize Discrimination in Housing," *American Buddhist*, October 1964, p. 2.

62. Kashiwagi, "Proposition 14," 2.

63. Sandra Izumizaki, "Proposition 14 Would Legalize Discrimination in Housing," *American Buddhist*, October 1964, p. 2.

64. "Help Our Suffering Buddhist Brethren in South Vietnam," *American Buddhist*, September 1963, p. 2.

65. Bishop Shinsho Hanayama, "Report—Office of the Bishop," 1963 BCA Annual Report, 1964, p. 19.

66. Hanayama, "Report—Office of the Bishop," 1963 BCA Annual Report, 19.

67. "Ministers Discuss Vietnam Crisis, Civil Rights and Other Issues at Annual Conference," *American Buddhist*, September 1963, p. 4.

68. "Aid for Vietnam Buddhist Reported at Board Meeting," *American Buddhist*, September 1963, p. 4.

69. "Delegates Commend President Johnson's Efforts for World Peace," *American Buddhist*, February 1964, p. 4.

70. "Report—Office of the Bishop," BCA 1964 Annual Report, February 1965, p. 19.

71. World Fellowship of Buddhists, *Report of the 8th General Conference*, Chengmai, Thailand, November 1965, p. 27.

72. Robert Self, *All in the Family: The Realignment of American Democracy since the 1960s* (New York: Hill and Wang, 2012), 3–6.

73. Janice Nakao, "WYBL Conference: Social Versus Religious Emphasis," *American Buddhist*, September 1964, p. 2.

74. "Young Buddhists Will Pick Two," *Fresno Bee*, June 29, 1969, p. 10.

75. CCYBA *Bussei Review*, 1962, p. 27, BCA Collection, JANM.

76. CCYBA *Bussei Review*, 1962, p. 32.

77. Marilyn Young, *The Vietnam Wars, 1945–1980* (New York: Harper Collins, 1991), 152.

78. "Notes from the Staff," *American Buddhist*, April 1965, p. 4.

79. Joanne Uyeda, "Decisions Facing Buddhists in 1965," *American Buddhist,* April 1965, p, 3.

80. Uyeda, "Decisions Facing Buddhists," 3.

81. Gary Yamamoto, "Sangha in Action," *CCYBA Carnival Capers,* 1966, pp. 10–11, BCA Collection, JANM.

82. Yamamoto, "Sangha in Action," 10–11.

83. Yamamoto, "Sangha in Action," 10–11.

84. Calvin C. Steinmetz, "Buddha Image vs. Buddhist Image," *American Buddhist,* August 1965, p. 1.

85. "Notes from the Staff," *American Buddhist,* August 1965, p. 4.

86. "Letter to the Editor," *American Buddhist,* October 1965, p. 4.

87. Cyril Zimmerman, "Buddhism and Social Change," *American Buddhist,* October 1965, p. 2.

88. Eugene Sasai, "Letters to the Editor: Buddhism and Social Problems," *American Buddhist,* December 1965, p. 2.

89. Sasai, "Letters to the Editor: Buddhism and Social Problems," 2.

90. Ricky Ito Taylor, "Are We Blaming Student Attitudes for Our Own Shortcomings," *American Buddhist,* July 1968, p. 3.

91. Transcript of interview with Patty Hirota, Asian American Political Alliance Oral History Project, 2018, pp. 1–3. Years later, Patty Hirota would come to appreciate her father's actions, given the constraints of forced incarceration, particularly on Buddhists. Thank you to Patty Hirota for providing further clarification regarding this time in her life; email from Patty Hirota to the author, January 30, 2022.

92. Transcript of interview with Patty Hirota, Asian American Political Alliance Oral History Project, 2018, pp. 1–3; email from Patty Hirota to the author, January 30, 2022.

93. Transcript of interview with Patty Hirota, Asian American Political Alliance Oral History Project, 2018, pp. 1–3.

94. Maeda, *Chains of Babylon,* 52.

95. Ryo Imamura interview by Stephen Fujita (primary) and Erin Kimura (secondary), segment 16, August 3, 1999, Olympia, WA, Densho Visual History Collection, Densho Digital Archive.

Conclusion

1. Alfred Bloom, "Shin Buddhism in America," in Charles S. Prebish and Kenneth Tanaka, eds., *The Faces of Buddhism in America* (Berkeley: University of California Press, 1998), 36.

2. "Buddhist Center to Break Ground," *East Bay Times,* May 4, 2005.

3. Bloom, "Shin Buddhism in America," 40.

4. A 1962 *Time* magazine article noted that approximately fifty-six temples representing 80,000 out of 100,000 US Buddhists belonged to the Jōdo Shinshū sect. These statistics likely combined Nishi and Higashi Honganji adherents. See Donald Harrington, "Buddhism in America," *Time,* October 26, 1962, p. 60. Recent estimates were taken from the BCA website, https://www.buddhistchurchesofamerica.org/about-bca, accessed February 29, 2021.

5. See, for example, Sharon Suh, *Being Buddhist in a Christian World, Gender and Community in a Korean American Temple* (Seattle: University of Washington Press, 2004); Wendy Cadge, *Heartland: The First Generation of Theravada in America* (Chicago: University of Chicago Press, 2004). For an early discussion of the proliferation of Buddhist groups, see

Charles S. Prebish and Kenneth Tanaka, eds. *The Faces of Buddhism in America* (Berkeley: University of California Press, 1998).

6. Helen Tworkov, "Many Is More," *Tricycle: The Buddhist Review,* Winter 1991, p. 4.

7. Ryo Imamura, "Letter to the Editor," *Tricycle: The Buddhist Review,* Fall 1992.

8. The fall 1994 issue of *Tricycle* included articles on dharma, diversity and race by bell hooks, Victor Mori, Russell Leong, Rick Fields, and Addie Foye. See *Tricycle: The Buddhist Review,* Fall 1994.

9. Nancy Lo and Becky Mah, interview with Mits and Sadame Kojimoto, BCSF Oral History Project, May 9, 1996, San Francisco, CA, 2–7, 11.

10. Keith Kojimoto and Elaine H. Kim, interview with Keith Kojimoto, 2018, Asian American Political Alliance Oral History Project, UC Berkeley, Ethnic Studies Library. Thank you to Keith Kojimoto for further clarifying some points in the interview. Keith Kojimoto, email to the author, January 26 and 31, 2022.

Bibliography

Manuscript and Archival Collections

Asian Pacific Resource Center, Los Angeles County Public Library, Rosemead, CA.
Bancroft Library, University of California Berkeley, Japanese American Evacuation and Resettlement Study (JERS).
Buddhist Study Center (BSC) Library, Honolulu, HI.
    BCA, Bureau of Buddhist Education, publications.
    Hompa Hongwanji Buddhist Temple Publications.
Densho Online Archive (densho.org).
Institute for Buddhist Studies Archives, Berkeley, CA, BCA Collection.
    Bay District YBA files.
    Bay District YBA newsletters.
    Bay District YBA scrapbooks.
    Berkeley YBA files.
    Central California YBA files.
    San Francisco YBA files.
Japanese American National Museum (JANM), Los Angeles, CA, Hirasaki National Resource Center, BCA Collection.
    BCA Administrative Records, board minutes, 1948–1967.
    BCA Annual Reports, 1960–1965.
    BCA General Administrative Records, 1946–1952.
    BCA National Board of Directors records.
    BCA newsletters.
    BCA Visitors—Lord Ohtani's Visit 1952.
    National Young Buddhist Coordinating Council (NYBCC) records.
    Reverend Kenryo Kumata World War II files.
    Western Young Buddhist League (WYBL) records.
    Young Buddhist Association (YBA) files.
Library of Congress, Washington, DC, World Fellowship of Buddhist (WFB) Conference proceedings and publications.
The National Archives and Records Administration (NARA).
    Office of Secretary of War, RG 107, College Park, MD.
    US Department of State, RG 59, College Park, MD.
    War Relocation Authority (WRA), RG 210, Washington, DC.

Pacific Citizen Digital Archives (pacificcitizen.org).

Stanford University, Special Collections, Palo Alto, CA, Allen Ginsberg Papers.

University of California, Davis, Special Collections, Davis, CA, Gary Snyder Papers.

University of Maryland, College Park, Special Collections, Mass Media and Culture, NBC's Wisdom Series.

University of Southern California, Doheny Memorial Library, Japanese-American Relocation Camp Newspapers.

Archival, Primary, and Unpublished Sources

BCA (Buddhist Churches of America). *Annual Report.* San Francisco: Buddhist Churches of America, 1959–1965.

BCA (Buddhist Churches of America). *Buddhist Churches of America: A Legacy of the First 100 Years.* San Francisco: Buddhist Churches of America, 1998.

BCA (Buddhist Churches of America). *Buddhist Churches of America, Volume 1, 75 Year History, 1899–1974.* Chicago: Nobart, 1974.

BCA (Buddhist Churches of America), Bureau of Buddhist Education. *Buddhist Service Book.* San Francisco: Buddhist Churches of America, 1967.

BCA (Buddhist Churches of America), Commission on Research and Publication. *Buddhism and Jodo Shinshu.* San Francisco: Buddhist Churches of America, 1955.

BCA (Buddhist Churches of America), Commission on Research and Publication. *Young Buddhist Companion.* San Francisco: Buddhist Churches of America, 1948.

Buddhist Church of San Francisco. *Buddhist Church of San Francisco, 1898–1978.* San Francisco: Buddhist Church of San Francisco, 1978.

A Challenge to Democracy. Film. War Relocation Authority, in cooperation with the Office of War Information and the Office of Strategic Service, 1944.

Elliot, Charles. *Japanese Buddhism.* London: Curzon, 1994 (reprint of 1935 monograph).

Fujiwara, Ryosetsu, Reverend. *A Standard of Shinshu Faith.* Jodo Shinshu Series No. 2. BCA Bureau of Education: San Francisco, 1963.

Goodrich, Joseph A. "Young Men's Buddhist Association of Japan." *Public Opinion* 33, no. 14 (1902).

Hanayama, Shinsho. *The Story of Juzu.* San Francisco: Buddhist Churches of America, 1962.

Hartono, Paulina M. "The Founding of the Institute of East Asian Studies at UC Berkeley." August 2012. Berkeley: UC Institute of East Asian Studies. ieas.berkeley.edu.

Imamura, Jane Michiko. *Kaikyo, Opening the Dharma: Memoirs of a Buddhist Priest's Wife in America.* Berkeley, CA: Self-Published, 1998.

Kashiwagi, Hiroshi. *Starting from Loomis and Other Stories.* Boulder: University of Colorado Press, 2013.

Kashiwagi, Hiroshi. *Swimming in the American: A Memoir and Selected Writings.* San Mateo, CA: Asian American Curriculum Project, 2005.

Kerouac, Jack. *Dharma Bums.* New York: Viking Press, 1958.

Kerouac, Jack. *On the Road.* New York: Viking Press, 1957.

Malalasekera, G. P. *The Buddhist Flag of South Asia.* Colombo: Buddhist Publishers, 1951.

Malalasekera, G. P., and K. N. Jayatilleke. *Buddhism and the Race Question.* Paris: UNESCO, 1958.

Masaoka, Mike, and Bill Hosakawa. *They Call Me Moses Masaoka: An American Saga.* New York: William Morrow, 1987.

Matsuura, Shinobu. *Higan: Compassionate Vow-Selected Writings of Shinobu Matsuura.* Berkeley, CA: Matsuura Family, 1986.

Miyabara, Sunao. *A History of the World Fellowship of Buddhists.* Bangkok: WFB Headquarters, 2000.

Nihon Kirsutokyo Kyogikai, Nihon Kirisutokyo Remmei, and Fellowship of Christian Missionaries in Japan. *Japan-Christian Yearbook.* Vol. 48. Tokyo: Christian Literature Society, 1959.

Sasaki, LaVerne Senyo. *Out of the Mud Grows the Wisteria: Life Journey and Essays of a Japanese American Jodo Shinshu Buddhist Minister.* San Francisco: Self-Published, 2017.

Shibutani, Tamotsu. "The Initial Phases of the Buddhist Youth Movements in Chicago." Japanese American Evacuation and Resettlement Study. Unpublished paper. Chicago: JERS Office, October 1944.

War Relocation Authority. *People in Motion: The Postwar Adjustment of the Evacuated Japanese Americans.* Washington, DC: GPO, 1947.

Watts, Alan. *Beat Zen, Square Zen, and Zen.* San Francisco: City Lights Books, 1959.

World Fellowship of Buddhists. *The Constitution of the World Fellowship of Buddhists.* Rangoon: The Fellowship Burma Centre, nd.

Yamaoka, Seigen H. *The Transmission of Shin Buddhism in the West.* San Francisco: Federation of Buddhist Teachers League, BCA, 2005.

Newspapers and Magazines

Albuquerque Journal

American Buddhist

American Legion Magazine

Bakersfield Californian, Bakersfield, CA

Berkeley Bussei

Bussei Review, Poston, AZ

Carnival Capers, Central California YBA

Chicago Daily Tribune

Corpus Christi Caller-Times, Corpus Christi, TX

Daily Independent Journal, San Rafael, CA

Daily Republican, Monongahela, PA

Delphos Daily Herald, Delphos, OH

Fowler Ensign, Fowler, CA

Fresno Bee, Fresno, CA

Gidra, Los Angeles, CA

Gila News Courier, Gila River, AZ

Greely Tribune, Greely, CO

Greenfield Daily Reporter, Greenfield, IN
Heart Mountain Echoes, Heart Mountain, WY
Kane Republican, Kane, PA
Life Magazine
Logansport Pharos-Tribune, Logansport, IN
Los Altos News, Los Altos, CA
Los Angeles Examiner
Los Angeles Herald-Express
Los Angeles Times
Manzanar Free Press, Manzanar, CA
Minidoka Irrigator, Hunt, ID
Mount Pleasant News, Mount Pleasant, IA
News-Herald, Franklin, PA
Newsweek
New York Herald
New York Times
New Yorker
Newell Star, Newell, CA
Nisei Vue, Chicago, IL
Northeast Times, Seattle, WA
Oakland Tribune
Ogden Standard-Examiner, Ogden, UT
Pacific Citizen
Poston Chronicle, Poston, AZ
Press Bulletin, Poston, AZ
Rafu Shimpo, Los Angeles, CA
Rohwer Outpost, Rohwer, AR
Sacramento Bee, Sacramento, CA
Salt Lake Tribune, Salt Lake City, UT
San Francisco Chronicle
Santa Cruz Sentinel, Santa Cruz, CA
Scene Pictorial Magazine, Chicago, IL
Seattle Times
Tacoma News Tribune, Tacoma, WA
Time
Topaz Times, Topaz, UT
Tricycle: The Buddhist Review
Tri-Ratna: Buddha, Buddhism, Buddhist, Fresno, CA
Tulean Dispatch, Tule Lake, CA
Washington Post
WFB News Bulletin, Bangkok, Thailand
World Buddhism, Columbo, Sri Lanka
YBA Times, Honolulu, HI
Young East, Tokyo, Japan

Oral Interviews

Interviews by the Author
John and Koko Doami, October 9, 2015, Cerritos, CA.
Isao Fujimoto, October 16, 2002, Davis, CA.
Kimi Hisatsune (nee Yonemura) and Clarence Hisatsune, October 18, 2002, San Francisco, CA.
Hiroshi Kashiwagi, San Francisco, CA, August 19, 1999, and October 17, 2002.
Albert Saijo, September 22, 2002, Volcano, HI.
LaVerne Senyo Sasaki, San Francisco, CA, April 22, 1996, and March 1, 1997.
Gary Snyder, February 7, 2002, Nevada City, CA.
Tomiye Sumner (May Nimura), May 30, 2016, Berkeley, CA.
Taitetsu Unno, November 18, 2002, Anaheim, CA.
Haruo Yamaoka, May 31, 2016, Berkeley, CA.
Asian American Political Alliance Oral History Project, 2018.
Patty Hirota, interview by Elaine H. Kim, 2018.
Keith Kojimoto, interview by Elaine H. Kim, 2018.
Buddhist Church of San Francisco Oral History Project, 1995–1997.
Tokuji Hedani, interview by Catherine Cofreros and Regina A. Lagman, San Francisco, CA, November 25, 1996.
Mits Kojimoto, interview by Becky Mah and Nancy Low, San Francisco, CA, May 9, 1996.
Kazuaki Kuwada, interview by Kaori Sano and Risa Shigemoto, San Francisco, CA, November 15, 1995.
Densho Visual History Collection, Densho Digital Archive
Ryo Imamura, interview by Stephen Fugita (primary) and Erin Kimura (secondary), segment 17, August 3, 1999, Olympia, WA.
REgenerations: Oral History Project, Rebuilding Japanese American Families, Communities and Civil Rights in the Resettlement Era. Vol. 2. Los Angeles, 2000.
Arthur Takemoto, interview by James Gatewood, May 19, 1998.

Unpublished Dissertations and Master's Theses

Leonett, Donna Lockwood. "Fertility in Transition: An Analysis of the Reproductive Experience of an Urban Japanese-American Population." PhD diss., University of Washington, 1976.
Nakagaki, Masami. "A Study of Marriage and Family Relationships among Three Generations of Japanese American-Family Groups." MA thesis, University of Southern California, 1964.
Ratanamani, Manimai. "History of Shin Buddhism in the United States." MA thesis, University of the Pacific, 1960.
Rust, William Charles. "The Shin Sect of Buddhism in America: Its Antecedents, Beliefs and Present Condition." PhD diss., University of Southern California, 1951.
Sasaki, LaVerne Senyo. "A Recommended One-Year Buddhist Curriculum for High School Seniors in the Buddhist Churches of America." MA thesis, University of the Pacific, 1965.

Spencer, Robert F. "Japanese Buddhism in the United States, 1940–1946: A Study in Acculturation." PhD diss., University of California Berkeley, 1946.

Swanger, Eugene, Rodgers, "The World Fellowship of Buddhists 1950 to 1966 C.E. Unitive and Divergency Factors in a Buddhist Quest for Unity." PhD diss., University of Iowa, 1971.

Secondary Sources

Ama, Michihiro. *Immigrants to the Pure Land: The Modernization, Acculturation and Globalization of Shin Buddhism, 1898–1941.* Honolulu: University of Hawai'i Press, 2011.

Amstutz, Galen. *Interpreting Amida: History and Orientalism in the Study of Pure Land Buddhism.* New York: SUNY Press, 1997.

Anderson, Benedict. *Imagined Communities: Reflections on the Origin and Spread of Nationalism.* New York: Verso, 1983.

Austin, Allen, W. "Eastward Pioneers: Japanese American Resettlement during World War II and the Contested Meaning of Exile and Incarceration." *Journal of American Ethnic History* 26, no. 2 (2007): 62–63.

———. *Quaker Brotherhood: Interracial Activism and the American Friends Service.* Urbana: University of Illinois Press, 2012.

Azuma, Eiichiro. *Between Two Empires: Race, History and Transnationalism in Japanese America.* New York: Oxford University Press, 2005.

———. *In Search of Our Frontier: Japanese America and Settler Colonialism in the Construction of Japan's Borderless Empire.* Oakland: University of California Press, 2019.

Bellah, Robert. *Tokugawa Religion: The Cultural Roots of Modern Japan.* New York: Free Press, 1957.

Bloom, Alfred. "The Unfolding of the Lotus: A Survey of Recent Developments in Shin Buddhism in the West." *Buddhist-Christian Studies* 10 (1990).

Bond, George D. *The Buddhist Revival in Sri Lanka: Religious Tradition, Reinterpretation and Response.* Columbia: University of South Carolina Press, 1988.

Bregman, Lucy, ed. *Religion, Death and Dying.* Vol. 3. Santa Barbara, CA: Praeger, 2010.

Brilliant, Mark. *The Color of America Has Changed: How Racial Diversity Shaped Civil Rights Reform in California, 1941–1978.* New York: Oxford University Press, 2010.

Briones, Matthew. *Jim and Jap Crow: A Cultural History of 1940s Interracial America.* Princeton, NJ: Princeton University Press, 2012.

Brooks, Charlotte. *Alien Neighbors, Foreign Friends: Asian Americans, Housing, and the Transformation of Urban California.* Chicago: University of Chicago Press, 2009.

———. "In the Twilight Zone between Black and White: Japanese American Resettlement and Community in Chicago, 1942–1945." *Journal of American History* 86, no. 4 (2000): 1661–1678.

Cadge, Wendy. *Heartland: The First Generation of Theravada in America.* Chicago: University of Chicago Press, 2004.

Chang, Kornel. "Circulating Race and Empire: Transnational Labor Activism and the Politics of Anti-Asian Agitation in the Anglo-American Pacific World, 1880–1910." *Journal of American History* 96, no. 3 (2009): 678–701.

Chatterjee, Partha. *The Nation and Its Fragments*. Princeton, NJ: Princeton University Press, 1993.

Cheah, Joseph. *Race and Religion in American Buddhism: White Supremacy and Immigrant Adaptation*. New York: Oxford University Press, 2011.

Cheng, Cindy I-Fen. *Citizens of Asian America: Democracy and Race during the Cold War*. New York: New York University Press, 2013.

Chiyoko King-O'Riain, Rebecca. *Pure Beauty: Judging Race in Japanese American Beauty Pageants*. Minneapolis: University of Minnesota Press, 2006.

Chow, Rey. *The Protestant Ethnic and the Spirit of Capitalism*. New York: Columbia University Press, 2002.

Daniels, Roger. *Asian America: Chinese and Japanese in the United States since 1850*. Seattle: University of Washington Press, 1988.

Davidann, Jon Thares. *A World of Crisis and Progress: The American YMCA in Japan, 1890–1930*. Bethlehem, PA: Lehigh University Press, 1998.

Dobbins, James C. *Jōdo Shinshū: Shin Buddhism in Medieval Japan*. Honolulu: University of Hawai'i Press, 2002.

Dower, John W. *Embracing Defeat: Japan in the Wake of World War II*. New York: W.W. Norton, 1999.

———. *War without Mercy: Race and Power in the Pacific War*. New York: Pantheon Books, 1986.

Dudziak, Mary L. *Cold War Civil Rights: Race and the Image of American Democracy*. Princeton, NJ: Princeton University Press, 2000.

Duus, Masayo. *Unlikely Liberators: The Men of the 100th and 442nd*. Honolulu: University of Hawai'i Press, 1987.

Fields, Rick. *How the Swans Came to the Lake: A Narrative History of Buddhism in America*. Boston: Shambala Press, 1992.

Frellsevig, Bjarje. *A History of the Japanese Language*. Cambridge, UK: Cambridge University Press, 2010.

Fujino, Diane C. *Heartbeat of Struggle: The Revolutionary Life of Yuri Kochiyama*. Minneapolis: University of Minnesota Press, 2009.

Fujitani, Takashi. *Race for Empire: Koreans as Japanese and Japanese as Americans*. Berkeley: University of California Press, 2011.

———. "The Reischauer Memo: Mr. Moto, Hirohito and Japanese Soldiers." *Critical Asian Studies* 33, no. 3 (2001).

———. *Splendid Monarchy: Power and Pageantry in Modern Japan*. Berkeley: University of California Press, 1998.

Galambos, Imre. "An English Participant in the Japanese Exploration of Central Asia: The Role of A.O. Hobbs in the Third Ohtani Expedition." In *Russian Expeditions to Central Asia at the Turn of the 20th Century*, edited by Irina Popova. St. Petersburg: Slavia, 2008.

Harris, Ian, ed. *Buddhism and Politics in Twentieth Century Asia*. New York: Continuum, 1999.

Hayashi, Brian Masaru. *Democratizing the Enemy: The Japanese American Internment*. Princeton, NJ: Princeton University Press, 2004.

———. *For the Sake of Our Japanese Brethren: Assimilation, Nationalism, and Protestantism among the Japanese of Los Angeles*. Palo Alto, CA: Stanford University Press, 1995.

Heine, Steven, and Charles Prebesh, eds. *Buddhism in the Modern World*. Cambridge: Oxford University Press, 2003.

Herzog, Jonathan P. *The Spiritual-Industrial Complex: America's Religious Battle against Communism in the Early Cold War*. New York: Oxford University Press, 2011.

Hirabayashi, Lane Ryo, Akemi Kikumura-Yano, and James A. Hirabayashi, eds. *New Worlds, New Lives: Globalization and People of Japanese Descent in the Americas and from Latin America in Japan*. Palo Alto, CA: Stanford University Press, 2002.

Hollinger, David. *Protestants Abroad: How Missionaries Tried to Change the World but Changed America*. Princeton, NJ: Princeton University Press, 2011.

Hong, Jane H. *Opening the Gates to Asia: A Transpacific History of How America Repealed Asian Exclusion*. Chapel Hill: University of North Carolina Press, 2019.

Hosokawa, Bill. *Nisei: The Quiet Americans*. Boulder: University of Colorado Press, 2002.

Howard, John. *Concentration Camps on the Homefront: Japanese Americans in the House of Jim Crow*. Chicago: University of Chicago Press, 2008.

Ichioka, Yuji. *The Issei: The World of the First Generation Japanese Immigrants, 1885–1924*. New York: Free Press, 1988.

Inouye, Karen M. *The Long Afterlife of Nikkei Wartime Incarceration*. Palo Alto, CA: Stanford University Press, 2016.

Ishii, Yoneo. Trans. Peter Hawkes. *Sangha and State: Thai Buddhism in History*. Honolulu: University of Hawai'i Press, 1986.

Iwamura, Jane. "Altered States: Exploring the Legacy of Japanese American Butsudan Practice." *Pacific World: The Journal of the Institute of Buddhist Studies* 3, no. 5 (2003).

———. *Virtual Orientalism: Asian Religions and American Popular Culture*. New York: Oxford University Press, 2011.

Jaffe, Richard. "Seeking Sakyamuni: Travel and the Reconstruction of Japanese Buddhism." *Journal of Japanese Buddhism* 30, no. 1 (2004).

Jacobson, Matthew Frye. *Whiteness of a Different Color: European Immigrants and the Alchemy of Race*. Cambridge, MA: Harvard University Press, 1999.

Jenks, Hillary. "Seasoned Long Enough in Concentration: Suburbanization and Transnational Citizenship in Southern California's South Bay." *Journal of Urban History* 40, no. 1 (2014).

Kashima, Tetsuden. *Buddhism in America: The Social Evolution of an Ethnic Religious Institution*. Westport, CT: Greenwood Press, 1977.

———. *Judgment without Trial: Japanese American Imprisonment during World War II*. Seattle: University of Washington Press, 2003.

Ketelaar, James. *Of Heretics and Martyrs in Meiji Japan: Buddhism and Its Persecution*. Princeton, NJ: Princeton University Press, 1990.

Klein, Christina. *Cold War Orientalism: Asia in the Middlebrow Imagination, 1945–1961*. Berkeley: University of California Press, 2003.

Kurashige, Lon. *Japanese American Celebration and Conflict: A History of Ethnic Identity and Festival, 1934–1990*. Berkeley: University of California Press, 2002.

———. "The Problem of Biculturalism: Japanese American Identity and Festival Before World War II." *Journal of American History* 86, no. 4 (2000).

Kurashige, Scott. *Shifting Grounds of Race: Blacks and Japanese Americans in the Making of Multiethnic Los Angeles.* Princeton, NJ: Princeton University Press, 2008.

Kwon, Heonik. *The Other Cold War.* New York: Columbia University Press, 2010.

Lowe, Lisa. *Immigrant Acts: On Asian American Cultural Politics.* Durham, NC: Duke University Press, 1996.

Maeda, Daryl. *Chains of Babylon: The Rise of Asian America.* Minneapolis: University of Minnesota Press, 2009.

Makoto, Hayashi, Otani Eiichi, and Paul Swanson, eds. *Modern Buddhism in Japan.* Nagoya: Nanzan Institute for Religion and Culture, 2014.

Man, Simeon. *Soldiering through Empire: Race and the Making of the Decolonizing Pacific.* Oakland: University of California Press, 2018.

Masatsugu, Michael K. "'Beyond This World of Transiency and Impermanence': Japanese Americans, Dharma Bums and the Making of American Buddhism during the Early Cold War Years." *Pacific Historical Review* 77, no. 3 (2008).

———. "Bonded by Reverence to the Buddha: Asian Decolonization, Japanese Americans and the Making of the Buddhist World." *Journal of Global History* 8, no. 1 (2013).

Matsumoto, Valerie J. *City Girls: The Nisei Social World in Los Angeles, 1920–1950.* New York: Oxford University Press, 2014.

May, Elaine Tyler. *Homeward Bound: American Families in the Cold War.* New York: Basic Books, 2017

McElya, Micki. *The Politics of Mourning: Death and Honor in Arlington National Cemetery.* Cambridge, MA: Harvard University Press, 2016.

Mettler, Megan. *How to Reach Japan by Subway: America's Fascination with Japanese Culture, 1945–1965.* Lincoln: University of Nebraska Press, 2018.

Meyerowitz, Joanne, ed. *Not June Cleaver: Women and Gender in Postwar America, 1945–1960.* Philadelphia: Temple University Press, 1994.

Mitchell, Scott A. *Buddhism in America: Global Religion, Local Contexts.* London: Bloomsbury, 2019.

Mollan, Marc C. "Honoring Our War Dead: The Evolution of Government Policy on Headstones for Fallen Sailors and Soldiers." *Prologue: The Journal of the National Archives* 35, no. 1 (2003).

Moriya, Tomoye. *Yemyo Imamura: Pioneer American Buddhist.* Honolulu: Buddhist Study Center Press, 2000.

Muller, Eric L. *American Inquisition: The Hunt for Japanese American Disloyalty during World War II.* Chapel Hill: University of North Carolina Press, 2007.

Nakamura, Kelli Y. "'They Are Our Human Secret Weapons': The Military Intelligence Service and the Role of Japanese-Americans in the Pacific War and in the Occupation of Japan." *The Historian* 70, no. 1 (2008).

Ngai, Mae. *Impossible Subjects: Illegal Aliens and the Making of Modern America.* Princeton, NJ: Princeton University Press, 2004.

Oda, Meredith. *The Gateway to the Pacific: Japanese Americans and the Remaking of San Francisco.* Chicago: University of Chicago Press, 2019.

Odo, Franklin. *No Sword to Bury: Japanese Americans in Hawai'i during World War II.* Philadelphia: Temple University Press, 2004.

Oh, Arissa H. *To Save the Children of Korea: The Cold War Origins of International Adoption.* Palo Alto, CA: Stanford University Press, 2015.

Prashad, Vijay. *The Darker Nations: A People's History of the Third World.* New York: New Press, 2007.

Prebish, Charles S., and Kenneth K. Tanaka, eds. *Faces of Buddhism in America.* Berkeley: University of California Press, 1998.

Preston, Andrew. "Peripheral Visions: American Mainline Protestants and the Global Cold War." *Cold War History* 13, no. 1 (2013).

Prothero, Stephen. *The White Buddhist: The Asian Odyssey of Henry Steel Olcott.* Bloomington: Indiana University Press, 1996.

Rafael, Vicente L. "The Cultures of Area Studies in the United States." *Social Text* 41 (1994).

Robinson, Greg. *After Camp: Portraits of Midcentury Japanese American Life and Politics.* Berkeley: University of California Press, 2012.

———. *By Order of the President: FDR and the Internment of Japanese Americans.* Cambridge, MA: Harvard University Press, 2001.

———. *Tragedy of Democracy: Japanese American Confinement in North America.* New York: Columbia University Press, 2009.

Rosenberg, Emily. *A Date Which Will Live: Pearl Harbor in American Memory.* Durham, NC: Duke University Press, 2003.

Schober, Juliane. *Modern Buddhist Conjunctures in Myanmar: Cultural Narratives, Colonial Legacies, and Civil Society.* Honolulu: University of Hawai'i Press, 2011.

Self, Robert O. *All in the Family: The Realignment of American Democracy since the 1960s.* New York: Hill and Wang, 2012.

Shibusawa, Naoko. *America's Geisha Ally: Reimagining the Japanese Enemy.* Cambridge, MA: Harvard University Press, 2006.

Simpson Christopher, ed. *Universities and Empire: Money and Politics in the Social Sciences during the Cold War.* New York: New Press, 1998.

Singh, Devin. *Divine Currency: The Theological Power of Money in the West.* Palo Alto, CA: Stanford University Press, 2018.

Sivasundaram, Sujit. "Ethnicity, Indigeneity, and Migration in the Advent of British Rule in Sri Lanka." *American Historical Review* 115, no. 2 (2010): 434.

Snodgrass, Judith. *Presenting Japanese Buddhism to the West: Orientalism, Occidentalism and the Columbian Exposition.* Chapel Hill: University of North Carolina Press, 2003.

Spalding, Elizabeth. *The First Cold Warrior: Harry Truman, Containment and the Remaking of Liberal Internationalism.* Lexington: University of Kentucky Press, 2006.

Spickard, Paul. *Mixed Blood: Intermarriage and Ethnic Identity in Twentieth Century America.* Madison: University of Wisconsin Press, 1991.

Sponberg, Alan. "A Report of Buddhism in the People's Republic of China." *Journal of the International Association of Buddhist Studies* 5, no. 1 (1982).

Stahl, Ronit. *Enlisting Faith: How the Military Chaplaincy Shaped Religion and State in America.* Cambridge, MA: Harvard University Press, 2017.

Suh, Sharon. *Being Buddhist in a Christian World, Gender and Community in a Korean American Temple.* Seattle: University of Washington Press, 2004.

Swearer, Donald. *The Buddhist World of Southeast Asia.* Albany: State University of New York Press, 2010.

Takahashi, Jere. *Nisei/Sansei: Shifting Japanese American Identities.* Philadelphia: Temple University Press, 1997.

Tuck, Donald R. *Buddhist Churches of America Jodo Shinshu.* Lewiston, NY: Edwin Mellon, 1987.

Tweed, Thomas A. *The American Encounter with Buddhism, 1944–1912: Victorian Culture and the Limits of Dissent.* Chapel Hill: University of North Carolina Press, 2000.

Von Eschen, Penny. *Satchmo Blows Up the World: Jazz Ambassadors Play the Cold War.* Cambridge, MA: Harvard University Press, 2006.

Whitfield, Stephen. *The Culture of the Cold War.* Baltimore, MD: Johns Hopkins University Press, 1996.

Williams, Duncan Ryūken. *American Sutra: A Story of Faith and Freedom in the Second World War.* Cambridge, MA: Harvard University Press, 2019.

Williams, Duncan Ryūken, and Tomoye Moriya, eds. *Issei Buddhism in the Americas.* Urbana: University of Illinois Press, 2010.

Woodard, William P. *The Allied Occupation of Japan and Japanese Religion.* Leiden: Brill, 1972.

Wu, Ellen. *The Color of Success: Asian Americans and the Origins of the Model Minority.* Princeton, NJ: Princeton University Press, 2013.

Yanagisako, Sylvia Junko. *Transforming the Past: Tradition and Kinship among Japanese Americans.* Palo Alto, CA: Stanford University Press, 1985.

Yonemura, Ayanna. *Race, Nation, War: Japanese American Forced Removal, Public Policy and National Security.* New York: Routledge, 2019.

Yoo, David K. "Enlightened Identities: Buddhism and the Japanese Americans of California, 1924–1941." *Western Historical Quarterly* 27 (1994): 3.

———. *Growing Up Nisei: Race, Generation and Culture among Japanese Americans of California.* Urbana: University of Illinois Press, 2000.

Young, Marilyn. *The Vietnam Wars, 1945–1980.* New York: Harper Collins, 1991.

Index

Page numbers in *italics* refer to figures and tables.

About the Author

Michael K. Masatsugu is an associate professor of history and director of the Program in American Studies at Towson University.

The Blind Writer: Stories and a Novella
SAMEER PANDYA

Ship of Fate: Memoir of a Vietnamese Repatriate
TRẦN ĐÌNH TRỤ
BAC HOAI TRAN AND JANA K. LIPMAN, TRANS.

Freedom without Justice: The Prison Memoirs of Chol Soo Lee
CHOL SOO LEE
RICHARD S. KIM, ED.

TADAIMA! *I Am Home: A Transnational Family History*
TOM COFFMAN